AF365313

A COMPANION TO MEKAS WALDEN

A GUIDE TO JONAS MEKAS'S DIARIES, NOTES AND SKETCHES

SCOTT HAMMEN

Eyewash
Books

PARIS EXPÉRIMENTAL

ISBN: 978-2-9582044-0-2

Copyright © 2022 by Scott Hammen.

All rights reserved.

No part of this book may be reproduced in any form or by any electronic or mechanical means, including information storage and retrieval systems, without written permission from the author, except for the use of brief quotations in a book review.

Whenever people ask me what it was like to live in New York in the '60s, I refer them to Mekas's *Walden*...

- Amy Taubin

CONTENTS

DEDICATION

Jonas Mekas changed film history by preserving certain fragments of his past on celluloid. But he also had an astonishing memory for events too insignificant to merit mention in his films or writing.

I first met him in 1976 at his home in New York City. I had seen the first edition of *Diaries, Notes, and Sketches* and wanted to interview him and write about it. He was generous with his time and we talked for a few hours.

We did not speak again until 1985 after a screening of his films in Massachusetts. Although he must have met hundreds of other admirers in the interim, he greeted me as if our conversation had not been interrupted for a decade.

I was in the crowd at his first major exhibition in Paris at the Jeu de Paume museum in 1999. Our conversation lasted a minute, surrounded by countless others who, like me, felt they knew Jonas through his films. Twelve years later, in 2011, I saw him again for a brief instant at the Centre Pompidou.

In January 2018, I said a last hello as he was signing copies of his book *A Dance with Fred Astaire*. He looked at me for a second and then mentioned a problem I had had with the article I wrote in 1976.

His life had spanned the better part of the 20th century and a good chunk of the 21st. He had survived the occupation of his Lithuanian homeland, lived in displaced persons camps in Germany, and been an immigrant day laborer on Long Island. And then he went on to change the way the world looked at the medium of film.

Of course all of those whose lives he touched still remember Jonas. What seems astounding is that he seemed never to have forgotten any of us.

This book is dedicated to his memory.

PREFACE

On the soundtrack of *Diaries, Notes and Sketches also known as Walden,* Jonas Mekas proclaimed, "I make home movies, therefore I live."

Because of who made the "movies" and where his "home" was, *Walden* was also an extraordinary panorama of cultural life in the 1960s. To watch it is to tour a vital place and time through the eyes of a remarkable poet.

It is not necessary to take the tour with a guide. But as one who has spent many happy hours exploring Mekas's *Walden,* I have found that its fascination increases with knowledge of its subjects.

Some of the people seen in *Walden* were already well-known when Mekas filmed them, others were later to become so, some were never to be. He knew that celebrities attracted audiences so the advertisement he placed in the *Village Voice* for the premiere of *Walden* in December 1969 featured a list of famous names, starting with the mayor of New York, John Lindsay, and a member of the Beatles, John Lennon.

But there were many of the non-famous too - those the ad describes as "countless others with names and without names"[1] who were just friends, colleagues, or accidental passers-by in Mekas's New York. The sub-title of a later extract from his film diaries, *Scenes from the Life of Andy Warhol* (1990), could just as well have described *Walden*: "Anthropological Sketches: Friendships and Intersections."

Mekas's personal feelings about the subjects of his "anthropological sketches" were rarely obvious. The video artist Wendy Clarke remembered him filming her wedding: "Jonas was very quiet so you didn't know he was there a lot. He was the perfect person to do this because he never took over and his presence was always somewhat removed."[2]

Walden turned out to be only the first of a series of publicly released excerpts from Mekas's film diaries. The period it chronicled, 1964 to 1969, was just one chapter in the saga of his life in New York.

A later release, *Lost Lost Lost* (1976) begins with sequences from his early years in New York, just after his arrival as a displaced person from Europe in 1949, and continues up until the period of *Walden*. Two later installments, *He Stands in a Desert Counting the Seconds of His Life* (1986) and *As I Was Moving Ahead Occasionally I Saw Brief Glimpses of Beauty* (2000) cover periods after *Walden*. In addition, Mekas released many of the sequences in his diaries as separate short films and finally, at the age of 90, presented a compilation of sequences he had not chosen to use in earlier editions of his diaries from 1960 to 2000: *Out-Takes From the Life of a Happy Man* (2012).

Consequently, the title *Diaries, Notes and Sketches* ended up describing the entirety of this activity and Mekas needed a way to distinguish the first publicly presented installment from its successors. When film labs started to confuse the reels of his different diary films Mekas recalled that "I had no choice but to rethink the titles. All of my film diaries are *Diaries, Notes, and Sketches*, but I now call the individual parts only by their specific names."[3]

So the choice of the title of Henry David Thoreau's 19th century literary classic was not fortuitous but neither did the respective works of the Lithuanian poet and New England moralist share many affinities (see Chapter 23). Mekas's overall title *Diaries, Notes and Sketches* is far more indicative of its impact on a generation of film artists.

Amateur filmmakers may have already been recording images of events in their daily lives and assembling them to show to family and friends as "home movies." But it was Mekas who permitted them to be imagined as an art form.

At first Mekas himself had considered his autobiographical images of New York as just preparatory "notes and sketches" for a narrative film - a story about the different stages of a woman's life beginning with her adolescence. A number of his "screen tests" of young girls in Central Park remain in *Walden*.

But when in 1968 the Albright-Knox Gallery in Buffalo commissioned a film from him, he decided to use "the material that was the easiest for me to put together."[4] The result, presented in its first edition at the end of the following year, opened a new chapter in the history of experimental film.

In general, the subjects of the chapters in this guide follow those noted by Mekas himself in a wonderful poster for the first version of *Walden* designed by George Maciunas. In a few cases it has proved impossible to identify images of the person Mekas noted, and, in other cases, recognizable figures are not explicitly mentioned. But, for the most part, the Maciunas poster provides an accurate list of the people and places visible in *Walden*.

For people whose biographies are already well-known, I have simply tried to provide some context for their appearance. For the less famous, I have sought to establish the salient facts of their life and to try to account, however speculatively, for how they crossed Mekas's path.

The image caption indicates the moment in *Walden* from which it was taken but many subjects appear repeatedly. And, while reel numbers are accurate, the exact minute and second of an appearance will vary according to the format in which the film is viewed

Mekas himself included time code on the original Maciunas poster for *Walden* and, in his introduction to it, wrote: "the Author won't mind (he is almost encouraging it) if Viewers will choose to watch only certain parts of the work (film), according to the time available to them, according to their preferences, or any other good reason."

PROLOGUE: STILL WINTER

In December 1963, Jonas Mekas returned to the Europe he had fled in 1949 to be on the competition jury of an experimental film festival in the Belgian seaside resort of Knokke-le-Zoute. Mekas had immigrated to New York under the terms of the Displaced Persons Act of 1948 which authorized Europeans displaced by the war to apply for permanent residence in the United States.

Since his arrival Mekas had become increasingly interested in film. He attended classes at the City University of New York taught by the pioneer of experimental film in Germany, Hans Richter, then began showing films himself. In 1954, he founded *Film Culture*, a magazine which would play a pivotal role in the post-war history of experimental film and, in 1958, he started writing a column called "Movie Journal" for the weekly newspaper *The Village Voice.*

Mekas had been invited to Knokke-le-Zoute as a juror but he clearly saw his role in far broader terms as an advocate of a new creative energy in his adopted land. In the summer of 1961, *Film Culture* had published "The First Statement of The New American Cinema Group." It stated that:

> The official cinema all over the world is running out of breath. It is morally corrupt, aesthetically obsolete, thematically superficial, temperamentally boring. Even the seemingly worthwhile films, those that lay claim to high moral and aesthetic standards and have been accepted as such by critics and the public alike, reveal the decay of the Product Film. The very slickness of their execution has become a perversion covering the falsity of their themes, their lack of sensitivity, their lack of style.[1]

The seaside resort casino of Knokke-le-Zoute was usually empty in winter. But there were tax advantages to hosting cultural events so, on Christmas Day 1963, its doors were opened for EXPRMNTL 3, the third festival organized by Jacques Ledoux, the director of the Belgian National Film Archive.

The festival selection committee had included *Flaming Creatures* (1963), a film by Jack Smith that Mekas had already shown in New York after warning viewers that it would "be called pornographic, degenerate, homosexual, trite, disgusting, etc.," and that "It is all that, and it is so much more than that."[2]

Flaming Creatures was initially chosen to be shown at the festival but, because of the possibility of obscenity complaints, it was withdrawn. The festival program explained:

During its final deliberation, the selection jury decided to state explicitly that the majority of its members "recognized the aesthetical and experimental qualities of the film FLAMING CREATURES by Jack Smith (USA, 1963) but had to ascertain unanimously that the showing of it was impossible in regards to Belgian laws."[3]

When Mekas learned of the last-minute decision, he was outraged:

At one point the Mekas contingent attempted to take over the projection facilities at the public screenings, armed with a print of *Flaming Creatures*. Though this attack was beaten off by casino employees and house detectives, who turned off the main electrical supply to the projection booth, the resultant uproar won a further gain for the anti-censorship forces...[4]

Upon his return to New York, Mekas gave further details in the following week's *Village Voice*:

I myself am not so sure about what really happened at Knokke during that stormy, confused, disappointed, sad, desperate week. It did different things to each of us. And there will be conflicting reports about it for years to come, about the flames over Knokke-le-Zoute: about how we smuggled *Flaming Creatures* into the projection room in the can of *Dog Star Man*; about our screenings in the hotel cellar amidst dusty old furniture, cobwebs, old newspapers; about how, on New Year's night, we stormed the Crystal Room and took over the projector, how the lights were cut off, and how I ran to the switchboard room, trying to push off the house detective, holding the door, trying to force the fingers of the bully who was holding the switch.

'People, do you want to see the film?' Barbara [Rubin] shouted from the projector platform, fighting like a brave general.

'Yes!' answered the people. It is too confusing what went on after that. Much pushing and shouting as the switch changed hands between me and the cop. It was about this time that the Minister of Justice arrived. The riot was getting more and more out of hand. The Minister made an attempt to explain the Belgian law. But when we asked if there was such a law forbidding the showing of films, he said there was no such law. 'Then fuck you!' shouted Barbara to the Minister of Justice of Belgium.

We made another attempt to project *Flaming Creatures* right on his face, but the light was cut off again....

Since the affair of *Flaming Creatures* has been blown across the world by now, and since there will be much more on the subject, I should tell you one thing. Our actions (by 'our' I mean Barbara Rubin, P. Adams Sitney, and myself) at Knokke-le-Zoute were motivated by our feelings against the suppression of any film or any human expression. During our press conference, as well as on other occasions, we made it clear that we were not fighting for this particular film, but for the principle of free expression.[5]

In one way Mekas was triumphant. He had returned to the Europe that he had escaped in 1949 at the head of another sort of American liberation army fighting for artistic freedom. At his side was the fearless Barbara Rubin whom he admired for "fighting like a brave general."

But this time the war was not just in Europe. It would continue back in his adopted home of New York.

At the Gramercy Arts Theatre under the banner of "Film-Makers' Showcase," he continued to show *Flaming Creatures* while avoiding mention of its name, advertising it simply as a "Surprise Program." But his caution was inadequate. A legal summons was issued prohibiting the showing of "unlicensed films." When the theater did not comply, its exhibition license was rescinded and the Film-Makers' Showcase evicted.

The administration of New York Mayor Robert Wagner was preparing to host a World's Fair in the summer of 1964 and had decided that the city's gay bars were detrimental to the city's image. Five years before the Stonewall Riots were to mark the launch of the struggle for LGBT rights, the city began to revoke the liquor licenses of selected bars, and send undercover police officers to entrap their customers. A theater showing *Flaming Creatures* was an obvious target as well.

Mekas moved the Film-Makers' Showcase to the New Bowery Theater, on 4th Street at St. Mark's Place where he subleased the space from Diane Di Prima and The American Theatre for Poets. There he announced another series of "Surprise Programs."

On March 2, an undercover policeman attended the screening and the following night, two NYPD detectives interrupted the program and arrested Mekas. The *Village Voice* reported:

> ... Without making themselves known, plainclothesmen watched *Flaming Creatures* when it opened last Monday night at the New Bowery Theatre, 4 St. Mark's Place. Presumably they did find the film objectionable - or those parts of it that

included shots of male sex organs and female breasts - because
the next night the film and four of those involved in its
showing were seized by the police. Mekas, a founder and
guiding light of the Film-Makers' Cooperative, was not at the
theater at the time, but when he was notified of what was
happening, he rushed down and demanded that he be arrested
too. The police obliged.[6]

The following week on March 12th, Mekas went to jail again:

Voice film critic Jonas Mekas spent another night in jail last
week, this time for showing the Jean Genet film *Un chant
d'amour,* a homosexual love story. One reason for the screening
of the Genet film on Friday night at the Writers Stage Theatre,
83 East 4th Street, was to raise money for a defense fund for
Mekas and three associates arrested two weeks earlier for
showing the Jack Smith film *Flaming Creatures* at the new
Bowery Theatre.

... He was arrested for the second time at about 1 a.m. Saturday
and taken to the Ninth Precinct house on East 5th Street,
where he had spent the night the last time.[7]

The *Flaming Creatures* trial began on June 2nd, 1964. On June 12th, the
Court convicted Mekas and his accomplices, Ken Jacobs and his wife
Florence Karpf. On August 7th, they were given a suspended sentence
of sixty days in the city workhouse.

On November 12th Mekas announced the formation of the Film-
Makers' Cinematheque as "a center for the enjoyment and study of
movies."[8] Its address was listed as that of the Writers Stage on East
4th St. where his arrest for showing the Genet film had occurred but
programs could not be publicly held there because it did not comply
with city regulations governing movie theaters.

Summarizing the events of this period in the January 7th, 1965 issue of the *Village Voice,* Mekas wrote that "a dark period in the New York film underground begins. No screenings for seven months. With no place to meet, film-makers' spirits go low. Clandestine screenings continue at the Co-op late into the summer, until the Co-op is raided and cops are placed nightly across the street."

The winter of 1965 was a dark time for Mekas. He had been serving as a soldier in a war for artistic freedom, a partisan fighter for film as a medium of personal expression. But the combat seemed endless.

Then something, perhaps a whiff of spring, brought him to a decision: "Instead of marching and shouting against things I didn't like, I decided to try to construct something new, outside the system."[9]

Maybe a new breeze reminded him of one of his first written diary entries, noted while fleeing Lithuania in advance of the Red Army in 1944: "I am neither a soldier nor a partisan. I am neither physically nor mentally fit for such a life. I am a poet."[10]

The leafless branches moving in the wind that Mekas filmed in Central Park late that winter now have the quality of an epiphany. They would be among the first images of the work of a poet not a soldier.

Three years later, he showed the first version of a new kind of film. Its title sequence read:

"DIARIES notes and sketches also known as WALDEN."

It contained little to indicate that its "Author" had been on the barricades in a war against censorship, declaiming his defiance of authority from a jail cell. Instead of partisanship, viewers would discover a new form of film poetry that was to expand the definition of personal film-making and inspire a new generation of artists.The first intertitles of *Walden* are euphoric, like the first lines of an epic poem

BUT THE WIND
WAS
FULL OF
SPRING

1 AUTHOR

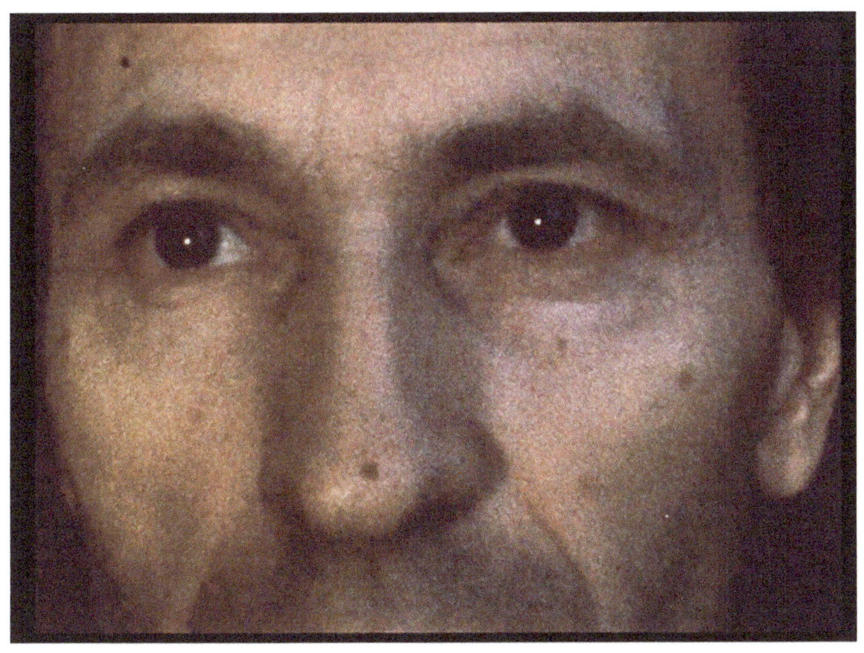

Reel 1 00:49

The very first few frames of the first reel of Jonas Mekas's *Diaries, Notes and Sketches* show its "Author" and, at the same time, indicate the new direction his film was about to take.

If it was a conventional film, its sequences would be long enough to allow viewers time to register their content. Mekas's first sequence lasted barely a second.

To preserve an illusion of objectivity, a conventional film narrative would conceal the mechanics of filmmaking and keep its maker out of sight behind the camera. Mekas begins with the camera on himself.

Walden went on to violate other norms as well, notably in its short bursts of just a few frames which fragmented and accelerated "normal" motion and its wandering camera motion which avoided concentrating on a single subject.

And the very length of the film rejected the basic convention of commercial exhibition - that its scenes should be watched in their entirety in a single linear stretch of roughly two hours.

In his introduction to the film, Mekas explicitly stated that viewers were encouraged to watch whatever parts they pleased for however long they chose in the same way as they would regard an immobile work of art. As a way to view the time-based medium of film, such freedom was unexpected.

The Author reappeared at regular intervals throughout *Walden*, each time a reminder that what was on the screen was not objective information but an intensely personal vision. It was a simple but profoundly liberating approach to filmmaking that would come to seem obvious in the decades that followed. But in 1969 it changed the way many of its viewers watched film.

2 SNOW

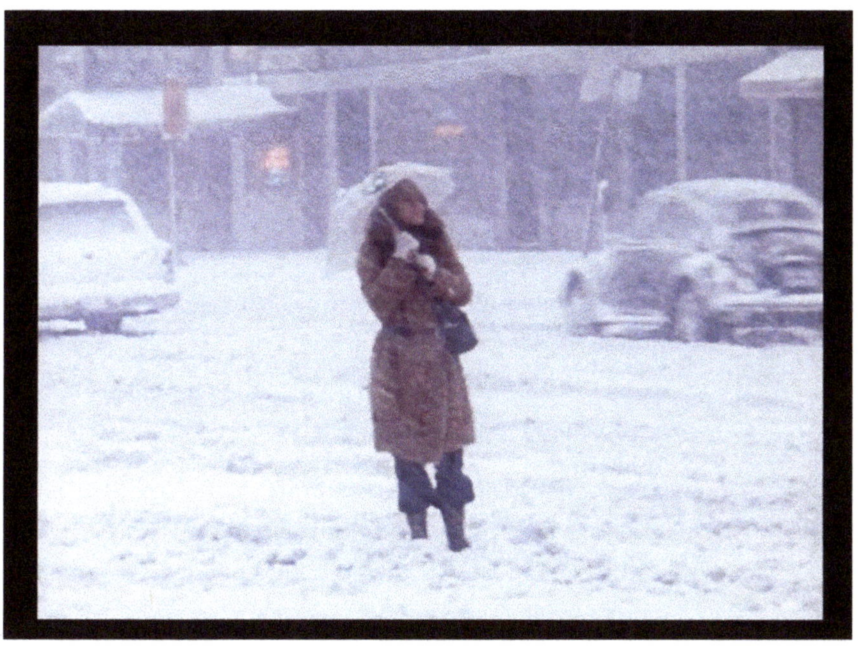

Reel 1 00:53

Mekas's New York is a city frequently covered in snow.

But in reality, even though in the 1960s snowfall in New York was not as rare as a warming climate would later make it, it was still not nearly as frequent as *Walden* would seem to suggest.

An explanation for the prominence of snowstorms in Mekas's imaginary New York was his nostalgia for the wintry landscape of his Lithuanian homeland. Mekas encouraged this interpretation in his 1973 interview with the *New Yorker* writer Calvin Tomkins:

> I thought I was shooting New York as it is but when I looked at the film I realized that my New York was a fantasy - that it does not really have so much snow. I was shooting my memories. Winter memories are very special to me. At home, everybody worked outside in the summer, but in the winter we all sat together in rooms, and so the memories of my childhood are very much of the winters.[1]

In a purely visual sense, this interpretation makes sense: when the city streets are hidden below a blanket of snow they can resemble the country fields of his home town when human life must submit to the whims of nature.

But this comment also explains that winter in Lithuania meant staying indoors. And interior scenes are indeed a frequent subject of *Walden*. But in New York Mekas obviously took great joy in being outdoors during and right after major snowfalls.

Walden's snow scenes were dense with celebratory activity - sledding and snowball fights - that were surely not always the reaction to snowstorms in rural Lithuania. Mekas's New York snowstorms are magical: the usually grey dirty streets turning pure white and their normally harried and ill-tempered inhabitants suddenly becoming playful as they were temporarily liberated from their normal routines.

There was nothing of the drudgery of a long winter of constant snow preventing people from working outside and forcing to gather indoors. Mekas's snowfalls were just the opposite: a joyous invitation to go outside and revel in the sudden escape from dreary routine.

3 FILM-MAKERS' CINEMATHEQUE

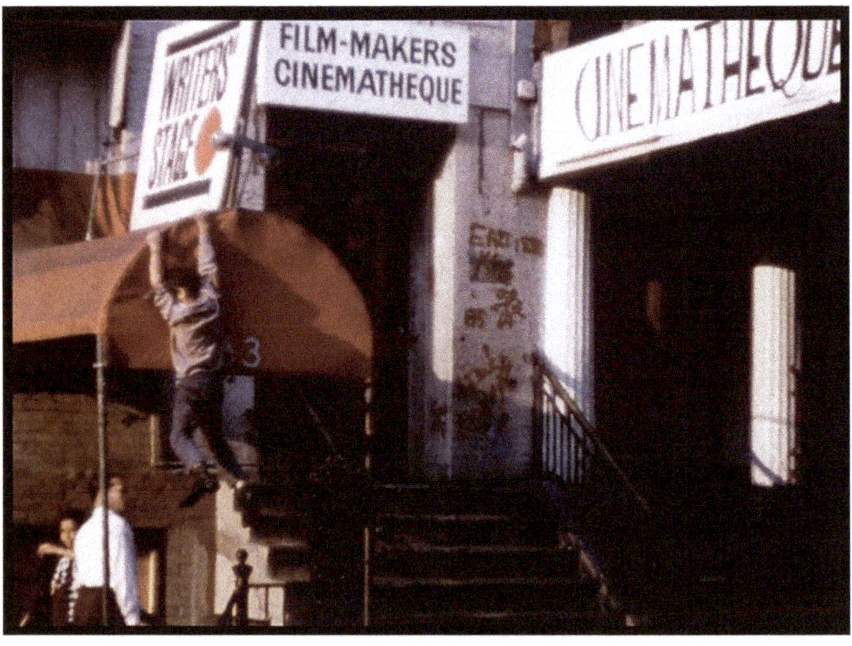

Reel 1 01:39

Although its signage on the street was prominent, the Film-Makers' Cinematheque at 83 East 4th St. turned out to be one of the most ephemeral of Mekas's multiple homes for his varied activities on behalf of the "New American Cinema."

The site was also the home of the "Writers' Stage," and in March of 1964 Mekas had rented it to show Jean Genet's *Un chant d'amour* (1950) to raise money for his legal defense after his arrest two weeks earlier for showing Jack Smith's *Flaming Creatures* (1963) at the New Bowery Theatre on Saint Mark's Place. He had correctly calculated that a film by a well-known writer would attract more support than one by the then little-known Jack Smith.

Eight months later on November 12, Mekas announced the formation of the "Film-Makers' Cinematheque" in the *Village Voice*. It was the continuation of programming he had previously called the "Film-Makers' Showcase" (not to be confused with his distribution efforts which were called the "Film-Makers Cooperative"). The announcement invited readers to become members of what was to be "a showcase of independent, underground, avant-garde cinema" and gave 83 East 4th St. as its mailing address.

On November 26, 1964, the Film-Makers' Cinematheque announced its first "members only" program featuring films by Warhol and others: "No single admissions will be sold...Memberships must be obtained in advance at the Film-Makers' Cinematheque, 83 East 4th St. by person or through mail."

At the end of December 1964, he issued a press release that noted:

> We are greatly aware that our current Monday midnight screenings are making it either undesirable or impossible for many to attend our screenings at the New Yorker Theater. Much work has been done during the past few months to ready our East 4th St. location for our membership. While we are able to say that our theatre is ready for screenings, we are waiting for action to be taken by the city on our

pending permits and licenses for occupancy. All we can do now is wait. The wheels of bureaucracy are turning slowly.

Meanwhile we shall have to continue at the New Yorker at our usual hour. The time and location of subsequent programs will be sent to you soon. Hopefully they will be at the Cinematheque on E. 4th St. Once located there we will have our screenings more often and at hours convenient for all.[1]

But it was not to be. Apparently the wheels of bureaucracy ground to a complete halt and no public programs were actually held at the 4th St. address. Yet Mekas retained the name Film-Makers' Cinematheque for programs at multiple locations around Manhattan for the rest of the decade until the founding of Anthology Film Archives in late 1970.

In 1979, Anthology was able to acquire and begin renovation of the Second Avenue Courthouse building and its two screening rooms opened to the public in 1988. It was less than 200 yards away from 83 East 4th St.

4 P. ADAMS SITNEY

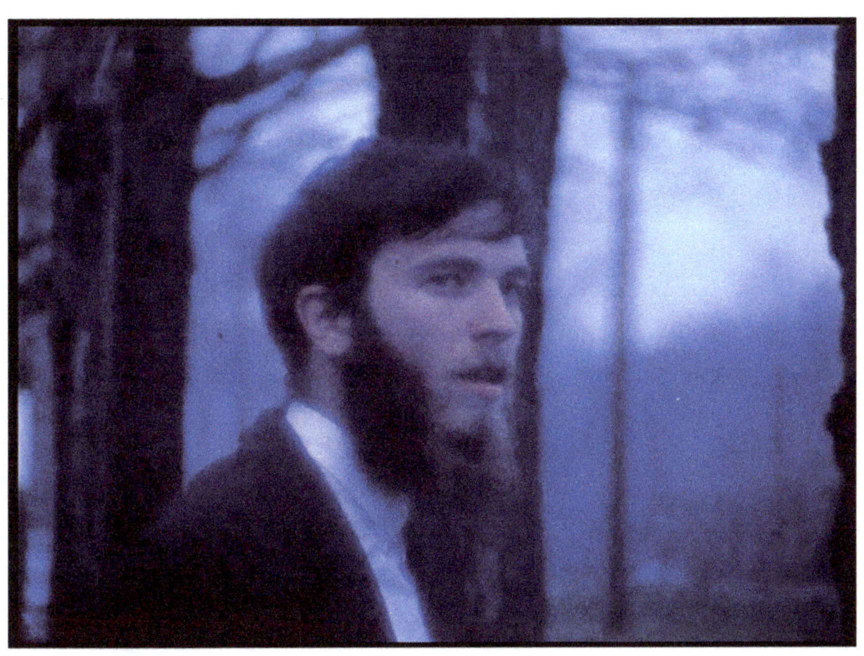

Reel 1 01:48

It is fitting that *Walden,* one of the major works of experimental film, documented the young adulthood of the scholar, writer and theorist who would, almost singlehandedly, establish the subject as a credible object of critical inquiry in American universities.

First published in 1974 by Oxford University Press, Sitney's *Visionary Film* would play a seminal role in the recognition of film as a subject of art history and his subsequent writing has been similarly influential.

He was barely out of his teens when *Walden* began to track major steps in his life: his departure from his childhood home in Connecticut (SITNEY DECIDES TO LEAVE NEW HAVEN, GOES TO NEW YORK), his decision to marry (SITNEY CATCHES THE GARTER, WILL HAVE TO MARRY NEXT), and then the ceremony itself (SITNEY'S WEDDING). One of *Walden*'s closing scenes concerned Sitney's literal transition to the role of patriarch (BLAKE SITNEY IS BORN).

Sitney was involved in every step of Mekas's struggle to establish a "New American Cinema" – first through exhibition (the Film-Makers Cinematheque) and distribution (the Film-Makers Coop) and then through Anthology Film Archives of which Sitney was a founding member.

But of even more lasting importance was Sitney's work as a critic and historian. In contrast to Mekas's own sometimes almost comically polemical approach in his weekly *Village Voice* columns, Sitney's writing was calm, scholarly, and eminently serious. And his *Visionary Cinema* surely reached a far wider audience than the films it described. In the pre-internet era, it was far easier to find Sitney's book than it was to see the films he so articulately defended.

Sitney's relative youth when he began would mean that his activity would extend beyond the lifetimes of most of his subjects. Over a half century after he appeared in the first minute of *Walden* (SITNEY IS FINGERPRINTED BY THE POLICE), Sitney's books - including *Eyes*

Upside Down and *The Cinema of Poetry* - continued to assert the rightful place of experimental film in the broader context of art history and criticism.

5 BARBARA & DAVID STONE

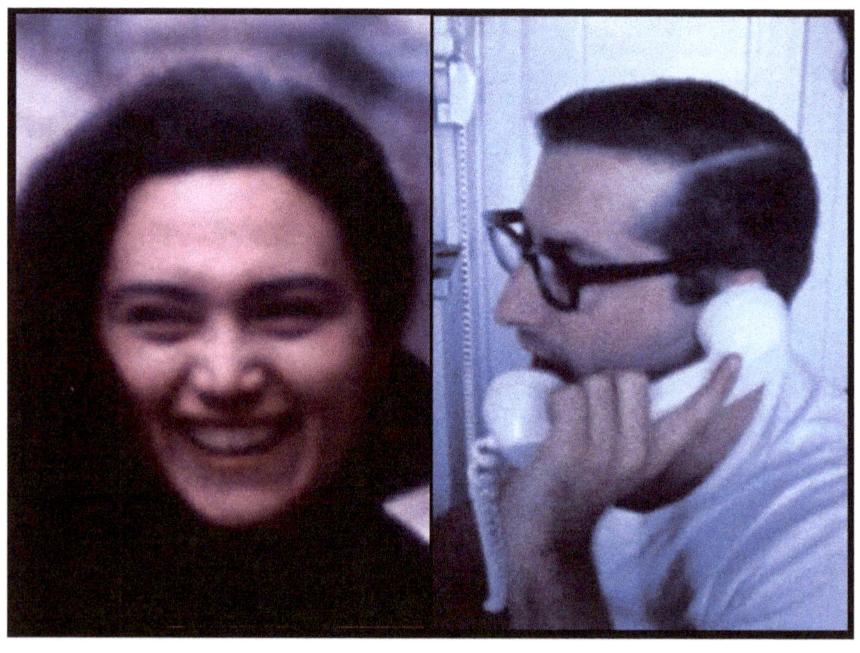

Reel 1 02:12

Despite his expressions of loneliness, Mekas seemed in *Walden* to be surrounded by a circle of devoted friends. And among the most visible were Barbara and David Stone.

Their friendship dated from Barbara's years as the circulation manager for *Film Culture* where she met David. They married in 1957. On September 28th, 1960, David was a co-signer of the "First Statement of the New American Group."

In 1961, the philanthropy of Jerome Hill enabled Mekas to send them as his representatives to the Festival dei Due Mondi arts festival in Spoleto Italy where the "New American Cinema" was exposed to Europeans for the first time. The Stones went on to produce Adolfas Mekas's first film *Hallelujah the Hills* in 1963 and Jonas's *The Brig* in 1964.

By the time of the opening sequences of *Walden*, the Stones had two small children, Alexandra and Jordon, and lived in an apartment overlooking Broadway (and the New Yorker Theater) on the Upper West Side. Judging by the frequency of their appearances in *Walden*, it seemed to have been a second home for Mekas.

Remembering David Stone after his death in 2011, critic Amy Taubin recalled:

> His and Barbara's sprawling, rent-controlled apartment on West 86th Street was a place where on any given night you might find Jonas Mekas, Michelangelo Antonioni, and the founding members of New York Newsreel arguing across huge potluck dinners.[1]

Defying the American ban on travel to Cuba, they made *Compañeras y Compañeros* (1970) with Adolfas Mekas and then left the U.S. As expatriates in London, they continued producing, distributing and exhibiting independent films for many decades. But during the years recorded in *Walden*, they were at the very center of Mekas's New York life.

6 CENTRAL PARK

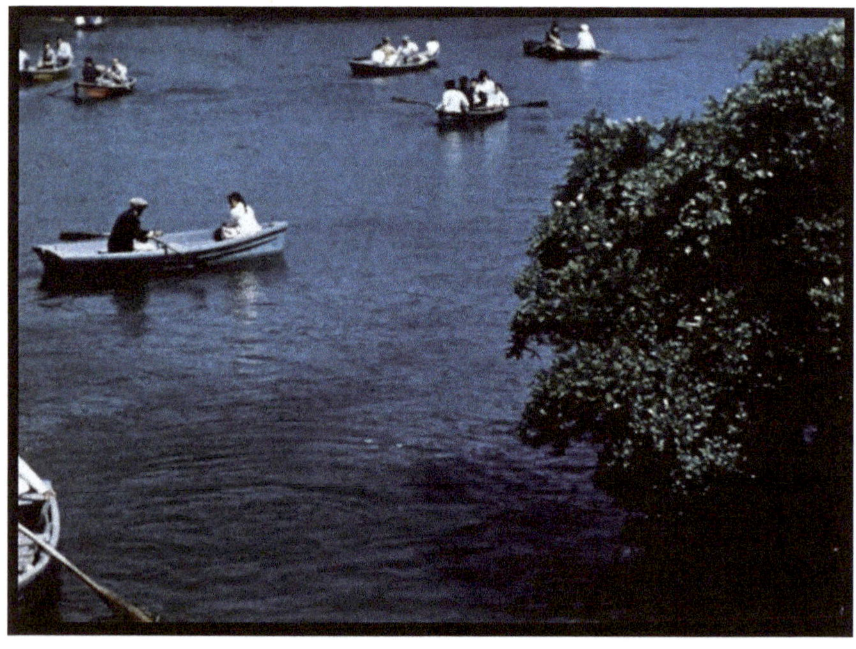

Reel 1 02:42

The name of Manhattan's largest park also described its role in *Walden*. It was central in an obvious geographical sense - the entrance at Columbus Circle where Mekas often filmed was literally midway between the Upper West Side where he lived for a while and frequently shared meals with the Stone family and downtown Manhattan where he wrote for the *Village Voice* and ran the Film-Makers' Cinematheque. But the park was also central to a major theme of his work - the celebration of natural spaces in a densely urban world.

Mekas's appropriation of the name of a pond in Concord, Mass-achusetts for the title of the first installment of his film diaries has inevitably led to analogies with Henry David Thoreau's book about his escape from society but there were more contradictions than similari-ties (see Chapter 23).

Central Park may have provided Mekas some respite from the noise and asphalt of Manhattan but it was not at all the escape from society Thoreau sought. Mekas's views of the park were often more crowded with people than those of the city streets surrounding it.

Thoreau retreated to Walden Pond in search of solitude but Central Park Lake had been designed by landscape architect Frederick Law Olmsted as a gathering place. As recorded by Mekas, it was filled with festive crowds, boaters in the summer and skaters in the winter. In March 1967 he filmed the "Be-In" organized by Parks Commissioner Thomas Hoving as part of a series of "Hoving Happenings" to get even more people to enjoy the city's green space.

Certain places and occasions seemed to trigger Mekas's impulse to take out his camera and begin shooting short bursts of frames. The entrances to Central Park, either from the Upper West Side at 90th St. or at Columbus Circle at 59th St. were such places.

7 BEVERLY GRANT & TONY CONRAD

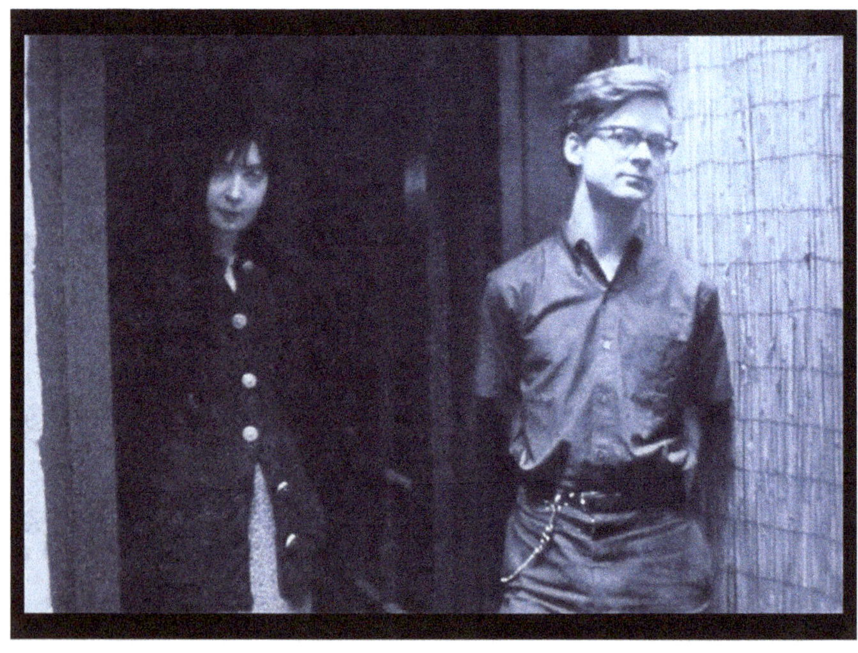

Reel 1 02:50

Beverly Grant had studied acting at the Stella Adler Studio, performed at Ronald Tavel's "Theatre of the Ridiculous" and played in a number of Jack Smith and Andy Warhol films, including the one which was later to be the source of Mekas's tumultuous battles against censorship, *Flaming Creatures* (1963). Its soundtrack was the creation of an artist she would later marry, Tony Conrad, who was sharing an apartment with Smith at the time.

Conrad had trained as a mathematician at Harvard and worked on computer programming which led him into electronic music in New York and the explorations of La Monte Young and John Cale in "The Theatre of Eternal Music."

During their married years in New York in the 1960s, Grant and Conrad were active in a myriad of creative endeavors from off-off Broadway theater to experimental music.

Conrad's first film *The Flicker* (1965), consisting of alternating black and white frames that produced a hypnotic effect when projected, became a landmark work in what critic P. Adams Sitney would later label "structural film." Mekas was instrumental in its making, providing Conrad with a camera and film.

In 1970 Grant and Conrad produced *Coming Attractions* which also used a flicker-like effect but within a narrative film structure. In 1972, they toured Europe together, establishing contact between the American "underground" and European film artists such as Malcolm Le Grice in Britain, Wilhelm and Birgit Hein in Germany, and Otto Muehl in Austria.

8 GIRLS IN THE PARK

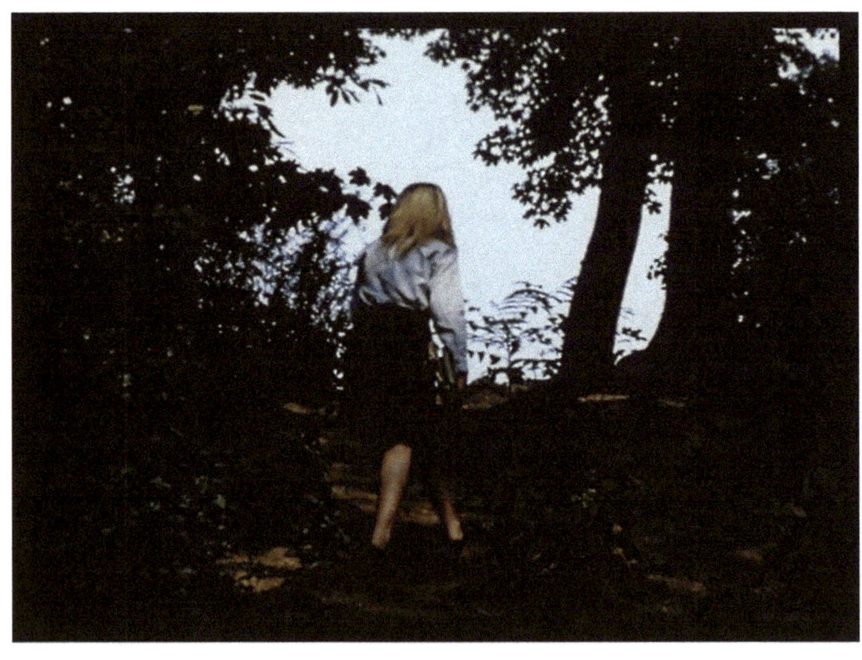

Reel 1 03:44

Mekas had been documenting his own life with a 16mm camera almost from the time he had arrived in the U.S. in 1949. But he did not appear to have thought of a first person diary as a valid form for a finished film until he received a commission from the Albright-Knox Gallery in Buffalo in 1967.

Instead he had made two feature-length narrative films, *Guns of the Trees* (1961) and *The Brig* (1964), and was planning a third:

> During the period when I was shooting the *Walden* material, I wanted to make a diary film of a teenage girl just leaving childhood and entering adolescence. I was collecting diaries and letters of girls of that age, and making many notes. I wanted to make a film - actually, a series of three or four films, one of a girl fifteen, one of a woman and a man twenty-five; then forty-five; then sixty-five. I never progressed beyond the notes. But on several occasions I took some shots with three or four girls whom I thought I would use in that film. I always filmed them in the park. Some of the young women were friends of friends....[1]

Clearly Mekas was still thinking of a third-person approach. From behind the camera, he would recount the story of a young woman keeping a diary - perhaps somewhat in the manner of George Steven's commercially successful 1959 film, *The Diary of Anne Frank*.

But his narrative feature was never made. Instead the test sequences of young girls served as a reminder of how close Mekas came to not making his simple but extraordinary discovery: a first person film diary had far more possibilities than a fictional story about an imaginary heroine.

9 BIBBE HANSEN

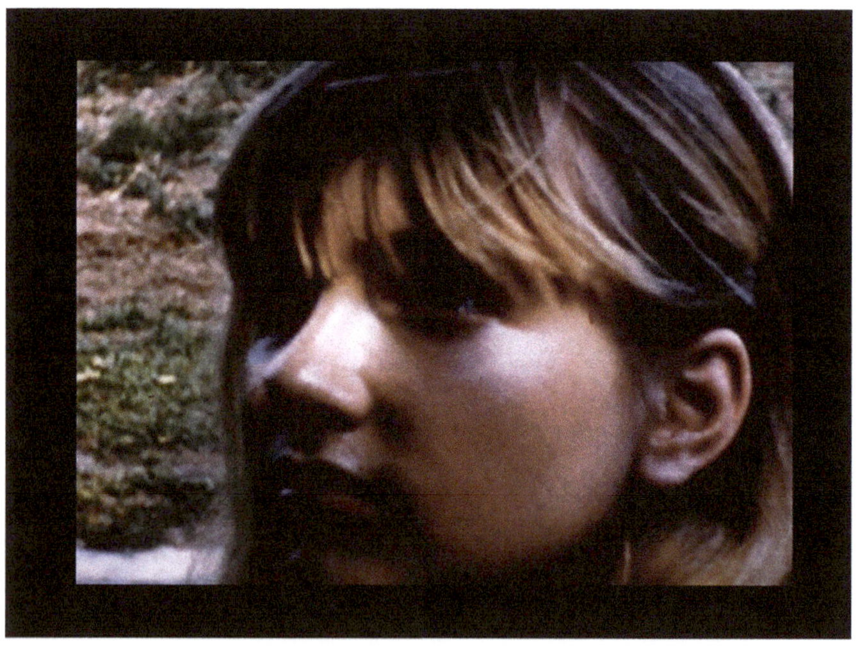

Reel 1 03:44

Bibbe Hansen was the only young woman Mekas mentions by name among the "friends of friends" he filmed in Central Park for a possible role in his never-to-be-made fictional film.

She was the daughter of Al Hansen, an early member of George Maciunas's art collective, the Fluxus. Al Hansen created performance pieces and happenings that included a famous one named in honor of another Fluxus collaborator, the "Yoko One Piano Drop." He was also an active participant in the Warhol entourage - doubtless a factor in Warhol's choice of his daughter for his film *The Thirteen Most Beautiful Women* (1964).

As an adult, Bibbe Hansen would keep her father's legacy alive by giving lectures and performances that explained and paid tribute to Al Hansen and Fluxus.

10 GENERAL POST OFFICE

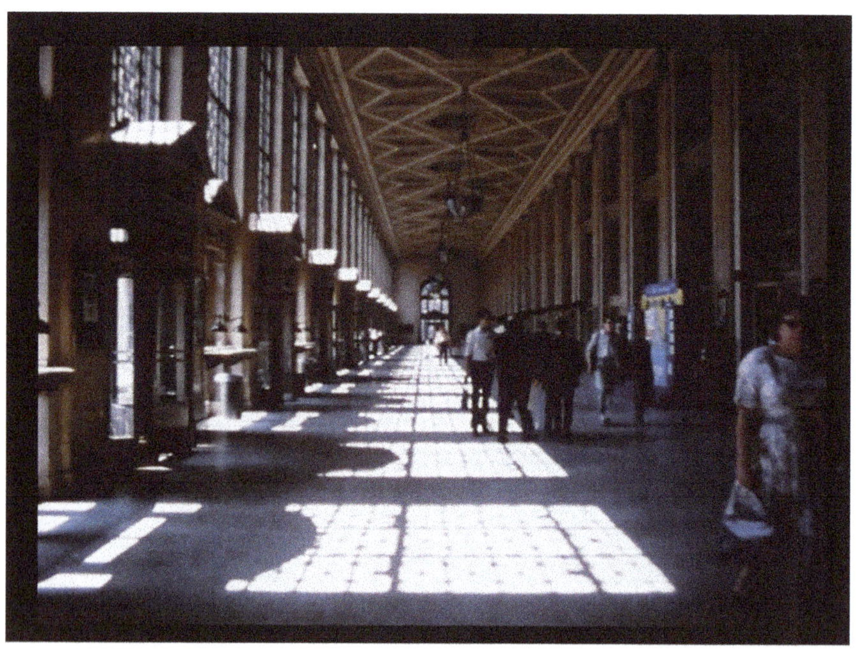

Reel 1 08:09

The chronology of his diaries (which Mekas did not always strictly respect in the final version of *Walden*) would indicate that he filmed the New York General Post Office in 1965.

Since its official designation as a New York City Landmark would not come until the following year, it is possible that he suspected the majestic structure was going to suffer the same fate as the one across the street, what had been New York's most magnificent building, Pennsylvania Station.

The demolition of Penn Station had begun in late 1963. By the time Mekas filmed the post office much of the train station had been reduced to rubble.

The Post Office's monumental facade on Eighth Avenue consisted of a majestic Corinthian colonnade that was meant to match the equally imposing colonnade of Penn Station. Both had been designed by the architectural firm McKim, Mead & White. As Mekas's views show, the interior featured an unbroken vista down a long gallery that parallels the colonnaded front.

When it was completed in 1910, Penn Station was considered a masterpiece of the Beaux-Arts style and one of the great architectural works of New York City. The equally impressive Post Office opened for business in 1914. But passenger travel by train had begun to decline after World War II, and in the 1950s, the Pennsylvania Railroad sold the air rights to the property and it was scheduled for demolition.

On August 2, 1962, a group of concerned citizens had protested its demolition in front of the station. They were supported by luminaries that included Philip Johnson, Aline Saarinen, Eleanor Roosevelt, Jane Jacobs, and Norman Mailer. But to no avail.

But, though too late to save the building, Images of its destruction fueled a public outrage that is often credited with igniting the historic preservation movement in the United States. Comparing the original

Penn Station with its replacement, the architectural historian Vincent Scully noted "One entered the city like a god; one scuttles in now like a rat."[1]

11 DAVID BROOKS

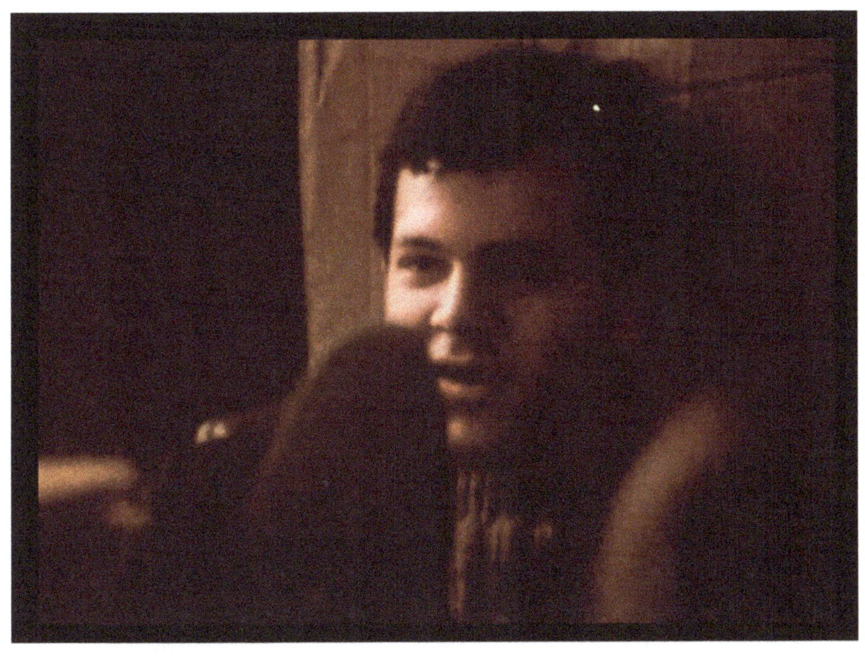

Reel 1 08:34

David Brooks might have become the most celebrated film artist to emerge from the group of young people that Mekas gathered to help with his multiple activities in the early 1960s.

Brooks's lyrically personal films used the medium quite differently from the more formal, concept-driven works which P. Adams Sitney was to describe as "structural film." Brooks' last and longest work, *The Wind is Driving Him Toward the Open Sea* (1968) was described by critic Fred Camper as a "sprawling, lyrical attempt to come to terms with the world's small beauties and large disappointments that is at once exhilarating and melancholy."

When Mekas named him the Executive Director of the newly-formed Film-Makers' Cooperative in 1962, the 18 year-old Brooks was enrolled at Columbia but soon abandoned his studies for filmmaking. He produced the Cooperative's first distribution catalogue but completed only a few films before his death in an automobile accident in 1969.

But those few were so close in spirit to Mekas's own that his description of them in the *Village Voice,* could be a statement of his intentions for his own new film, *Walden*:

> The film is as poetic as its title...David Brooks manages to fuse in it a number of different techniques which till now have been used only in non-narrative, poetic films - techniques such as single frame, free, impressionistic camera movement, almost total plotlessness, etc. The other thing that I like about *The Wind* is a fascinating melancholy that surrounds it. It's a narrative of moods, of reflection, of things lost, gone, like autumn leaves - no tragedy, really, only a mood of melancholy, of sadness - of friends, of ways of life, of cultures gone, of ages coming and going - these are just some of the notes that the film strikes. Romanticism? Perhaps.[1]

12 HARRY SMITH

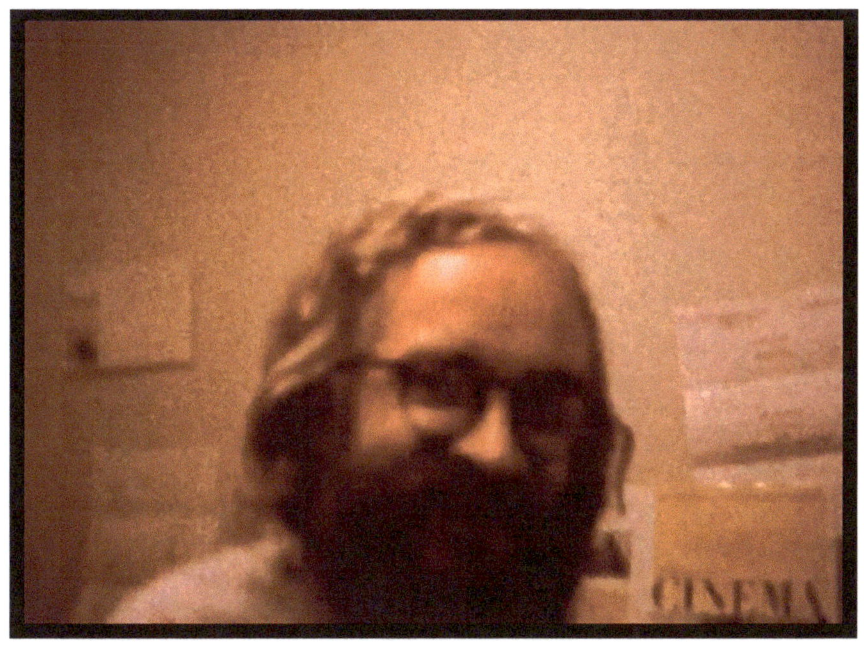

Reel 1 08:40

Any one of Harry Smith's multiple passions would have made him a notable figure in 20th century American culture.

He was an anthropologist and musicologist. When still a teenager in the Pacific Northwest, he recorded the songs and religious rituals of Native American tribes and built an extensive collection of their sacred objects. Later, he travelled the country collecting the earliest recordings of traditional folk music and himself making some of the only recordings ever made of its greatest practitioners. It resulted in the *Anthology of American Folk Music* which became the point of reference for the musicians who revived American folk music in the 1960s. He also befriended and championed major figures of progressive jazz.

But despite his singular contribution to music, Smith considered painting his primary interest and, by extension, what he described as "color music" which he had decided could be expressed in film. He had already been experimenting with applying painterly techniques directly to the physical surface of film when he arrived in San Francisco in the late 1940s and met the artists of the "West Coast avant-garde" - among them Jordan Belson, Hy Hirsch, and the exiled German pioneer of "visual music," Oskar Fischinger.

The first of his series of *Early Abstractions* made between 1946 and 1952 premiered with live jazz accompaniment in May 1950 as part of the Art in Cinema series curated by Frank Stauffacher at the San Francisco Museum of Art. Mekas was later to write about Smith's series that:

> You can watch them for pure color enjoyment; you can watch them for motion - Harry Smith's films never stop moving; or you can watch them for hidden symbolic meanings, alchemic signs. There are more levels in Harry Smith's work than in any other film animator I know.[1]

Smith arrived in New York in 1952 where he would spend most of the rest of his working life and continue making extraordinarily rich films in addition to his intense involvement in occult sciences, music, and painting.

Much of his prodigious creative activity was conducted in his small room at the Chelsea Hotel and later at the home of Allen Ginsberg who tried to provide for him. But Smith was disdainful of the practical demands of daily life, bartering away much of his art work and incurring debts that were left to Ginsberg to pay. His survival depended entirely on the generosity of his few devoted friends of which Mekas was unfailingly one. He died in 1991 at the Chelsea Hotel.

13 WEDDINGS

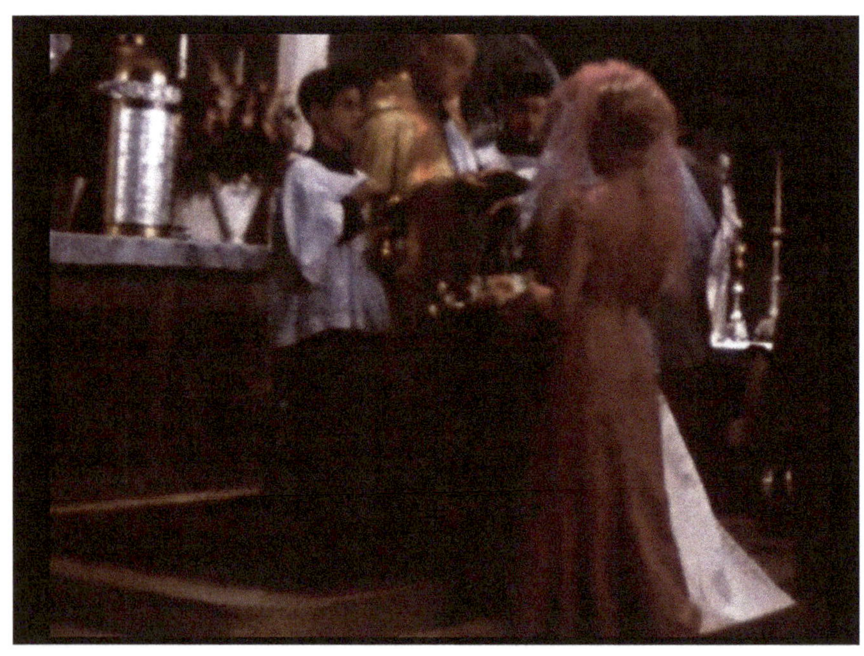

Reel 1 09:04

Walden is rich in wedding celebrations. There are those of Mekas's brother, Adolfas, of his collaborator, P. Adams Sitney, of Wendy, daughter of fellow filmmaker Shirley Clarke, and his wealthy friend, photographer Peter Beard.

> There are a lot of weddings in my diaries. A wedding is a big event in anybody's life; it's colorful and there's always a lot of celebration. As a child, I remembered for years my sister's wedding. Where I come from, weddings go on for a week or two. Occasions like that attract me. There are, of course, no such weddings here. But I film them anyway, hoping to find the wedding of my memory.[1]

The most significant one for Mekas personally was surely the first shown, his brother's, for it marked the end of their life together after the painful years in displaced persons camps in Germany and those spent struggling to survive in their early years in New York. Immediately following it, Mekas's physical loneliness can be felt in the scenes of his half-empty apartment just after Adolfas moved out.

But the wedding celebration itself seems to have been joyous, a chance to celebrate with both friends from his old life - fellow Lithuanian poets Leo Adams and Algirdas Landsbergis and those of his new one. Visible among the latter were Barbara Rubin, P. Adams Sitney, and Ed Emshwiller.

The other weddings may have been less personal but Mekas captured the festivities devotedly - a measure of the importance he still attached to the ritualized occasion as a way to reinforce bounds of community and friendship. They played the same role for him in New York as they had in rural Lithuania.

14 POLA CHAPELLE

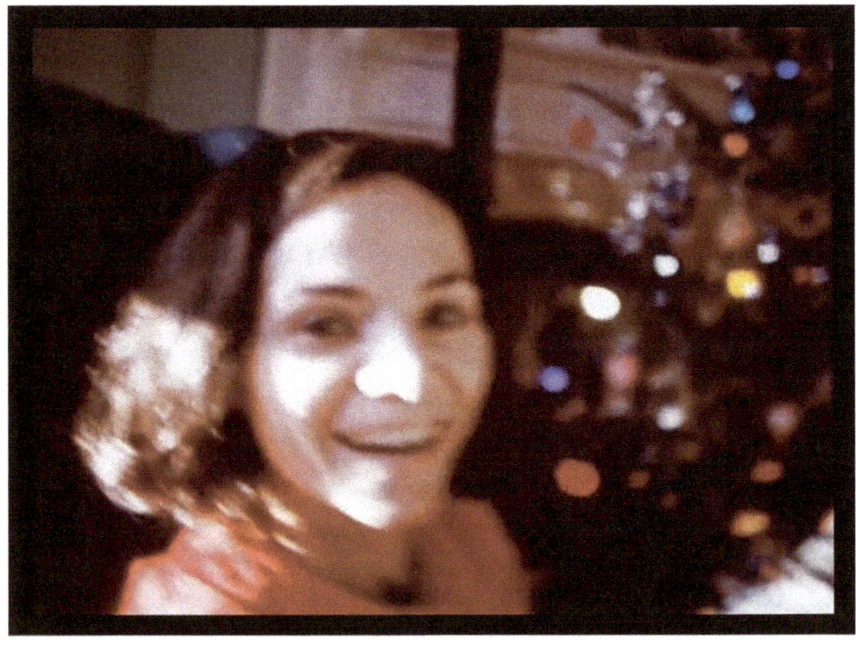

Reel 1 09:29

When Mekas began to edit his film diaries, he started with sequences from the beginning of 1965, the year his life had been changed by the marriage of his brother Adolfas to Pola Chapelle. Their wedding ceremony is the first significant event that he recorded but images of his charismatic sister-in-law would recur throughout *Walden*.

Chapelle was a professional singer who both appeared in and provided music for Adolfas's films. She had had a career as a cabaret singer, recorded an album of folk songs she had learned while on tour in Italy, and was the musical director and a production assistant for a variety of Adolfas's film projects as well as those of other Mekas friends including Storm de Hirsch's *Goodbye in the Mirror* (1965).

In 1969 she founded and curated INTERCAT '69: The First International Cat Film Festival at the Elgin Theatre, assembling films about cats from an impressive array of film artists that included Robert Breer, Joyce Wieland, Standish Lawder, Alexander Hammid and Maya Deren.

Chapelle accompanied Jonas and Adolfas on their first trip back to Lithuania in 1971 which each of them documented on film. She not only recorded the sound for Jonas's *Reminiscences of a Journey to Lithuania* (1972), and Adolfas's *Going Home* (1971), but shot her own record of the trip, *Journey to Lithuania* (1971).

She continued several of Adolfas's ventures after his death, notably his Hallelujah Editions, "Publisher of the Unpublishable," which included three volumes of *The Adolfas Diaries*, the daily journal of Adolfas in Lithuania and Germany, from 1941 to 1946.

15 ADOLFAS MEKAS

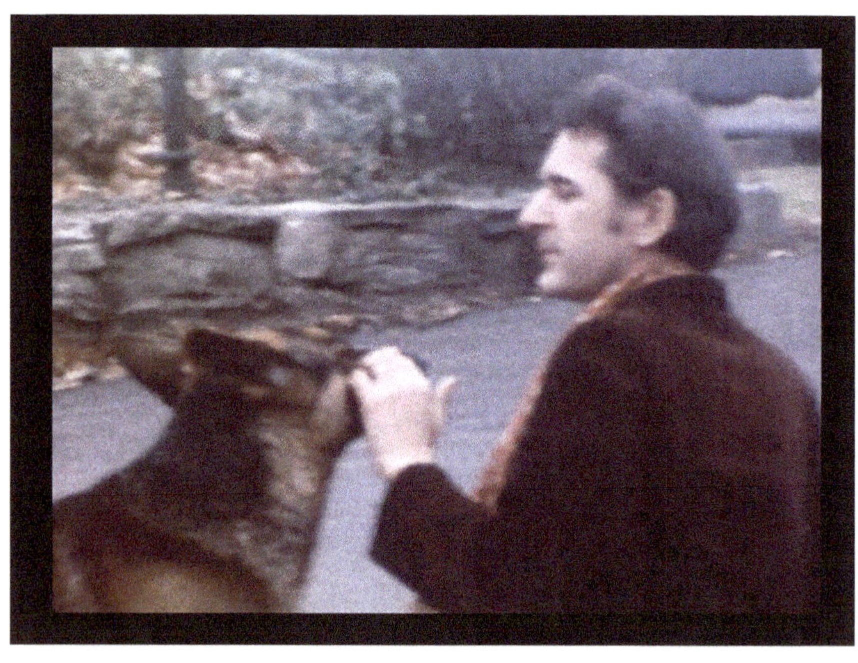

Reel 1 09;55

Mekas's younger brother had shared his exodus from their native Lithuania, his time in a German displaced persons camp and, finally, exile in the U.S. starting in 1949. Shortly after their arrival, the brothers purchased a Bolex 16mm camera and threw themselves into a variety of film activities in New York.

One of their projects was the magazine *Film Culture* whose first issue appeared in 1954. Others included the feature length films *Guns of the Trees* (1961) and *Hallelujah the Hills* (1963), and the filmed performance of the Living Theater production of *The Brig* (1964) directed by Judith Malina.

As documented in *Walden*, Adolfas's marriage to Pola Chapelle in 1965 and his moving out of the apartment he shared with Jonas proved to be a pivotal event in Jonas's development of the diary film.

While his brother was inventing a new form of personal filmmaking, Adolfas's ambitions focussed on the realm of traditional narrative and documentary film. But he remained a recurrent presence in his brother's diaries, appearing in key sequences such as the excursion to New Jersey to make an "underground" film for Gideon Bachman's German television crew, or in the visit to Hans Richter's country home in Connecticut.

Adolfas founded his own press, Hallelujah Editions, and published three volumes of his own written diaries detailing the brothers' lives in internment camps in Lithuania and Germany.

But his crowning achievement was in the academic world. When he died in 2011, P. Adams Sitney contributed to his obituary published in *The Brooklyn Rail*:

> He took a job at Bard College to hold himself over for a year or two and stayed on for some four decades. What he came to call "The People's Film Department" was his theater of hijinks; for he surprised even himself with his enormous didactic gifts, his startling administra-

tive skill, and his unceasing fount of comic invention. His own fractured education and his nearly total disregard for academic decorum made him the ideal professor. Nowhere in the archives of film is there an invented character who could come near the brilliant, lovable, outrageous mischief that consistently turned his classrooms into arenas of magic. He taught generations how to see and act.[1]

16 ED EMSHWILLER

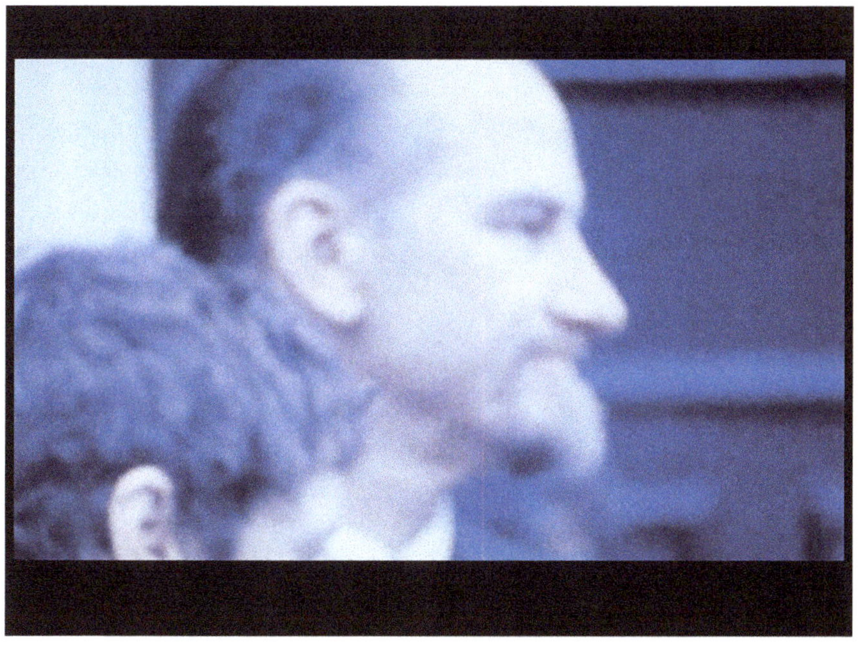

Reel 1 11:03

When Ed Emshwiller attended Adolfas Mekas's wedding in 1965, he was renowned not just as a science fiction illustrator (he had won multiple Hugo Awards from the World Science Fiction Society), but also as both an accomplished film artist in his own right and a cinematographer on films by others.

Though formally trained as a painter, Emhswiller seemed unconcerned with notions of hierarchy among art forms. From the early 1950s, he was known for cover paintings and text illustrations of science fiction books and magazines. In 2007, the Museum of Popular Culture in Seattle inducted him into their Science Fiction and Fantasy Hall of Fame.

In 1959 he began experimenting with extending his abstract paintings through time by filming them with a moving camera and accompanying the result with improvisational jazz. The result was his first film: *Transformation.*

The same year he made *Dance Chromatic,* the first example of how his unusual grace as a cameraman could complement and enhance the movements of dancers. He was soon in demand as a cinematographer, notably for Adolfas Mekas's feature *Hallelujah the Hills* (1963) and D.A. Pennebaker's *Don't Look Back* about Bob Dylan's 1965 tour of England.

On his own Emshwiller went on to make a number of masterful 16mm films often in collaboration with dancers - notably *Lifelines* (1960) *Thanatopsis* (1962) and *Relativity* (1966). But his imagination continued to push him into new forms of image-making and, in 1972, he became one of the first artists-in-residence at the Television Laboratory at WNET/Thirteen, New York, and began to explore video technology.

Of his first effort there, *Scape-Mates* (1972), the New York Times television critic John J. O'Conner wrote:

The result, suggesting both eerie landscape and claustrophobic escape, works impressively, going beyond experiment to solid achievement. One note: It demands a color-TV set. Apparently, Mr. Emshwiller has been impressed with the medium of video. He is quoted as saying: "It's a terrific way to choreograph visual material. It gives an artist access to dimensions that previously, could not be visually expressed."[1]

In 1979, he made *Sunstone*, a pioneering foray into 3-D computer-generated video. When he died in 1990, he was the dean of the School of Film/Video at the California Institute of Arts and working at their Computer Animation Lab, exploring the possibilities of digital imagery decades before most other artists.

17 LEO ADAMS

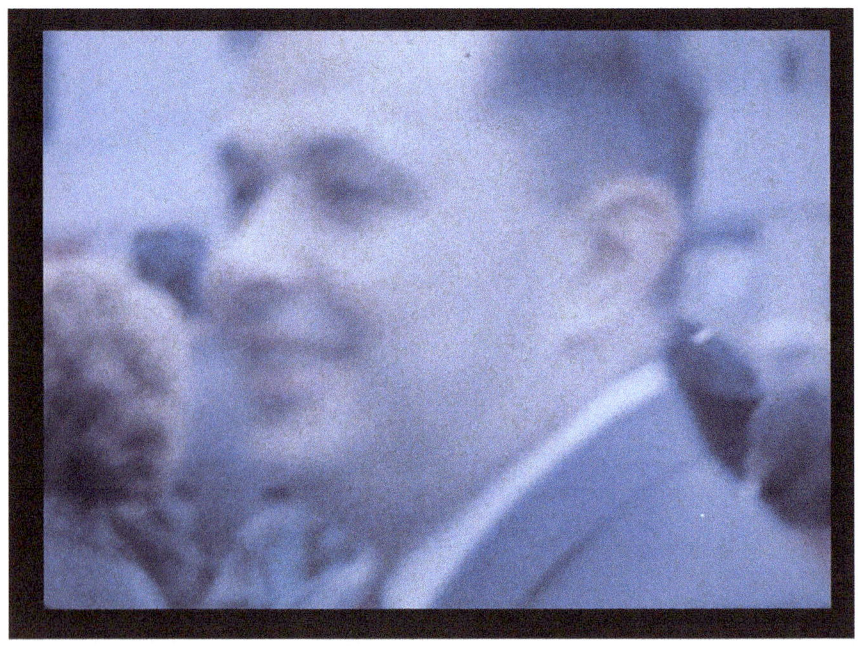

Reel 1 11:05

Adolfas Mekas's wedding was the occasion for a New York reunion of the Lithuanian avant-garde literary scene that had survived multiple Displaced Persons Camps in Germany. The Mekas brothers had met Leo Adams and fellow poet Algirdas Landsbergis while living in such a camp in Wiesbaden, Germany in the fall of 1945. By 1947 they had all been transferred to another camp in Kassel where they somehow requisitioned a mimeograph machine and established *Zvilgsniai,* a publishing house and literary journal.

They produced four mimeographed issues with Jonas Mekas as editor-in-chief and Adolfas Mekas, Leo Adams, and Algirdas Landsbergis as assisting editors. *Zvilgsniai* also published *Proza,* a selection of Lithuanian post-war novels, including one by Jonas and Landsbergis. Most of the group's publications were designed by Leo Adams.

On October 10, 1950, a year after their own arrival, the Mekas brothers welcomed Adams to New York.

In his adopted country, Adams continued to write in Lithuanian using the pen name Leonas Lėtas (Leo the Slow) as well as his original Lithuanian name, Vytautas Leonas Adamkeviciaus for his poems.

Their reunion at Adolfas Mekas's wedding in 1965 was a happier time than their first years in New York about which Mekas wrote:

> It hurts very much not to have anybody here that I could really talk with, except two or three old friends. Leo, Algis, Adolfas - we have nothing to say to each other anymore, we sit silent now, like three mountains, we have said everything to each other. [1]

18 ALGIRDAS LANDSBERGIS

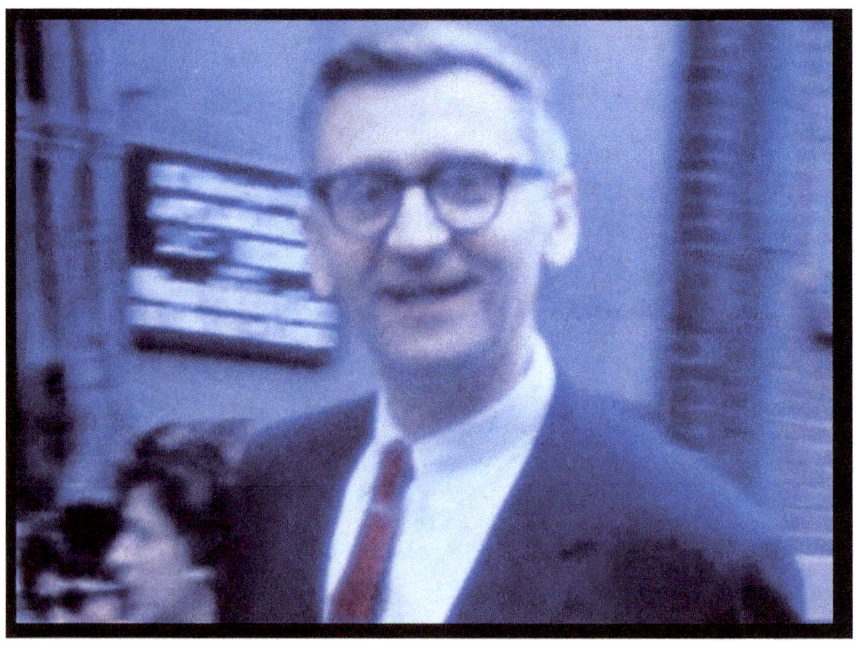

Reel 1 11:08

Algirdas Landsbergis was the fourth member, along with Leo Adams and the Mekas brothers, of the quartet of exiles who had dedicated themselves to the advancement of Lithuanian literature, first in German Displaced Person camps until 1949, and then in the United States.

Landsbergis was the first of the group to arrive in America and was on hand to welcome the Mekas brothers to New York on October 29, 1949. There the brothers' interests soon turned to film but his remained resolutely literary.

Along with Mekas, Landsbergis had been able to study at the University of Mainz while still in Germany and, once in New York, continued studying at Columbia. He worked in journalism and broadcasting, and taught literature, all the time continuing to write stories, plays, and a novel, mostly in his native Lithuanian. He was active in PEN, the international writers' association dedicated to defending writers in exile.

His 1954 novel *Kelionė* (*Journey*) was described as "in the spirit of the Beat generation, like Jack Kerouac's *On the Road* (1950)"[1] and described a community of exiles thrown together in a displaced persons camp in postwar Germany.

19 TRAIN TRAVEL

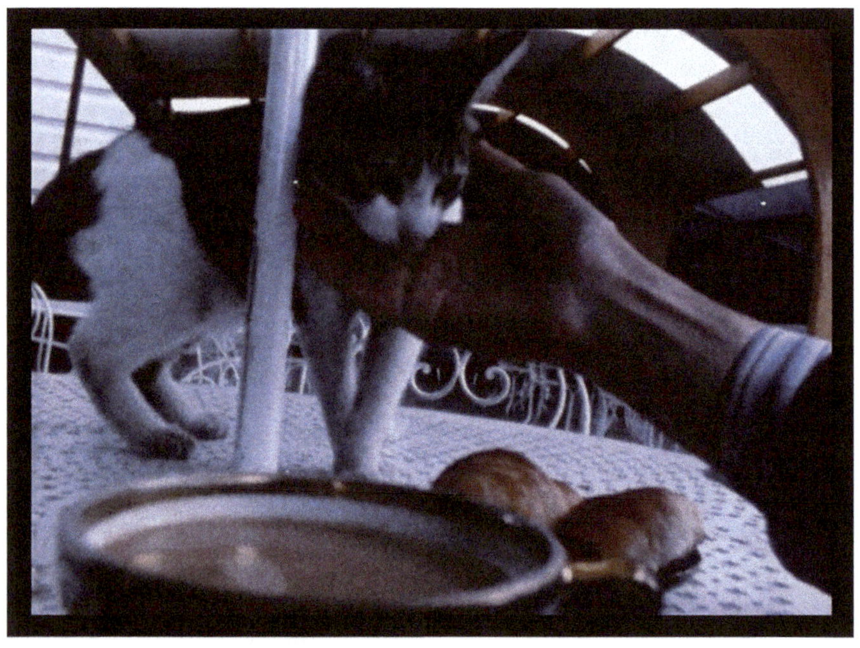

Reel 1 13:18

Just before the scenes of the wedding of Pola Chapelle and Adolfas Mekas an intertitle reads MORBID DAYS OF NEW YORK & GLOOM. It is followed by shots of their half-empty apartment with the intertitle "AL MOVES OUT." Mekas had lived with his brother since his arrival in the U.S. Now he was alone and the tone seemed set for morbidity and gloom.

And then suddenly he is at a cafe eating a croissant on the terrace of the Marseilles train station. On the soundtrack he sings "I am searching for nothing. I am happy."

The sequences are not in chronological order. Before being invited by the Albright-Knox Gallery to compose what would become *Walden*, Mekas had extracted sections of footage he had shot in 1966 and put them into distribution as four separate short films: *Cassis, Notes on the Circus, Hare Krishna,* and *Report from Millbrook* (see Chapter 36).

He later decided to include the four sections into the larger diary film of *Walden* but not in order. He inserted *Cassis,* shot in June 1966, before *Notes on the Circus,* which was shot in May, and directly after his brother's wedding, shot in 1965, and then preceded it with BREAK-FAST IN MARSEILLES. The reason seems to be to signal a major change in mood.

Mekas had spent the first 27 years of his life in Europe, the last of them under grim conditions in Germany. And when he returned for the first time in 1963, it was to do battle with state censorship at Knokke-le-Zoute on the wintry coast of Belgium.

But this return to Europe is a flight in the other direction. The morbidity and gloom was back in New York. At the Marseille train station are the simple pleasures of morning coffee and Mediterranean light. And the prospect of another train ride, a recurring source of joy in *Walden.*

Mekas was on his way to visit his old friend Jerome Hill in the small port of Cassis and had likely just arrived in Marseille by train from

Paris. Here he would have had to change to a local train heading east along the Côte d'Azur. Cassis would be the train's first stop; the second, La Ciotat, was perhaps the most famous train station in the history of film.

L'Arrivée d'un train en gare de La Ciotat was shot by the Lumière brothers in 1895. The story, probably apocryphal, was that when the Lumières projected it in the room they had rented for the occasion in Paris, the audience panicked and stampeded to the exits, fearing they were about to be crushed by the approaching train.

The story has survived not because it is literally true but because it evoked an underlying truth about the power of projected moving images. In the opening titles of *Walden*, Mekas dedicated his film to the Lumière brothers.

And, like the Lumières, Mekas understood the affinities between film and train travel. Just after his train voyage to Cassis, Mekas filmed his ride back to New York City from a visit to St. Vincent College near Pittsburgh and another as he travels to Timothy Leary's retreat in Millbrook, N.Y. The longest of such sequences recorded his travel to the home of Stan and Jane Brakhage outside Denver, Colorado.

Despite the precipitous decline in the quality of passenger rail travel in the U.S. during the 1960s, almost all of his trips outside of New York recorded in *Walden* were by train and they are among the most joyfully lyrical sequences in the film.

20 CASSIS

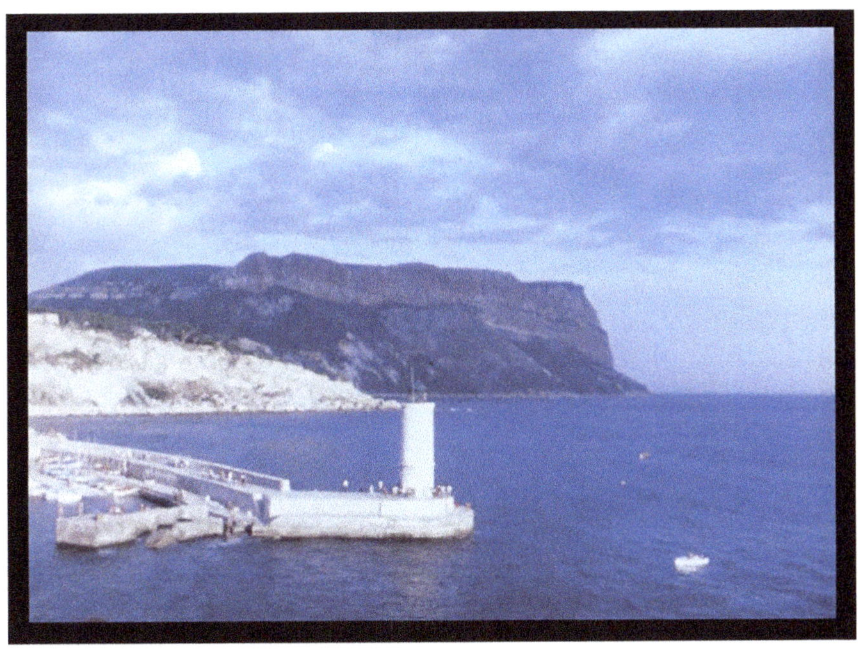

Reel 1 14:13

It was not the first time that the sponsor of Mekas's trip to France, Jerome Hill, had come to his rescue at dark moments.

Hill's financial support had enabled Mekas to continue publishing *Film Culture* when he could not pay its printer, and then helped the Film-Makers' Cooperative and the Film-Makers' Cinematheque to survive. Hill would later make Anthology Film Archives possible.

In 1937 Hill's inherited fortune had allowed him to purchase a majestic property overlooking the harbor of the port of Cassis near Marseilles. He regularly spent his summers there at work on his multiple creative passions - painting, music, and film, all of which he practiced with considerable skill.

On the grounds of his villa he had built an outdoor theater where he invited music and theater groups to perform. One of the latter was Judith Malina's and Julian Beck's Living Theater. In the summer of 1966, Hill commissioned them to stage their production of *Frankenstein* and asked Mekas, who had filmed the Living Theater's 1964 production *The Brig*, to come to Cassis to record the performances.

Mekas described the event as "the greatest theatre experience of my life."[1] Decades later, he edited his footage of the Living Theater's four-hour production into a 90-minute film he called *Memories of Frankenstein* (1996).

But at the time what clearly interested Mekas more than theater was the studio on Hill's property, a former Napoleonic-era guardhouse that had previously been used by the painter Paul Signac. In 1889 Signac had painted a view from its balcony: *Cassis Cap Canaille*.

Shot from exactly where Signac had painted, Mekas's film poem, *Cassis* was a lyrical time-lapse sequence of boats leaving and entering the harbor from dawn to dusk, an animated reincarnation of *Cassis Cap Canaille* and a very long way from New York's gloom.

21 STAN BRAKHAGE

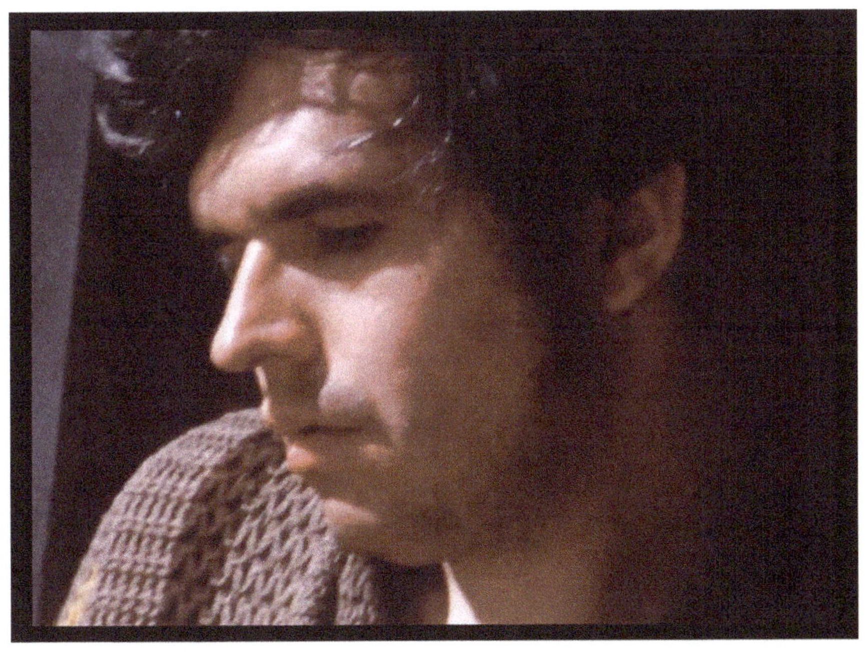

Reel 1 17:46

From his earliest "psychodramas" made when still in his teens to, a half century later, his majestic abstract films made by scratching and painting directly on the surface of the film, Brakhage's monumental output is one of the most significant in the history of experimental film. And throughout his years as a columnist for the *Village Voice* from 1959 to 1971, Mekas never stopped saying so.

On October 26, 1961, Mekas wrote in his *Movie Journal* column in the *Village Voice*:

> I will begin by stating that Brakhage is one of the four or five most authentic film artists working in cinema anywhere, and perhaps the most original film-maker in America today.[1]

Shortly afterward, he bestowed on him the *Film Culture* Fourth Independent Film Award for *The Dead* (1960) and *Prelude* (1961), writing that Brakhage's films showed "an intelligence and subtlety that is usually the province of the older arts" and, on August 2nd 1962, as part of his "Filmmakers Festival" at the Charles Theater, Mekas organized the "World Premiere" of Brakhage's *Anticipation of the Night* (1958).

Like Mekas, Brakhage also wrote about film and his texts, *Metaphors on Vision* first published in 1963 and later *A Motion Picture Giving and Taking Book* in 1971 reached through words a generation of artists who may not have been able to see his films.Brakhage was not just an ally in Mekas's defense of film art but, as his multiple appearances in *Walden* attest, also a friend. He was visible in the first reel at Sitney's wedding and in the last at Anthology Film Archives. And the longest single episode in *Walden* documents a visit to Brakhage's mountain home in Rollinsville, Colorado.

22 CARL DREYER

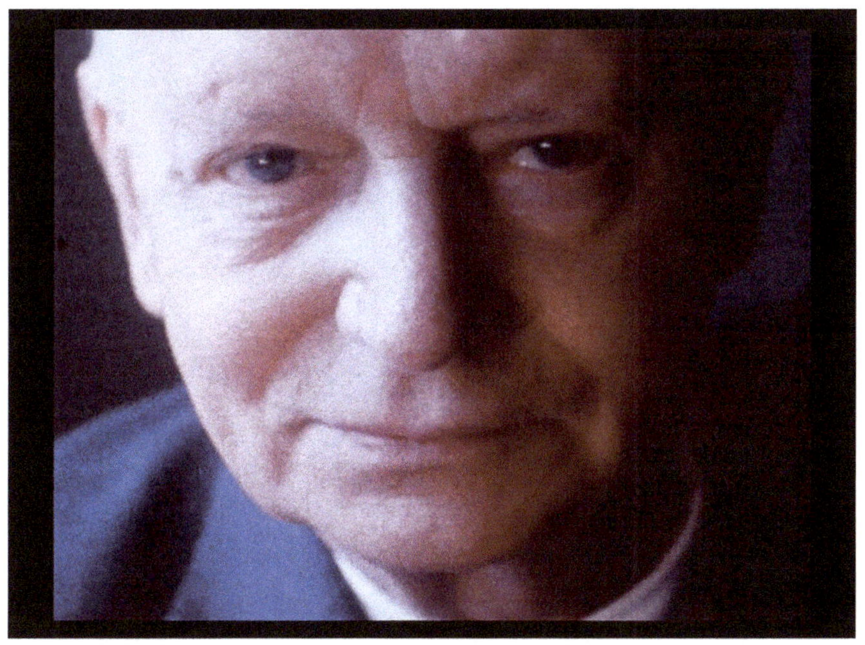

Reel 1 20:09

When Mekas visited him at the Plaza Hotel at Fifth Ave and 62nd St, the 76 year-old Danish director Carl Theodore Dreyer was in New York to present his final film, *Gertrud* (1964), at the 1965 New York Film Festival.

Critical reactions to *Gertrud* were generally negative. In the *New York Times*, Stanley Kaufmann reported that the film proved that Dreyer was "out of touch. Worse, his technique is the least fluently cinematic of any work of his that I know."[1]

In the *Village Voice*, Mekas too reported on *Gertrud* but not like the *New York Times*:

> From all of the films shown at the festival, it was by far the most perfect artistic statement, the most perfect expression of an artist's moral and aesthetic attitude. Every detail, every motion, every word in *Gertrud* has its right place, its own voice, and contributes to the whole and is beautiful.[2]

Mekas's view can be seen as evidence of his wide-ranging, inclusive approach to film in general but surely also reflected his contrarian reaction to the critics in the mainstream press who largely ignored the films he loved.

Despite Mekas's praise, Dreyer's often lugubrious narrative style could not have been farther either in spirit or technique from both the films Mekas usually championed and those he made himself. *Gertrud* favored dialogue over visual elements and long virtually motionless sequences of actors talking. But critical disdain united Dreyer's total abstinence from camera movement with the anarchic vitality of Mekas's bursts of single frames.

23 THOREAU'S WALDEN

cenery of Walden
autiful, does not a
oncern one who h
nore; yet this pond
s to merit a partic
een well, half a mile

Reel 1 21:18

Images of pages from Henry David Thoreau's *Walden or Life in the Woods* appear at intervals in Mekas's *Walden,* a constant reminder of his attachment to the book.

As mentioned in the preface, the choice of *Walden* as a title was partly pragmatic: the need of film labs to distinguish the reels of his first diary film from other parts of his diaries. But its choice originated in Mekas's abiding affection for Henry David Thoreau's 1847 literary classic, *Walden or Life in the Woods.*

Mekas recalled having read Thoreau's book in translation while still a displaced person in Germany, then rediscovering it when he arrived in New York. As a solitary man's reflections on the redemptive quality of nature, the text had an obvious appeal to him.

But however inspiring Mekas found Thoreau's reverence for nature, his own was very different - rooted both in the pain of exile from his rural Lithuanian homeland and his joy at finding elements of nature in the urban environment. But even if Mekas was moved by isolated traces of nature, he was fundamentally in love with the city of New York. Thoreau was not.

In a letter to Ralph Waldo Emerson from New York in 1843, Thoreau wrote:

> I don't like the city better, the more I see it, but worse. I am ashamed of my eyes that behold it. It is a thousand times meaner than I could have imagined...The pigs in the street are the most respectable part of the population.[1]

Thoreau detested urban life and found massed humanity repugnant. Mekas was unfailingly tolerant and sympathetic to the idiosyncrasies of his fellow humans and found in them endless sustenance for his art. His nostalgia for nature in the Lithuania of his childhood did not preclude a passionate defense of the eccentric denizens of his adopted city.

And while the essay form of Thoreau's *Walden* was firmly rooted in a long literary tradition, the form of Mekas's *Walden* signaled a radical break with the narrative conventions of its medium.

Mekas's first-person viewpoint and often staccato succession of single frames had rarely been seen before by filmgoers and had a liberating effect on a younger generation of artists. And nature of this liberation is far better described by the overall title of Mekas's work – *Diaries, Notes and Sketches* – than the title he borrowed from Thoreau.

24 AMY TAUBIN

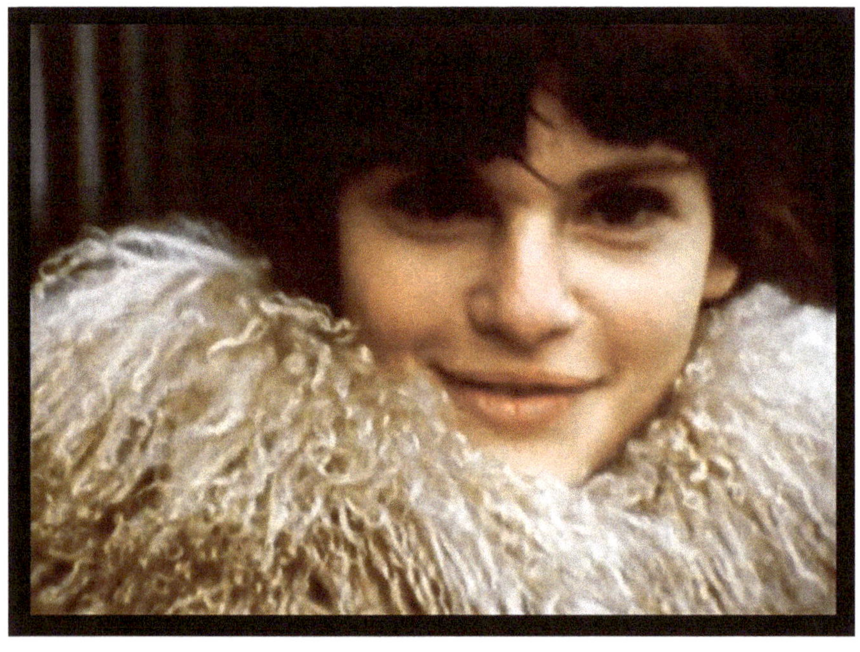

Reel 1 21:22

"Whenever people ask me what it was like to live in New York in the '60s, I refer them to Mekas's *Walden*,…"[1] wrote the critic Amy Taubin in *Artforum* in 2017 reviewing a new edition of Mekas's collected "Movie Journal" columns for the *Village Voice*.

In this review and in her obituary after Mekas's death in 2019 also in *Artforum*, Taubin articulated his contribution: "He changed so many lives. He gave people a way to identify themselves: as filmmakers or film viewers or film scholars or film critics who care most about films that are in a world apart, a world that Jonas Mekas built."[2]

While they may well be implicit in her tone, Taubin is more reticent about her personal connections to Mekas saying only that she "was drawn into Jonas's orbit through his criticism."[3] This is undoubtedly true as far is it goes; as a film critic who paid as much attention to the work of film artists as to the products of the film industry, Taubin kept the spirit of Mekas's advocacy alive into a new century.

But she did not mention her marriage to the avant-garde theater artist Richard Foreman that lasted from 1961 to 1972, simultaneous with Mekas's tenure at the *Village Voice*. Mekas himself was to reminisce in 2016:

> When we were still screening at the Gramercy Arts Theater,[4] this guy always used to come in with a young woman, Amy Taubin. He was always in a very heavy fur coat, like a bearskin coat, and they came to almost every screening. That's how I met them and that's how we became friends.[5]

And in the ad Mekas published for *Walden*'s world premiere in December 1969, it is Taubin, not Foreman, who was mentioned by name. To promote his film as best he could, Mekas listed the most famous names first - the Mayor of New York, John Lindsay, the Beatle John Lennon - and puts Taubin right after Timothy Leary.[6]

Taubin crossed Mekas's path frequently in the years documented in *Walden,* but it was surely also her startling beauty that explains the frequent close-ups of her that punctuate the film. They recall the other shots of young women that Mekas made as screen tests for his never-to-be-made fictional film of a young woman's diary.

But it could not have been Taubin's physical beauty that made her Mekas's choice as his successor when he stopped writing his *Movie Journal* column for the *Village Voice.* Although she had never written about film before, he obviously recognized the talent that would make her, a half century later, his most insightful and articulate critic and a defender of his legacy as board member of Anthology Film Archives.

25 MILLBROOK

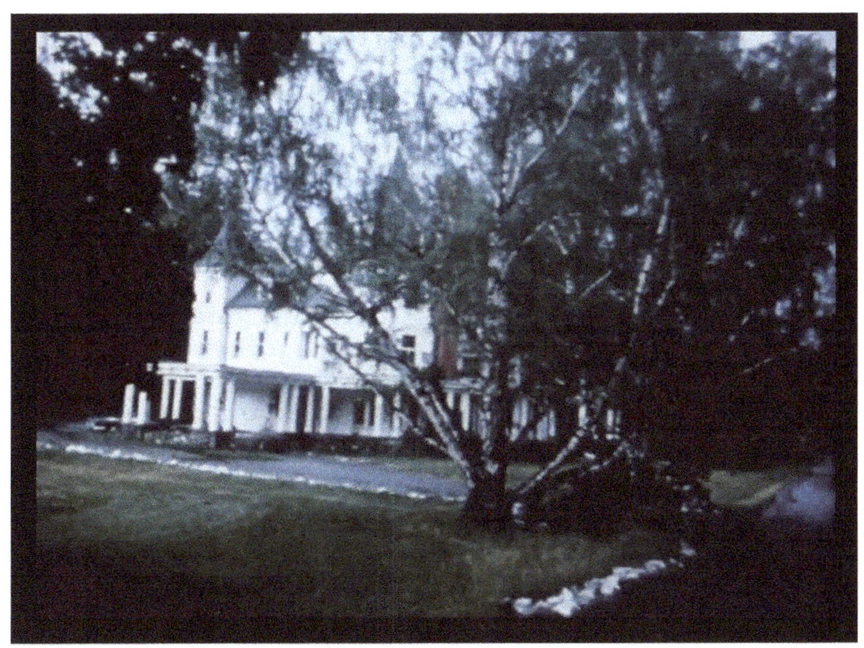

Reel 1 22:15

Timothy Leary's invitation to Mekas to visit the headquarters of the League of Spiritual Discovery in Millbrook, New York certainly included the opportunity to take the drug that shared its initials, Lysergic Acid Diethylamide. An article on his visit reported:

Mekas recalled a brief walk he took with Leary, who offered to supervise him if he wanted to try LSD. "I said no, I do not want to take LSD, because my greatest drug experience was Rimbaud," Mekas said, referring to the French poet. "Rimbaud sent me to inner spaces, and no matter what I try, nothing did what Rimbaud did to me." They walked in silence back to the mansion, and Leary didn't bring up LSD again. Instead of tripping, Mekas read and shot footage for the rest of his time in Millbrook.[1]

Given Rimbaud's own notorious fondness for mind-altering substances, Mekas's claims of abstinence are less than convincing. But Leary could not have wished for a more effective publicist. Before incorporating the footage he had shot on his visit into *Walden*, Mekas released *Report from Millbrook* as a "newsreel" describing Leary's activities as "Reflecting the Social, Political and Moral Climate of Our Times."[2]

A number of notable artists, musicians and writers had already visited and, for a few years in the mid-1960s, the 19th century mansion in Millbrook, N.Y. became the epicenter of a national cultural revolution.

Built as a hunting lodge for robber barons in 1912, the estate was purchased by the Hitchcock family, heirs to the Andrew Mellon fortune, in 1963. One of them, Margaret Mellon "Peggy" Hitchcock, had been introduced to psychedelic drugs by Leary and Richard Alpert at Harvard. In 1965 she rented them the estate for a dollar a year and they moved in with the announced intention of pursuing scientific research into the possibilities for pharmacologically assisted spiritual development.

When Mekas visited in the summer of 1965, the Hitchcock mansion was already coming to be seen as an incubator for the exploding "drug culture." Intense media attention was focussed on Leary's League of Spiritual Discovery and, although its gatherings were comparatively sedate, the estate began to attract many uninvited visitors as well as increasing surveillance from law enforcement authorities.

In the spring following Mekas's visit, a squad of police officers entered the house in the middle of the night to search for illegal drugs. They found very little but continued their intense surveillance until Leary, Alpert and followers were eventually evicted.

The original soundtrack for *Report from Millbrook* (1966) consisted of a police press conference on the raid. A *Village Voice* ad announced:

AMERICA TODAY
A New Series of Journalistic Film Programs Reflecting the Social, Political and Moral Climate of Our Times, the Feelings, Issues, and Events of the Day As Seen by Today's Independent Film-Makers
Program No. One
Jonas Mekas's Newsreel: Report from Millbrook
An interview with the Sheriff of Millbrook on the arrest of Dr. Timothy Leary in the summer of '66.[3]

But when he reincorporated the footage into *Walden*, the sound was completely different from the "Newsreel": instead it consisted of Mekas with his accordion singing a Lithuanian song and then reading from a text by the 16th century Spanish mystic St. John of the Cross. The theme of the sequence had changed from a record of social conflict to one of pastoral calm.

26 TIMOTHY LEARY

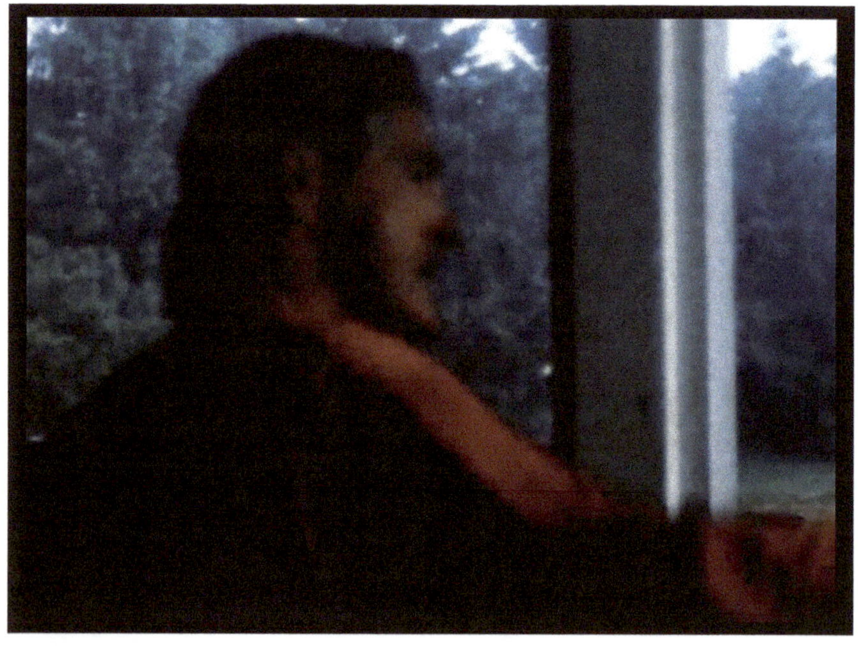

Reel 1 22:17

Harvard psychology professor Timothy Leary had been investigating the use of psychedelic drugs for religious enlightenment. But when he heard Allen Ginsberg read his poem "Lysergic Acid," he decided it had a role to play in the arts as well.

Ginsberg's view was that if prominent artists and intellectuals testified to the value of hallucinogenic drugs, it would create institutional support for preserving their legality. Leary would later say, "From the time that Ginsberg showed up on my doorstep, everything changed. After that, the project was different, my life was different, and I was on a different path."[1]

Leary was soon to become the most prominent public advocate for the consumption of Lysergic Acid, and coin the phrase that became the motto of the cultural revolution of the 1960s: "Turn On, Tune In, Drop Out."

From the beginning, the research of Leary and his colleague Richard Alpert had attracted media attention and raised concerns among their academic colleagues about the legitimacy and safety of their experiments, particularly their practice of joining their subjects in the ingestion of the drugs they were studying. Harvard eventually fired Leary and Alpert and they arrived in Millbrook soon afterwards.

After Leary's eviction from the Millbrook estate (see Chapter 25), he continued his advocacy of the benefits of mind-altering drugs, confrontations with the legal system, and penchant for sharing the media spotlight with celebrities up to - and including - the moment of his death in 1996. He reappears in *Walden* at Yoko Ono and John Lennon's Montreal Bed-In in 1969 (see Chapter 118).

27 SHEPARD SHERBELL

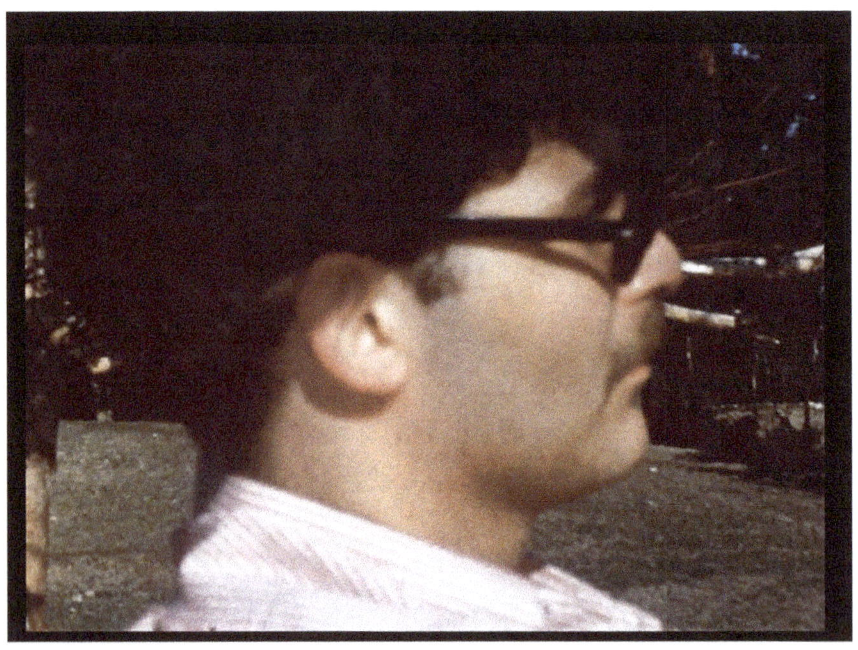

Reel 1 26:14

The presence in Millbrook, New York of the documentary photographer Shepard Sherbell was a sign that something important was happening. For Sherbell and his camera always seemed to be eyewitnesses to the major events of the late 20th century.

Why exactly he was at the Hitchcock Mansion at the same time as Mekas is not clear but judging from the scenes in *Walden*, Sherbell seemed to have been at Mekas's side throughout his visit to Millbrook.

Sherbell was primarily based in London at the time where he captured iconic images of the British rock musicians, among them the Beatles, the Rolling Stones, and the Who, whose popularity in the U.S. was exploding.

In the 1970s, Sherbell turned his attention to American political life, photographing presidents at the White House, prominent senators, and congressmen. He covered national Democratic and Republican conventions and the candidates they nominated.

Later he travelled the world photographing seemingly every major global conflict and world-changing event. He spent several years in Moscow documenting the dissolution of the Soviet Union in the early 1990s. On September 11, 2001 Sherbell and his camera were at the World Trade Center.

Given his propensity for being at critical places at decisive times, Sherbell's presence at Mekas's side at Millbrook in 1965 could be seen as certification that the "psychedelic era" in American culture was near its apogee.

28 RICHARD ALPERT

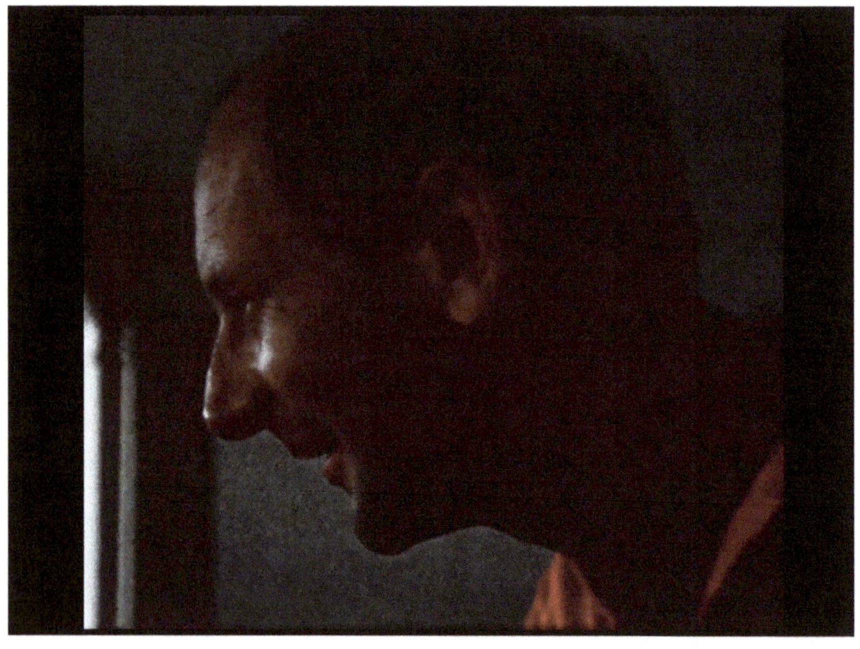

Reel 1 26:23

The clinical psychology professor Richard Alpert was fired from the Harvard University faculty in May 1963 for allegedly giving the psychedelic drug psilocybin to students. At the same time his colleague Timothy Leary was dismissed because he had "failed to keep his classroom appointments." It was the end of the "Harvard Psilo-cybin Project."

Together Alpert and Leary founded the International Federation for Internal Freedom (IFIF) and moved to Mexico where Leary had discovered the use of psilocybin in the religious rites of the indigenous Mazatec people. There the IFIF started a community devoted to researching the effects of mind-expanding hallucinogens but local authorities proved inhospitable and they were deported.

Later in 1963, the IFIF found a new home in Millbrook, New York (see Chapter 25) and Alpert and Leary renamed the IFIF the Castalia Foundation. The Foundation was again renamed, this time as the League for Spiritual Discovery and Alpert gave lectures at its center in New York City. He then went to India to study under a Hindu guru. There he took the Hindi name, Ram Dass (Servant of God) and, after eviction from the Hitchcock estate, went on to pursue his spiritual activity on the West Coast and eventually Hawaii.

29 RALPH METZNER

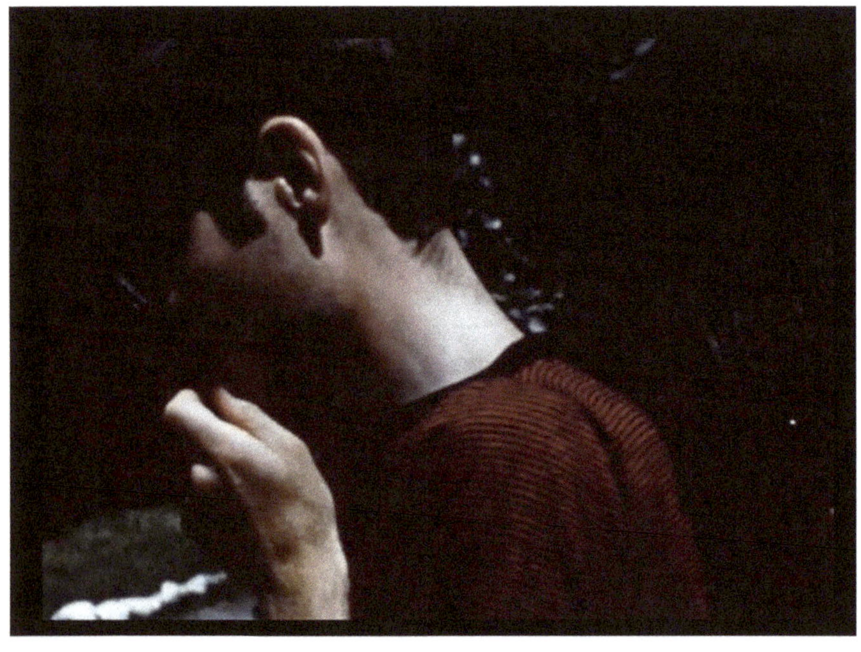

Reel 1 27:10

Less prominent in the media frenzy surrounding the activity of Timothy Leary and Richard Alpert was another of their Harvard colleagues, Ralph Metzner. After their academic employer lost patience with their controversial research, Metzner joined Leary and Alpert at the Hitchcock Estate in Millbrook, New York in 1963.

Born in Germany, Metzner had received a Ph.D. in Psychology from Harvard in 1962 and had worked as a graduate student with Leary and Alpert on the therapeutic uses for hallucinogenic drugs. But from the beginning his work had a more traditionally academic foundation than his two more charismatic colleagues.

He was credited as a co-author with Leary of their first "Statement of Purpose of the International Federation for Internal Freedom" in 1963 but probably did all of the actual writing. When in June of 1963, the group published the first issue of the *Psychedelic Review*, Metzner was listed as its main editor, with Leary and Alpert in secondary roles as "contributing editor" and "consulting editor" respectively.

And Metzner was the only one of the three who actually contributed an article to the *Psychedelic Review*, a highly clinical study called "The Pharmacology of Psychedelic Drugs." Its examination of the actual molecular structure of psychedelic drugs offered a far more scientific perspective than the messianic one of his colleagues.

In August 1964, Metzner again shared authorship credit with Leary and Alpert when they published, *The Psychedelic Experience: A Manual Based on The Tibetan Book of the Dead*. But unlike his colleagues, he neither became a Hindu mystic nor an international fugitive but continued to lecture and publish on the intersection of psychotherapy and spirituality for the rest of his life.

30 GREGORY MARKOPOULOS

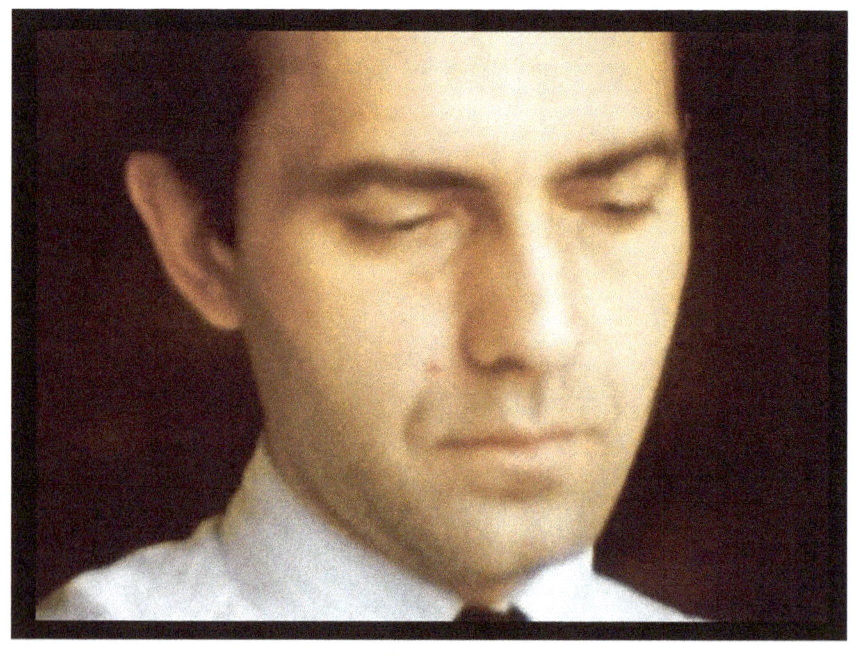

Reel 1 28:47

Had Gregory Markopoulos remained in New York after 1967 he would likely have been recognized as among the important film artists at work there. But his self-imposed exile in Europe in that year and subsequent refusal to have his films shown or even written about delayed the recognition of his stature for years.

Beginning in 1961, Markopoulos wrote regularly for Mekas's *Film Culture,* often about his own work. Mekas, in his *Village Voice* column of June 7, 1962, wrote under the title ON GREGORY MARKOPOULOS:

> Markopoulos' name is not new to those who have followed the experimental-independent cinema for the past decade. His trilogy, *Psyche-Lysis-Charmides* (1947-48), which I saw again a few weeks ago, remains one of the classics of experimental cinema. There is poetry, sensitivity in his work that is very personal, very special. He puts into his films those delicate feelings and thoughts of which most of us are either afraid or unaware.[1]

A year later he added:

> I still see the images of *Twice a Man* (1963). The film keeps growing in my memory. Gregory has put into this film so much of himself and so much of unseen, fresh-born lyricism. There are sequences which take your mind away, they are so rich, so splendorous; they burst out into bouquets of colors, meanings, sensuousness, and poetry.[2]

Mekas interviewed Markopoulos again for the *Village Voice* on April 14, 1966 about the last film he made in New York, *The Illiac Passion* which featured a gallery of notable figures of the "underground" scene, including many - Beverly Grant, Andy Warhol, Gerard Malanga, Jack Smith - who were also visible in *Walden.*

The final *Village Voice* interview with Markopoulos was published on February 2, 1967 shortly before his exile began. Mekas wrote that he found *Himself as Herself* (1967) "his most perfect, most dramatic, most personal work to date."[3]

When Markopoulos and his partner Robert Beavers moved to Europe, he withdrew all his films from distribution, even insisting that all mentions of his work be removed from what had become the most widely-read book on the subject of avant-garde film, P. Adams Sitney's *Visionary Film*.

For almost three decades his work was virtually never seen as he worked on what he called *Eniaios*, an exhaustive compilation of his life's work. At his death in 1993, Markopoulos had edited nearly 80 hours of 16mm color film. But *Eniaios* had never been printed for projection.

Through the Herculean efforts of Robert Beavers, who had become an important film artist in his own right, *Eniaios* has been gradually restored and projected at four-year intervals at Temenos, an open air theater in rural Greece.

Beavers describes the event on the Temenos website:

> Markopoulos wished to create a deeply personal and rewarding cine-matic experience for his spectators. He chose the site near Lyssaraia, his father's birthplace, for its natural beauty and conceived the Temenos as a space uniquely in harmony with the film as an instru-ment of philosophical and psychological revelation. The spectator's journey to the Temenos anticipates the more extraordinary journey that takes place in front of the projection screen. The serene pace and gradual development of the film allows the viewer to perceive his or her own emotions in dialogue with the filmmaker's concentrated, fleeting images. It is what Markopoulos designated "the intuition space." Each screening begins with the setting of the sun and continues for approximately three hours under the movement of the heavens.[4]

31 BOLEX

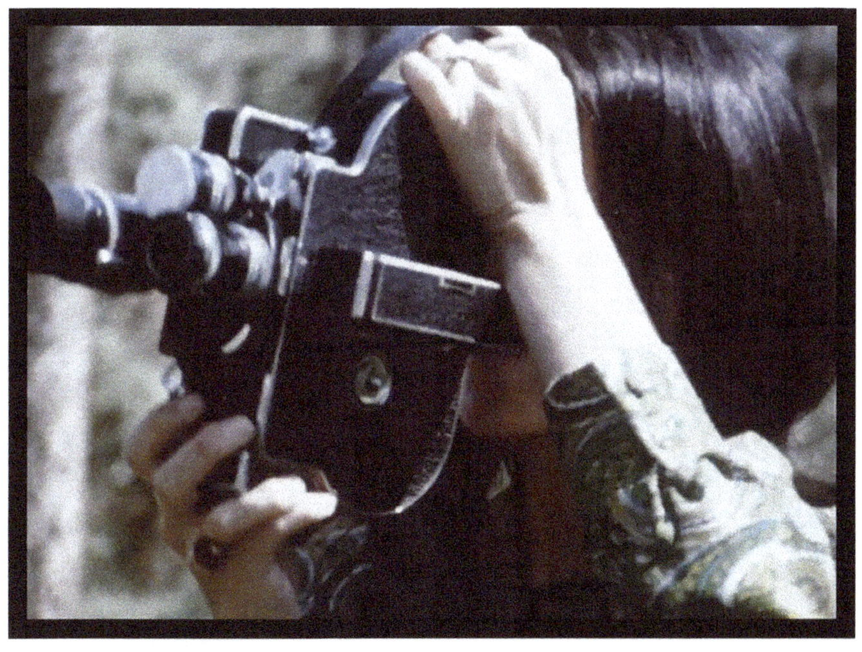

Reel 1 28:51

It was not a coincidence that the 16mm film camera that *Walden* shows Markopoulos using to shoot his film *Galaxie* (1966) was almost identical to the one Mekas had in his own hands. Later, Mekas filmed himself with it on the train to Colorado to visit Stan Brakhage who used the same camera. It was called a Bolex.

The name derived from that of another eastern European immigrant, Yakov Bogopolsky born in Kiev on 31 December 1895.[1] By 1924 he had emigrated to Switzerland, shortened his name to Bolsky, and begun developing a 35mm film camera called the Cinématographe Bol. In 1930 he sold his patents to the watchmaking company Paillard which perfected a 16mm camera they began marketing as the Bolex in 1935.

The Bolex would remain the essential tool for filmmaking outside the Hollywood industry for four decades. It was standard equipment not just for filmmaking in the fields of education, science, and industry but for making art as well. In fact, the entire history of experimental film in America can be linked to this one robust product of Swiss engineering.

In 1949, a few months after Mekas and his brother arrived in New York, Paillard founded a subsidiary in the city to distribute their cameras in the U.S. As soon as he was able to save a little money from his meager wages, Mekas bought a Bolex camera and began to film the daily life of Lithuanian immigrants in Williamsburg.[2]

Meanwhile Paillard Products Inc. opened a showroom on Madison Ave and began publishing a magazine, *The Bolex Reporter*, to promote their camera. It touted the use of its product in many industries, but recognized that artists were important customers too. Its 1966 issue focussed on the "The New American Cinema Group" and its choice of subjects could have been taken from Mekas's film diaries: Marie Menken, Naomi Levine, Ken Jacobs, Stan VanDerBeek, Gregory Markopoulos, Robert Breer, Robert Frank, David Brooks, Jack Smith, Gerald Malanga, Andy Warhol and, of course, their author himself.

When a major retrospective of Mekas's work was held on the occasion of his 90th birthday at the Serpentine Gallery in London in 2012, a large display case was devoted to an array of his heavily-used Bolex cameras. They had been his primary tools for over 50 years.

32 BLEECKER STREET

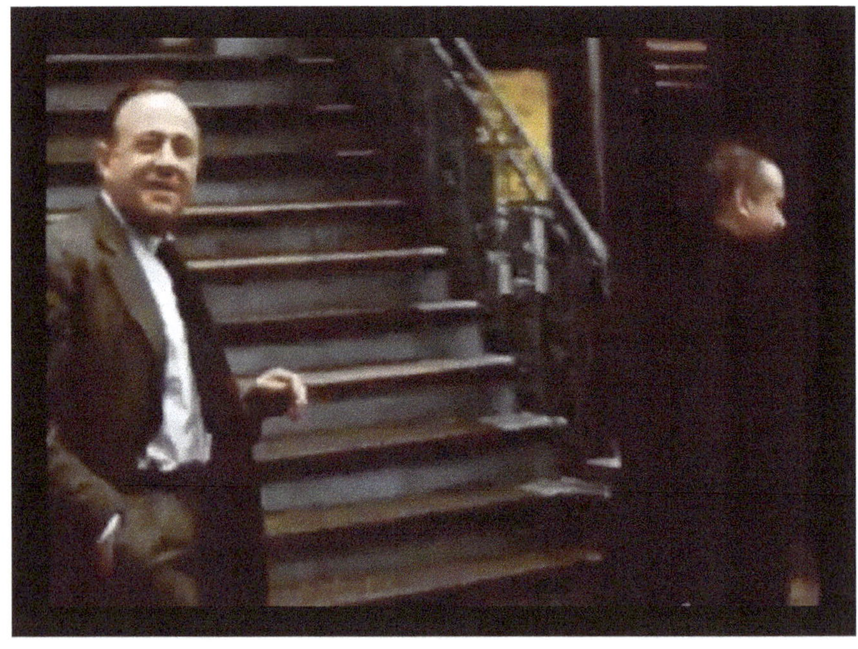

Reel 1 30:01

The short block of Bleecker St. between Thompson St. and LaGuardia Place was home to three landmarks of the cultural life of the 1960s. At one end was the nightclub The Village Gate at 160 Bleecker St. where Allen Ginsberg and the Kreeping Kreplachs had called a press conference to announce that a new era had begun.

In the middle was The Bitter End at 147 Bleecker St., originally a coffee shop where the Jim Kweskin Jug Band first performed. The group included Mel Lyman who shared Mekas's apartment for a while at the time before founding the Fort Hill Community in Boston. The band provided the soundtrack for *Notes on the Circus* (1966) which was later incorporated into *Walden*. The Bitter End was the epicenter of the 1960s "folk revolution" in music as well as a launching pad for many of the era's most famous comedians among them Lenny Bruce, Woody Allen, and Mel Brooks.

Directly across the street was the Bleecker Street Cinema whose influence on America's discovery of the "art" film (often simply meaning not made in Hollywood) was comparable to that of The Bitter End in music and comedy. The 200-seat theater was founded in 1960 and run by filmmaker and political activist Lionel Rogosin as a way to show *Come Back Africa*, his 1959 film about South Africa under apartheid that no existing exhibitor would agree to show.

The programming that followed gave visibility to new trends in international film production - particularly the French "Nouvelle Vague." But whether for financial or aesthetic reasons - or most likely both - the Bleecker St. Cinema was never really aligned with "underground" film as championed by Mekas.

For several months in early 1963, Rogosin hosted some of Mekas's itinerant screenings but their collaboration was not smooth. In his June 13 column of that year Mekas wrote:

> You may have noticed that the Monday midnight screenings at the
> Bleecker Street Cinema, held by Film-Makers' Co-op and *Film Culture*

for the past few months, have been cancelled. You may be wondering what happened and why. The truth is, we have been thrown out. The Bleecker Cinema people did not like our movies. They thought the independent cinema was ruining the 'reputation of the theatre.' Dig that![1]

It was true that the kind of films Mekas showed, particularly when they provoked obscenity charges, were not compatible with the theater's business objectives but the estrangement was not total: a *Village Voice* ad announced a benefit screening of Ron Rice films organized by Mekas's Film-Makers' Cinematheque at the theater on January 24th 1965.

In May of 1965 Mekas reported in his column about a meeting with Louis Marcorelles, the editor of the French magazine that had launched the "Nouvelle Vague," *Cahiers du Cinéma*. It included Lionel Rogosin and Louis Brigante whom Mekas filmed across the street from Bleecker Street Cinema in front of The Bitter End.

33 LIONEL ROGOSIN

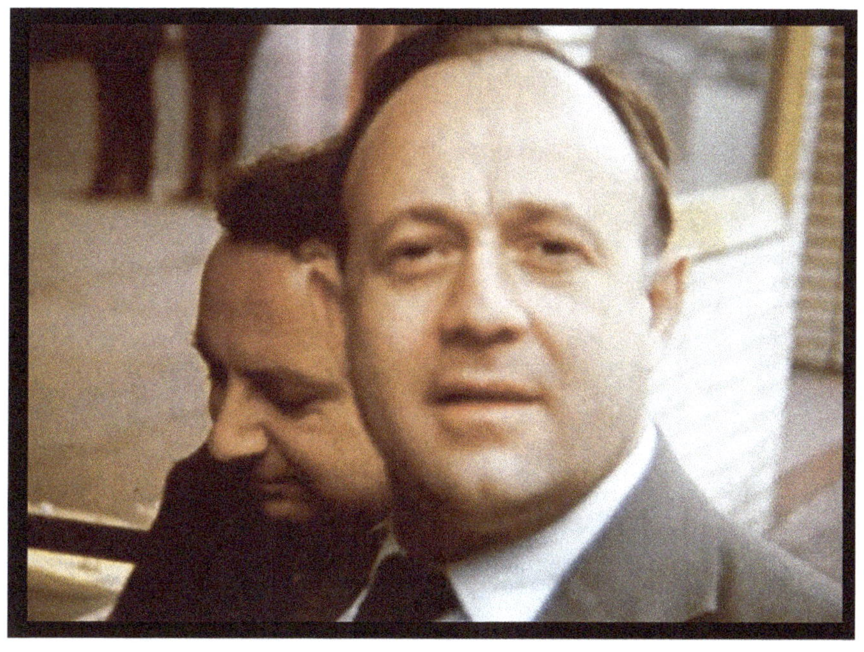

Reel 1 30:02

Lionel Rogosin was a founding member with Mekas of the New American Cinema Group. In September 1960 the group had issued a manifesto declaring its resistance to censorship and dedication to personal expression in film and it met frequently at Rogosin's Bleecker Street Cinema in its early days.

Rogosin made his first film, *On The Bowery*, in 1954 not far south of the cinema which he bought six years later and ran for fourteen years. The film was a stark view of the lives of people on the street whose name had become a synonym for urban dereliction. Its portrayal of an America rarely seen in commercial films drew attention particularly in Europe where it was named "Best Documentary" both at the 1956 Venice Film Festival and by the British Academy of Film and Television Arts.

Rogosin's style as an independent filmmaker was straightforward and compassionate. And the problems of his subjects - homelessness, racial discrimination, alcoholism, and poverty - were not frequently visible on movie screens.

His next film, *Come Back Africa* (1959) was made farther from home, on location in Johannesburg, but, given the cordial diplomatic relations between the U.S. and South Africa, was no less a challenge to the status quo. Having convinced government authorities that he was making a benign musical travelogue, Rogosin focussed his camera on the cruelty of official apartheid. Through a combination of documentary footage and fiction, *Come Back Africa* exposed the brutality of the official policies of white South Africa.

But despite its powerful impact, Rogosin could find no American distributor for the film so he decided to exhibit it himself. Signing a ten-year lease on the old Renata Theater in Greenwich Village, he renovated and reopened it as the Bleecker Street Cinema. *Come Back Africa* premiered there on April 4, 1960.

Rogosin's priority however was his own filmmaking and programming at the Bleecker St. was delegated to a succession of managers who kept the theater financially viable by programming primarily European feature films for which there was a reliable audience. Mekas's "underground" cinema offered no such fiscal stability and thus, except for a brief period in 1963, was not a part of the Bleecker St.'s repertoire.

Rogosin sold the Bleecker St. in 1974 and continued his struggle to produce politically and socially engaged films around the world. He died in Los Angeles in 2000.

34 LOUIS BRIGANTE

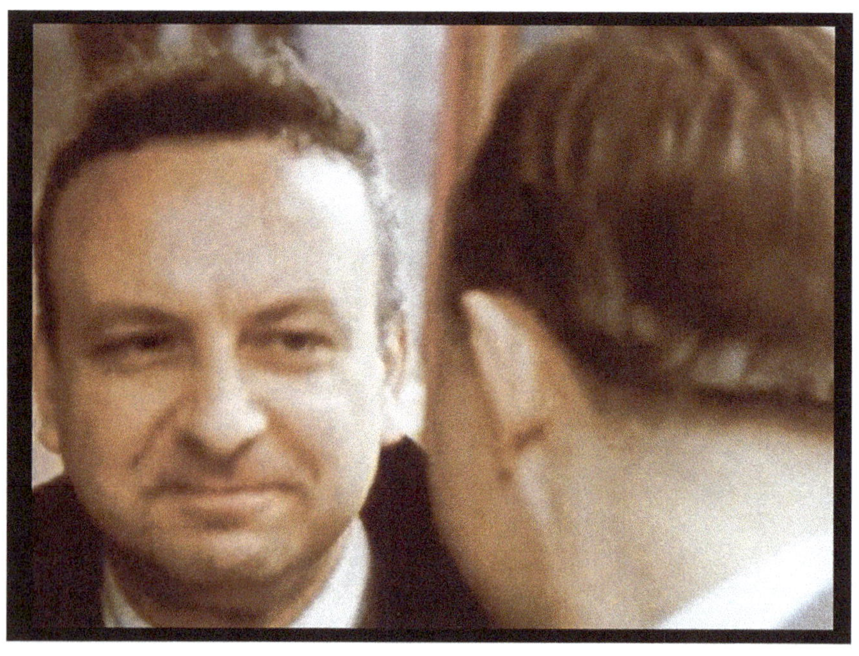

Reel 1 30:04

It is appropriate that in the credits of Mekas's first film, *The Brig* (1964), Louis Brigante was listed as an "unspecified assistant." He seemed always to be involved in a multitude of projects but in "unspecified" ways, doing whatever needed to be done behind the scenes, only acknowledged in small print if at all.

Perhaps the greatest beneficiary of his help, was his life-long companion, Storm de Hirsch, a major film artist who has herself been unjustly neglected.

Brigante was credited over the years as a literary editor, a publisher, a film director, a translator, a cinematographer, an actor, a film editor. The first trace of his service to Mekas was in January 1955 when the inaugural issue of *Film Culture* listed him alongside Jonas and Adolfas Mekas on the editorial board.

In his book *The Cinema of Poetry*, Sitney credited Brigante with his discovery of the writing of Pasolini:

> It was *Film Culture* yet again that led me to the theoretical work of Pier Paolo Pasolini. I served on the editorial board beginning with Issue 24 (Spring 1962). In that number one of my coeditors Louis Brigante translated a text he titled "Literary and Stylistic Figures".[1]

In the early 1950s, Brigante published a small magazine, *Intro. A Quarterly of Literature and the Arts*. In addition to its quarterly issues, *Intro* also published a poetry series, *The Round Quarter Series of New Poets & Artists*.

He was the translator of *Italian Fables*, a collection of Italian folktales published in 1956 by Italo Calvino and in 1963 translated *Screenplays of Michaelangelo Antonioni: L'Avventura, Il Grido, La Notte, L'Eclisse*.

For his first film, *The Brig* (1964) Mekas mentions Brigante along with Ed Emshwiller as "our little crew," loading the cameras and surely performing many other tasks as well. He assisted his wife as director and editor of her feature film *Goodbye in the Mirror* (1965). Adolfas Mekas credits him as his co-editor in *Hallelujah the Hills* (1963), Pola Chapelle lists him in the cast of her film *A Matter of Baobab* (1970). And Lionel Rogosin credits him with the cinematography and editing of his last film *Arab Israeli Dialogue* (1974).

Finally the Film-Makers Coop catalogue contains two films made by Brigante himself: *Assemblage* (1967) and *Objective Correlative* (1969). The former is cited by film historian William Wees as an example of the significant role of found footage in experimental film.[2] Even in his own films, Brigante put the work of others ahead of himself.

35 MIKE JACOBSON

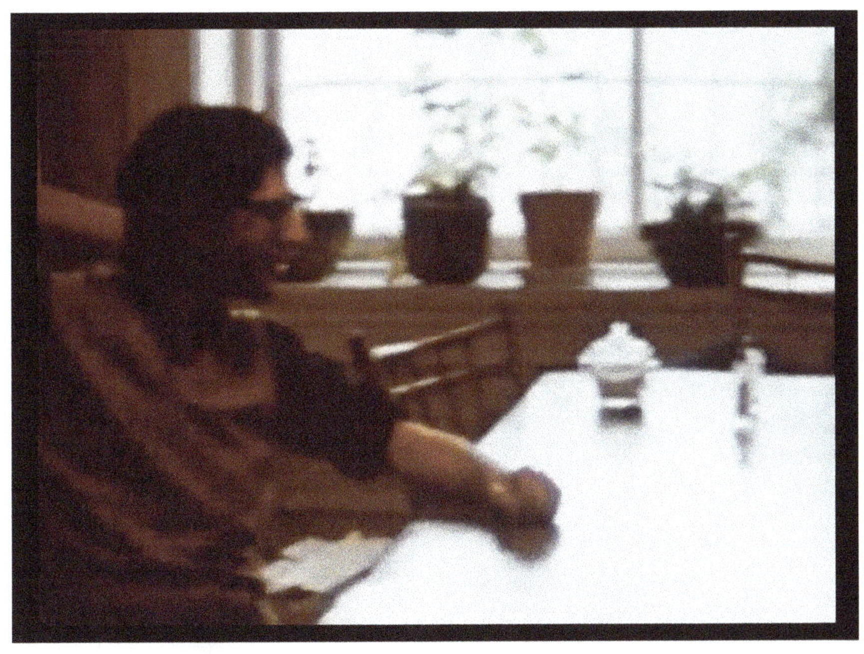

Reel 1 30:10

In a brief period of creative activity while enrolled as an NYU graduate student between 1965 and 1969, Mike Jacobson made a series of film loops which critic Wheeler Winston Dixon described as "a gorgeous series of loop variations" and a "dazzling series of visual mosaics."[1]

Jacobson's work was featured in a series of expanded cinema performances in the summer of 1967 at the Film-makers Cinematheque in the Wurlitzer Building on 42nd St. and he had his "First One Man Show" on June 10, 1969 at the Film-makers Cinematheque at the Jewish Museum.

In his *Village Voice* column of February 13, 1969 Mekas wrote:

> I really liked Mike Jacobson's little film called *Esprit de Corps* (1965) which was shown last weekend at the Gotham Art Theatre. There was a positive, life-inspiring energy locked in this little unpretentious film. Probably, it was the only life-generating film playing in New York that evening - or that week.[2]

Then Jacobson seemed to have stopped filmmaking and subsequently worked as an advertising copywriter.

In 2015 he began publishing his writing in *Unbroken,* a quarterly online journal where he listed himself as a "former independent film-maker" who writes "various kinds of prose pieces."[3]

36 CIRCUS

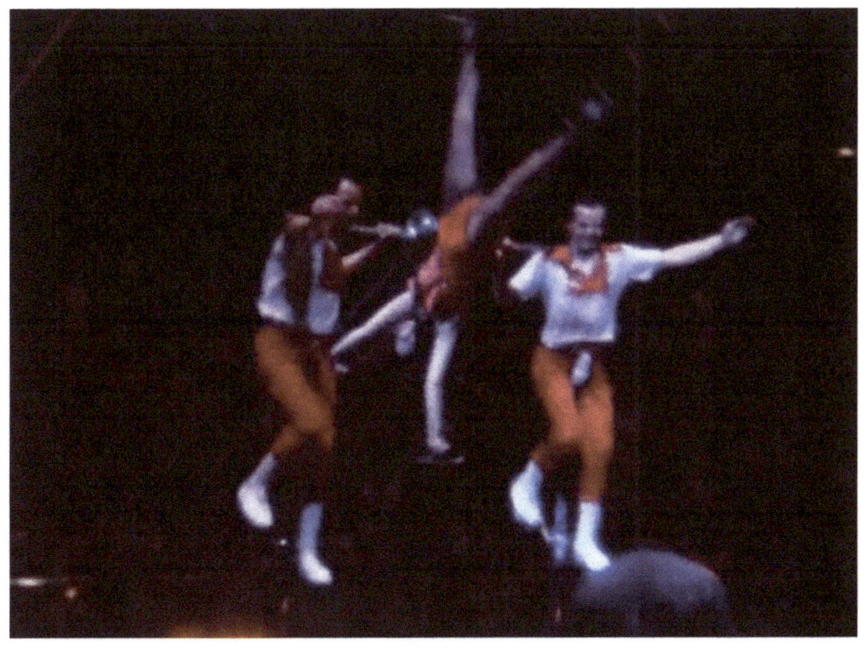

Reel 2 00:34

"The Greatest Show on Earth" was the self-proclaimed description of the Ringling Brothers Barnum and Bailey Circus. For almost a century its New York performances were held in the succession of large arenas called Madison Square Garden.

The first venues were actually on Madison Square on Broadway between 5th Avenue and 23rd St; the last one was at 8th Avenue and 33rd. But the circus's longest-lived New York home, from 1925 to 1968, was at Madison Square Garden's second location on 8th Avenue between 49th and 50th Streets. It was here on May 16, 1966 that Mekas shot the footage he released as a short film called *Notes on the Circus*.

The show changed little over the years. An account by writer Roger Angell of what he saw as a small boy in the 1920s describes the subjects of Mekas's film four decades later:

> The opening parade inside Madison Square Garden was a blur of circling horses and waving performers, jugglers and acrobats and fat ladies, world-famous trapeze and high-wire artists in capes and tights, and tiara'd young women confidently astride the lofty necks of elephants.[1]

As mentioned (see Chapter 19), Mekas released four separate films in 1966 that were later integrated into *Walden* but not in chronological order. Although it was the first of the four to be shot, *Notes on the Circus* was inserted as the third, after *Cassis* and *Report from Millbrook*. This may be of little consequence to *Walden* as autobiography but it obscures the importance of the circus sequences to the development of Mekas's personal vision.

Mekas's earliest footage, shot in the 1950s and eventually presented later in *Lost, Lost, Lost* (1976), was shot in an unobtrusive style that would be virtually impossible to distinguish from that of other documentary filmmakers. But there would be no such difficulty in identifying the maker of *Notes on the Circus*.

Its short bursts of single frames, its exuberant, unpredictable pans and zooms seemingly unhinged from any need to realistically document its subject, its superimpositions, its raucous soundtrack by the Jim Kweskin Jug Band untethered from the images, its celebration of the pure sensation of colors and light, all make *Notes on the Circus* a compendium of what would later be recognized as Mekas personal filmmaking style.

Mekas's view of the circus would have a huge effect on later film artists. It was a declaration that the film medium could be used outside the traditional rules of "correct" cinematography and montage. And the very idea that a film could consist simply of "Notes" and needed no narrative structure for its imagery was liberating. Even if, in retrospect it is clear that Mekas's vision owed much to Marie Menken and her *Notebook* (1963), Mekas was much better known and so his liberating message in *Notes on the Circus* had a much longer reach.

37 BARBARA RUBIN

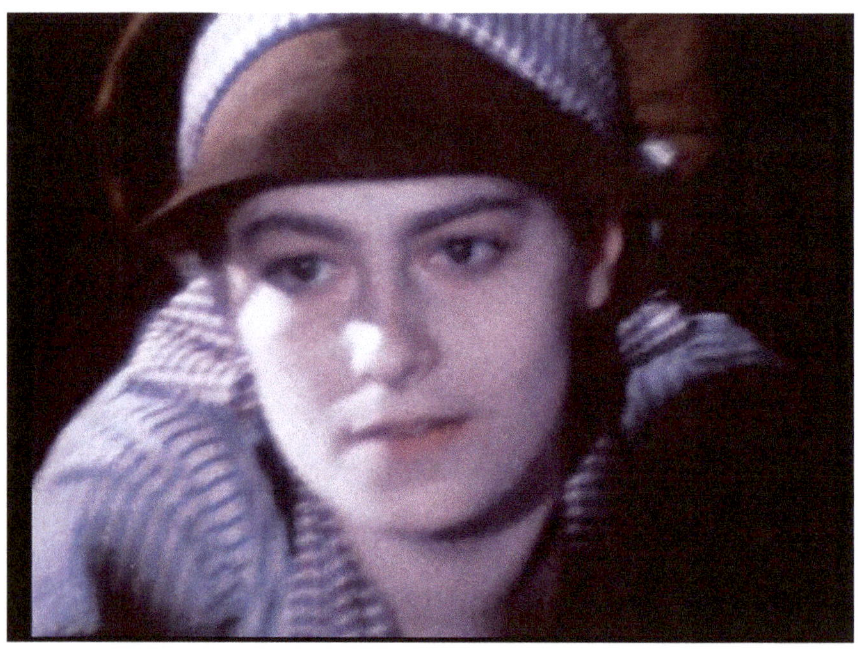

Reel 2 13:01

The Kreeping Kreplach press conference in June 1966 was organized by Barbara Rubin who, a year earlier, had also managed the hugely successful "International Poetry Incarnation" with Allen Ginsberg and an array of "Beat" poets. Held on June 11, 1965, the event had drawn an audience of more than 7000 to the Royal Albert Hall in London.

The press conference, held to announce a sequel to that event, had few resources behind it besides Rubin's energy but that was enough - as she had amply demonstrated by her actions at the unauthorized projection of *Flaming Creatures* (1963) at the Knokke-le-Zoute festival in December 1963 (see Prologue).

In his review of a 2019 documentary on her life by Chuck Smith, *Barbara Rubin and the Exploding New York Underground*, the critic J. Hoberman wrote:

> Barbara Rubin (1945-1980) may have been something less than a great artist, but she was also something more. Rubin was zeitgeist-made material, a young woman who embodied her historical moment in the process of working out a unique destiny. In earlier centuries and perhaps even this one, Rubin might have been understood to be a woman possessed. An agitator and a mystic ... Rubin made scenes the way other people made movies - although she did make those as well.[1]

Mekas was devoted to Rubin during her few but eventful years in the limelight. They first met soon after her discharge from a sanitarium; her uncle had asked Mekas if he could find her a job at the Film-Makers' Cooperative. Her arrival on the scene coincided with the first screenings of *Flaming Creatures*.

Mekas wrote in his *Village Voice* column of July 25, 1963 that:

> Barbara Rubin, from the Order of Fools, bursting and burning with hallucinations, shooting her first movie, with the excitement of a holy nun, feverishly engaged to rip out fragments of veiled revelations from

her subconscious and the world, the sensory experiences and visions of the sad loveless century, pouring her heart out.[2]

As Hoberman pointed out, she "more or less invented the idea of film as installation and projected film as a performative medium."[3] She practiced what would come to be called "performance art." She was instrumental in organizing Warhol's "The Exploding Plastic Inevitable" in which the music of the Velvet Underground was combined with visual effects, dance, and other spontaneous "happenings." She rarely projected her own film, *Christmas on Earth* (1963), in the same way twice.

In the early 1970s Rubin retreated from the New York scene, marrying and moving to France to live in a religious community. She died there of a postnatal infection in 1980 at the age of only 35. She had left her films with Mekas with the request that he destroy them. Fortunately, he did not comply.

38 AL ARONOWITZ

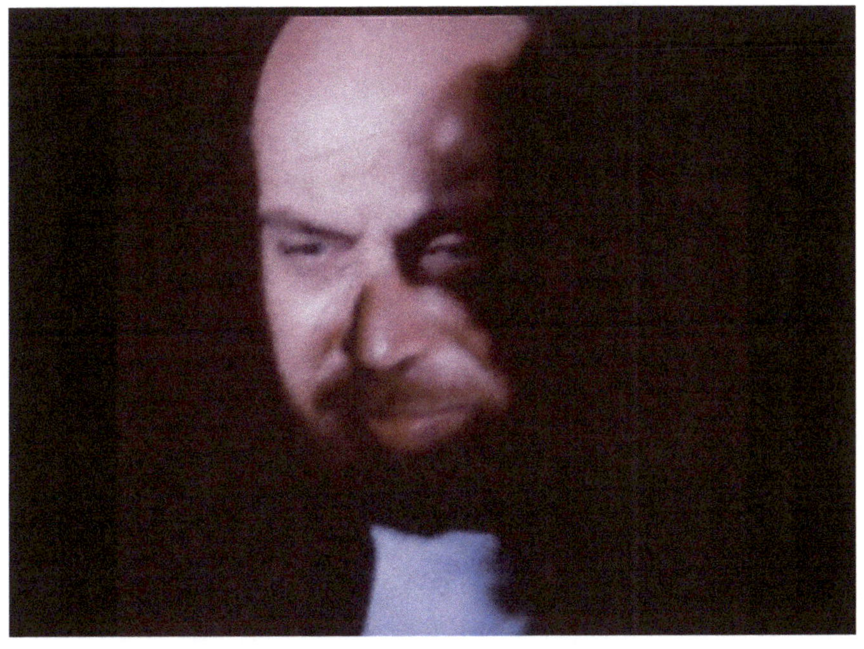

The Kreeping Kreplach Non-Profit Cultural International Foundation of Purple People Art Combine (its name, Allen Ginsberg conceded, was subject to change) had invited journalists to their press conference to inform them of an upcoming event in London:

> The first activity of the Combine will be to stage a rock and roll, film festival at Royal Albert Hall in London on June 17th and 18th. The festival will exhibit the talents of filmmakers Jonas Mekas, and Andy Warhol and the musical talents of The Fugs, The Velvet Underground, The Flowers, The Chambers Brothers, and Donovan.[1]

As probably all involved realized, the announcement contained a large dose of wishful thinking. But, credible or not, it was exactly the kind of news that interested Al Aronowitz.

Aronowitz reported on the popular music business for the *New York Post* and in 1959 had written a twelve-part series on the writers called "the Beats." He had covered the New York arrival of the Beatles in March 1964 and credited himself with having introduced them to Bob Dylan. His regular column for the *Post* was called "Pop Scene."

Aronowitz had a keen eye for the commercial potential of the New York avant-garde. He arranged for The Velvet Underground's first paid performance at a suburban high school in New Jersey in December 1965 and became their manager until he was supplanted a few weeks later by Andy Warhol.

He was a pioneer in the new field of "rock journalism" whose eventual main purveyor, *Rolling Stone* magazine would be founded less than a year later in 1967. But he never seems to have been too scrupulous about the ethical line between journalist and entrepreneur. He was managing several rock groups when he was fired by the *New York Post* in 1972 for conflict of interest.

A review of Aronowitz's reminiscences comments that "It certainly takes a bit of hubris" to say that, as Aronowitz apparently did, "the

'60s wouldn't have been the same without me."[2] But, like the Kreeping Kreplachs whose press conference he reported on, Al Aronowitz did not suffer from a lack of hubris.

39 TULI KUPFERBERG

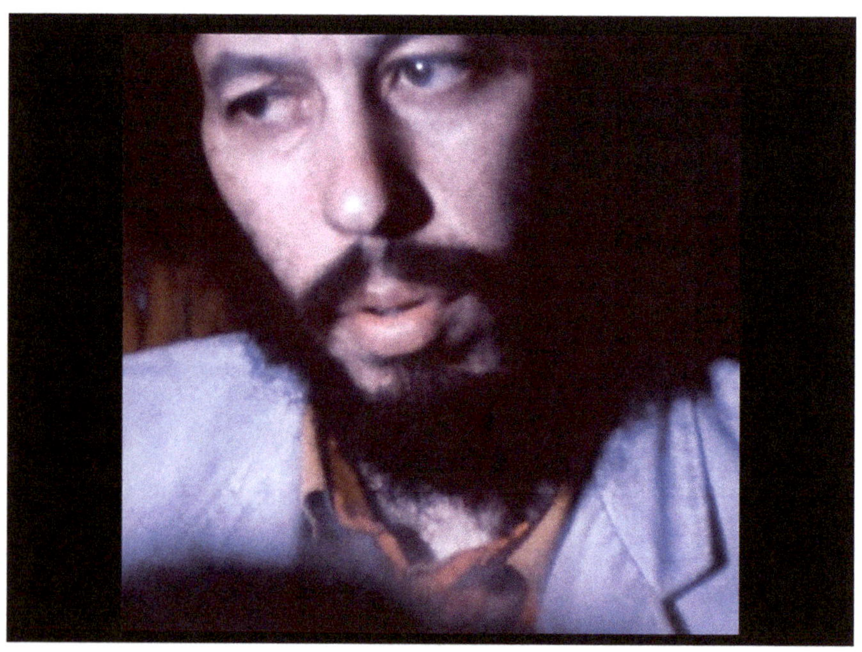

Reel 2 13:08

When the Kreeping Kreplachs assembled for a press conference at the Village Vanguard on Bleecker Street on June 7, 1966, they were speaking to the entire world. They announced that "the whole culture has moved and changed; a new generation has grown up."

But if their message was global, their origins were not. A number of the poets, musicians, and artists assembled on Bleecker St. were not far from their childhood homes.

Tuli Kupferberg and Peter Orlovsky were from a nearby neighborhood and Ginsberg was born just across the river in Newark. They came from places where Yiddish was still spoken and the word "kreplach" would not need the translation that Kupferberg offered the assembled journalists: "a Kreplach is what a Jewish mother calls her son when he decides to go into the arts instead of taking a job that will earn some money."

Born Naphtali Kupferberg, he grew up on Manhattan's Lower East Side. The political and musical activity of adjacent Greenwich Village drew him in early and he began publishing poems and humorous observations in *The Village Voice.*

At Ed Sanders's Peace Eye Bookstore, a former kosher delicatessen on East 10th Street, Kupferberg and Ed Sanders formed The Fugs, a rock band whose often scatological lyrics on their favored subjects of sex, drugs, and radical politics put them on the front lines of the assault on conventional culture that the Kreeping Kreplachs announced.

Their first album, "The Village Fugs Sing Ballads of Contemporary Protest, Points of View and General Dissatisfaction," appeared in 1965. And Kupferberg's iconoclastic energy never faltered over the following decades. The Fugs disbanded in 1969 but reunited in 1984 and resumed performing. In 2004 the *Times* reported:

> Back in the 1960s the Fugs were profane pranksters who skipped the euphemisms in their determination to make love, not war. In two sets

on Thursday the Fugs offered a whiff of that ephemeral 1960s moment when it seemed that pleasure could be revolutionary.[1]

In January 2010, after Kupferberg suffered a serious stroke, a number of major figures in New York music, including Lou Reed and Phillip Glass, organized a benefit concert to raise money for his medical expenses. Kupferberg was not physically able to attend but his 10-second video message to the concertgoers was reported in the *New York Times*: "'Now go out there and have some fun,' he said, with a strange smile. 'It may be later than you think.'"[2]

He died six months later.

40 ALLEN GINSBERG

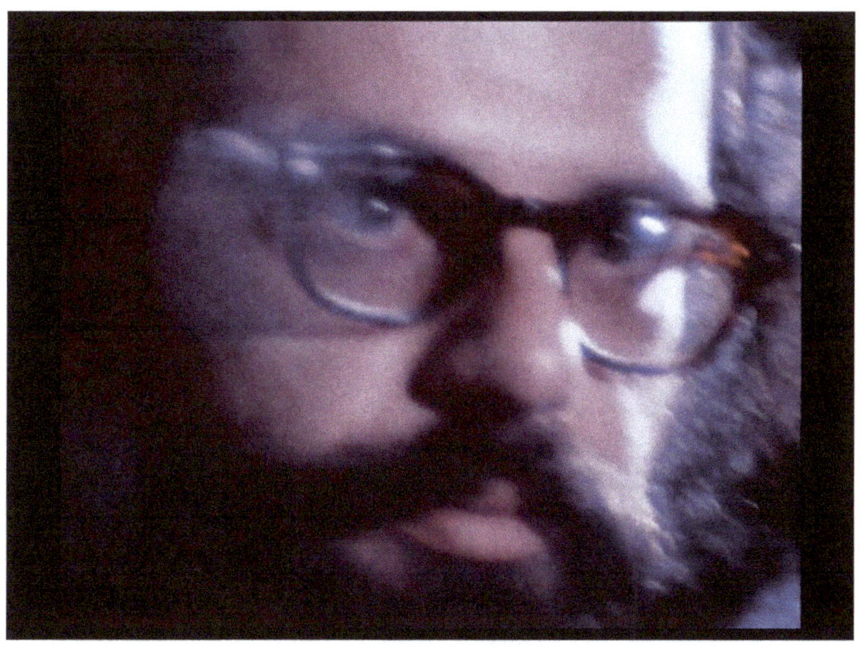

Reel 2 13:09

At center stage at the press conference of the Kreeping Kreplachs at the Village Vanguard on June 7, 1966, was Allen Ginsberg. He was the éminence grise, the natural spokesman for the East Village poets, musicians, and artists gathered to announce to the mainstream press that "the whole culture has moved and changed; a new generation has grown up."

Born and raised nearby in New Jersey, Ginsberg seemed to unite all of the elements of the cultural maelstrom brewing in the East Village - poetry, music, politics, religion. His appearance at an event guaranteed its import and consequent media attention.

Unlike the other Kreplachs who were mostly still unknown, Ginsberg had achieved celebrity decades earlier. He had close ties to all the Beat poets and novelists, - Jack Kerouac, William Burroughs, Gregory Corso - dating from the early 1950s in New York and then in San Francisco where his most famous work *Howl* was published in 1956.

In the late 1950s and early 1960s, Ginsberg travelled widely in Europe, including several years in Paris with other American expatriates including Burroughs and Corso, who shared cheap lodgings at what came to be known as "The Beat Hotel" in Paris.

In the spring of 1965 Ginsberg was reading his poetry on a European tour with Bob Dylan and they had performed to a sold-out audience at the Royal Albert Hall in London. The tour was documented in D. A. Pennbaker's film *Don't Look Back* (1967).

The London success inspired Ginsberg and his (and Mekas's) close friend and accomplice, Barbara Rubin, to book the same venue for an all-poetry event and on June 11,1965, in London, Ginsberg had presided over the "International Poetry Incarnation." In retrospect the event has come to be seen as marking a sort of transformation of the 1950s introspective beatnik culture into the more extraverted counter-culture of the 1960s.

At the time Mekas started filming the sequences which he would incorporate into *Walden*, Ginsberg was back in New York living in the East Village. Mekas recalled:

> I think I met Ginsberg at the Living Theater just after the theater had moved up to 6th Avenue and 14th Street from lower Broadway. I don't know what the event was but I remember introducing myself and we had some conversation.
>
> Later when I moved to East 13th St. I discovered that Allen lived there too just a block away and so we used to see each other more often. He visited me when I was editing *Guns of the Trees*. He read some of his poetry for the soundtrack and he used to come and watch me doing the editing.
>
> But before I formally met him, I remember I was filming an event at the Living Theater, maybe in '57, and he stopped me. It was not in the air at the time to just show up someplace and film and I had an old camera that made a lot of noise, a great "rrrrrrr!" So, when I pulled out the camera while Allen was reading his poetry and started filming, the noise bothered him and he yelled at me: "Stop it!"

Twenty years later, when he saw the footage that I had managed to get that evening, he said, "Oh! You should have filmed more!" And I said, "Yeah Allen, but it was you who stopped me!"[1]

It is ironic that Mekas's first memory of Ginsberg was his asking him to stop filming since, in the years that followed, Ginsberg was among the most frequently filmed figures in American counter-culture. Whatever the event - protest marches, sit-ins, rock concerts - throughout the following three decades, Ginsberg seemed always to be in front of the cameras.

But in the end, it was Mekas who had the last word. In the segment of his video diary, *Scenes from Allen's Last Three Days on Earth as a Spirit*

(1997), Mekas filmed at Ginsberg's deathbed, recording the last farewells of family and friends.

41 PETER ORLOVSKY

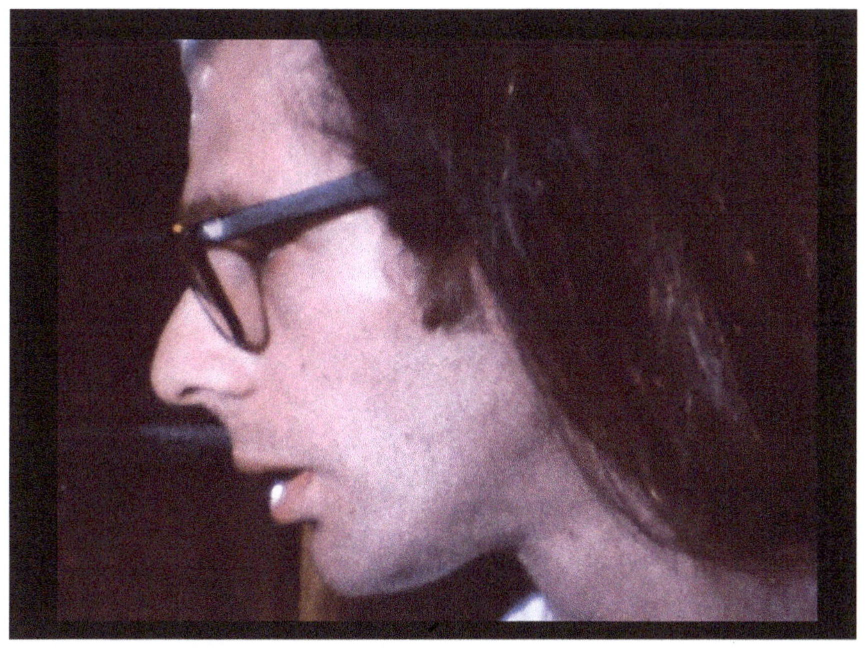

Reel 2 13:13

Like his fellow Kreeping Kreplach, Tuli Kupferberg, Orlovsky was born and raised on the Lower East Side of New York City, the son of Yiddish-speaking immigrants. Though they were both from New York, he actually met Ginsberg in San Francisco in December 1954. They were partners for four decades until Ginsberg's death.

It was during their years in Paris, living in what became known as the "Beat Hotel" with fellow expatriates William Burroughs and Gregory Corso, that Ginsberg encouraged Orlovsky to begin writing poetry. His work would eventually be widely published and anthologized.

In addition to his appearances, usually at Ginsberg's side, in Mekas's diary films, Orlovsky was prominent in the first "beat" film, Robert Frank's *Pull My Daisy* (1959) and was the subject, along with his brother Julius, of Frank's *Me and My Brother* (1969).

Julius Orlovsky had been diagnosed with catatonic schizophrenia and institutionalized at a psychiatric hospital on Long Island since 1950. In January 1965, though Julius's condition was unimproved, his brother and Ginsberg assumed responsibility for caring for him themselves in their East Village apartment. Julius accompanied the two to the Kreeping Kreplach press conference in June 1966.

In addition to caring for Julius, it surely required additional strength and courage for Orlovsky and Ginsberg never to disguise their partnership wherever they went. Even if open homosexuality did not draw attention in New York, the couple frequently traveled to places in the world where it was officially illegal.

42 ED SANDERS

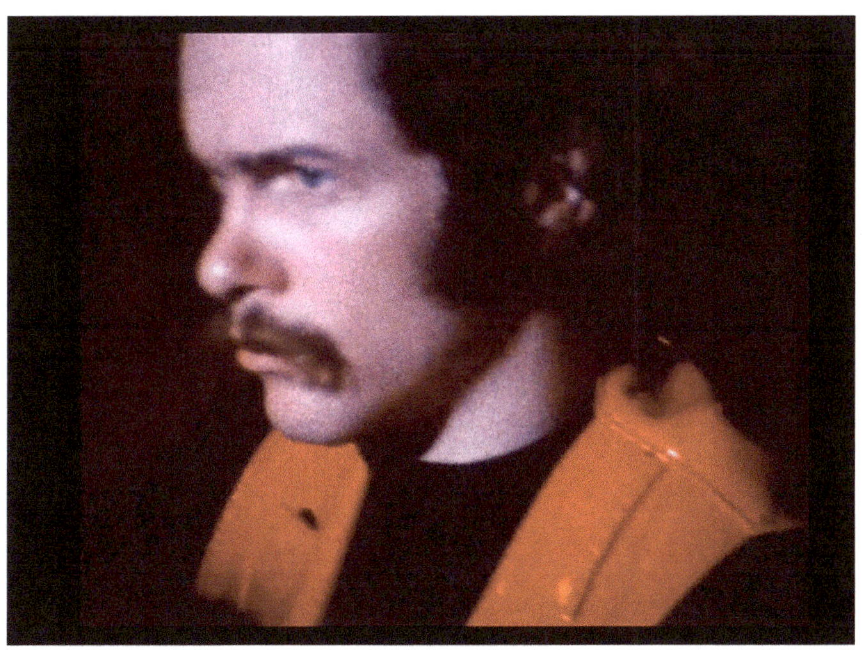

Reel 2 14:06

Ed Sanders was not, like his fellow Kreeping Kreplachs, a native of the Lower East Side. He had landed there as a refugee from what he had found oppressive in his native Midwest.

He had left the University of Missouri and enrolled at New York University where he studied classical Greek while pursuing a parallel life as publisher of *Fuck You: A Magazine of the Arts*. He was the proprietor of the unofficial headquarters of the counter-culture, the Peace Eye Bookstore, and co-founder of the rock band The Fugs with Tuli Kupferberg. Testifying at the infamous "Chicago Seven" trial in 1970, Sanders identified himself to the judge as a "poet, songwriter, leader of a rock-and-roll band, publisher, editor, recording artist, peace-creep."[1]

Inspired by Mekas's *Guns of the Trees* (1962) and Allen Ginsberg's recitation of his "Sunflower Sutra" on its soundtrack, Ed Sanders decided to buy a 16mm camera and throw himself into "underground" filmmaking. But the footage of his planned exposé of Lower East Side amphetamine addicts was confiscated when the police raided his bookstore in January 1966 and charged him with obscenity. His career as a filmmaker went no further but the publicity surrounding his arrest opened other possibilities.

Six months after the Kreeping Kreplach press conference recorded in *Walden*, Sanders was on the cover of *Life Magazine*. Its issue of February 17, 1967 displayed his face in close-up and the title of the cover story: "HAPPENINGS/ the worldwide underground of the arts creates THE OTHER CULTURE."

He recalled 1967 as:

> …an interesting year. It contained this interlude called the Summer of Love, where in San Francisco and New York City - but also places in the Midwest where the Fugs toured - there were these love-ins. We would go to little towns in the Midwest on tour, and there would be a crowd of younger people who were holding a love-in…we decided to

hold a demonstration at the very heart of the war - that is, right at the Pentagon. And the Fugs were charged with organizing an exorcism of the Pentagon.[2]

Sanders may not have grown up in a New York neighborhood where mothers used Yiddish pejoratives to criticize their sons but he had still risen to the rank of a true Kreeping Kreplach.

43 RONNA PAGE

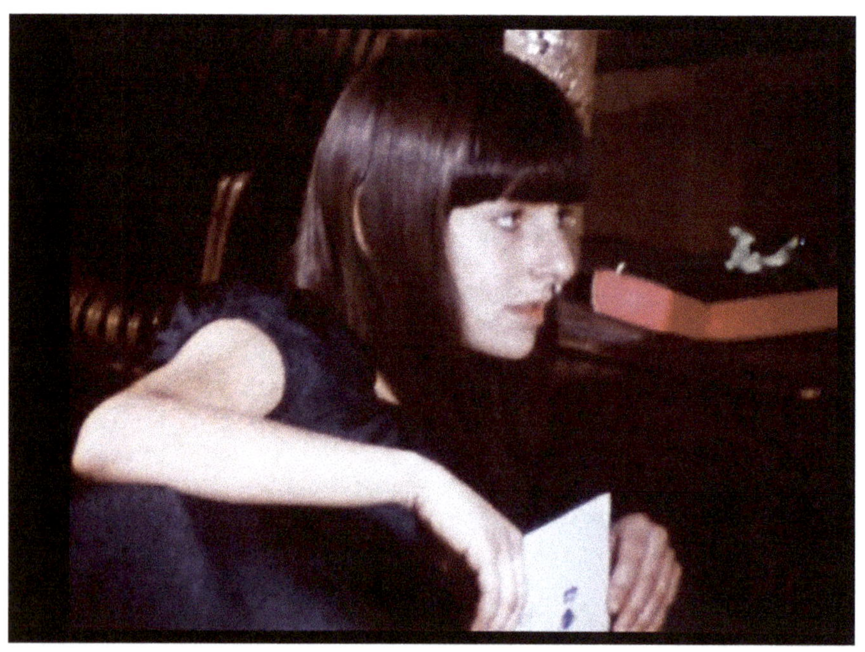

Reel 2 15:28

Ronna Page appears first in *Walden* very briefly next to Andy Warhol at the Kreeping Kreplach press conference on June 7, 1966. At the end of the same year, Mekas filmed Barbara Rubin filming Page in a sequence entitled "Barbara & Ronna, shooting, under a Christmas tree."

Mekas had introduced Page to Andy Warhol who gave her one of his *Screen Tests* (1964-66), number 252. And she appeared subsequently in several Warhol films, most notoriously in a sequence of *The Chelsea Girls* which had been taken from a previous Warhol production, *The Pope Ondine Story* (1966).

Ondine was the screen name of Robert Olivo, a flamboyant personality who had previously appeared in a number of other Warhol films. In the scene with Page, Ondine, having just injected himself with amphetamine, becomes enraged when she accuses him of being a phony and abruptly slaps her. Warhol recalled that:

> It got so real that I got upset and had to leave the room – but I made sure to leave the camera running…This was something new. Up until this, when people got violent during any of the filmings, I always turned the camera off and told them to stop, because physical violence is something I just hate to see happening, unless, of course, both people like it that way. But now I decided to get it all down on film, even if I had to leave the room.[1]

The scene was instrumental in boosting the notoriety of *The Chelsea Girls*. It attracted such large crowds that Warhol decided to move its showings from Mekas's Cinematheque in the basement of the Wurlitzer Building to more commercial movie theaters, first in New York, then in other American cities.

44 ANDY WARHOL

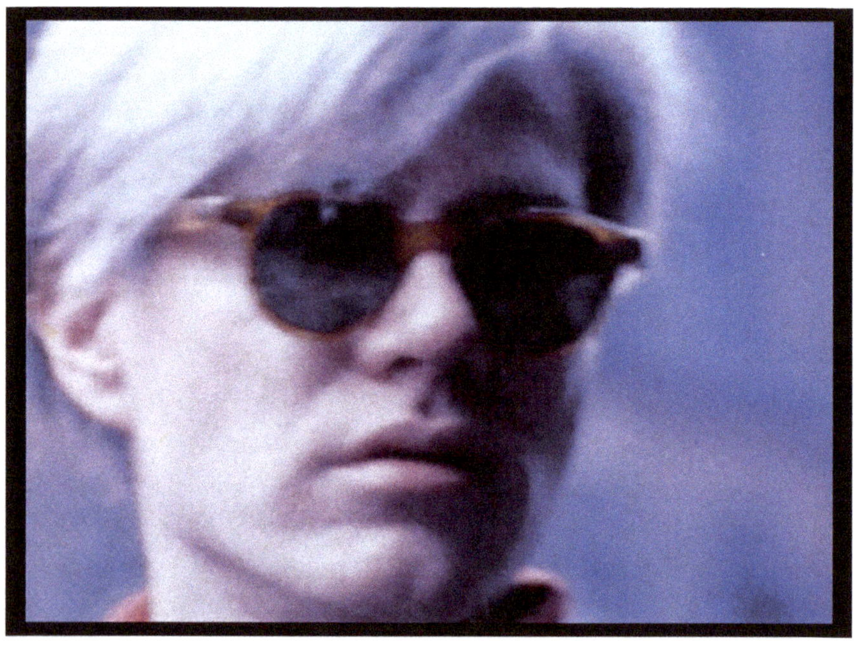

Reel 2 15:30

Warhol and Mekas seemed to have little in common. The former was a magnet for journalists, an inexhaustible subject of articles and interviews, the latter struggled constantly, often in vain, to attract any attention at all to his frequently sparsely attended film screenings. One became enormously wealthy in the art market, the other had to deal with the financial challenges of the organizations he created for his entire life.

Both were filmmakers. But Mekas took his camera everywhere and shot in short bursts of frames that, when projected, accelerated "normal" motion. Warhol took his camera nowhere; he planted it in his studio and recorded virtually no motion at all. Mekas's films made daily life look lively and constantly changing, Warhol's celebrated monotony - *Sleep* (1963) recorded a static subject for over 5 hours; *Empire* (1964) for 8 hours.

But there were close links.

After the Film-Makers' Cooperative started in January 1962, Mekas began showing films in the loft at 414 Park Ave South where he was also living. When Naomi Levine first mentioned Warhol to Mekas by name, he replied:

> 'Warhol? I don't know him, he's your friend?' And she says, 'You don't know Warhol? He has been sitting here in your loft for months, watching films…why don't you know Warhol?' There had been so many people sitting on the floor (we had no chairs) watching those movies that I hadn't had time to meet them all. But when I saw Warhol at Naomi's party, I recognized that he had in fact been there all the time."[1]

Their paths intersected constantly. While Warhol's wealth and fame started with his "Pop Art" silkscreens and paintings (his first New York solo exhibition was in November 1962), he worked in a wide variety of media, including film.

He started filming *Sleep* in July 1963 and Mekas wrote about it in his column in the *Village Voice* entitled ON ANDY WARHOL before it was even finished:

> It doesn't have to be a great or a complex work of art to be a witness of a passionate movement forward. Andy Warhol, for instance, is in the process of making the longest and simplest movie ever made: an eight-hour-long movie that shows nothing but a man sleeping. But this simple movie will push Andy Warhol - and has pushed me, and a few others who saw it, some of it - further than we were before. As simple as it is, it is a movement forward that carries others with it. Therefore it is beautiful like anything that is alive. Anything that is alive is beautiful - that is my statement for the week.[2]

The world premiere of *Sleep* was at the Film-Makers Cinematheque on January 17, 1964. Subsequent Warhol films would all be shown by Mekas, culminating in *The Chelsea Girls* (1966) which attracted so large an audience that it eventually left the basement Cinematheque and moved to a bigger theater.

Warhol, one of the most successful artists of the 20th century, endowed a foundation to distribute his fortune after his death. Mekas struggled to the end to raise funds for his Anthology Film Archives. But, Mekas recalled in a late interview, "We remained friends."[3]

45 WALTER BOWART

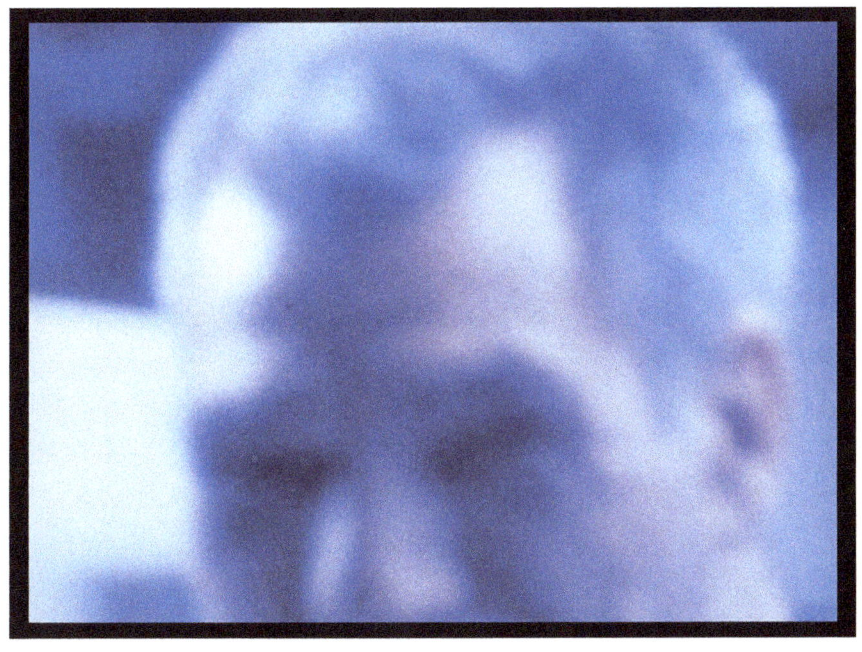

Reel 2 15:34

The Village Voice, based on Christopher Street in the West Village, may have published Mekas's calls for a revolution in film but by the middle of the 1960s, it had become too staid for many in the neighborhood further east.

The East Village was already home to Ed Sander's Peace Eye Bookstore where he started *Fuck You: A Magazine of the Arts* in 1962. But Sanders' objectives were not overtly commercial. *The East Village Other* however, founded by Walter Bowart in October 1965, wanted to compete with *The Village Voice* as a business.

The *"EVO"* had only existed for six months at the time of the Kreeping Kreplach press conference but had already been noticed as "a New York newspaper so countercultural that it made *The Village Voice* look like a church circular."[1] And it was clearly aimed at a younger generation than its West Village neighbor.

The Village Voice had only been founded in 1955 but the literary bohemian tradition of the West Village dated back to the early years of the century. The East Village as a center of cultural radicalism was a relatively new phenomenon, fueled by the eastward migration of those who could not afford the rising rents of the West Village.

Bowart was already part of their culture. The name for his regular column in the *EVO* was "Turn On, Tune In and Drop Out," Timothy Leary's rallying cry to the new generation. Testifying before the Senate Special Subcommittee on Juvenile Delinquency in Washington in the spring of 1966 on the question of whether to make LSD illegal, Bowart recommended that senators try it first.

The reach of the *EVO* was extended nationally when Bowart founded the Underground Press Syndicate at about the same time as the Kreeping Kreplach press conference. The syndicate agreed to allow its members to freely share all their contents, greatly lowering the financial barriers to starting new counter-culture publications in other cities across the country.

The graphic design of the *EVO* was as iconoclastic as its writing and its issues were a vector of what came to be called "psychedelic art." Its cartoonists included Robert Crumb and Art Spiegelman, pioneers of "underground comix" and the emergence of the graphic novel.

Bowart left New York just a few years later in 1968. The *EVO* only survived until 1972 but, for its short existence, it mirrored the unique quality of its time and place.

46 GERARD MALANGA

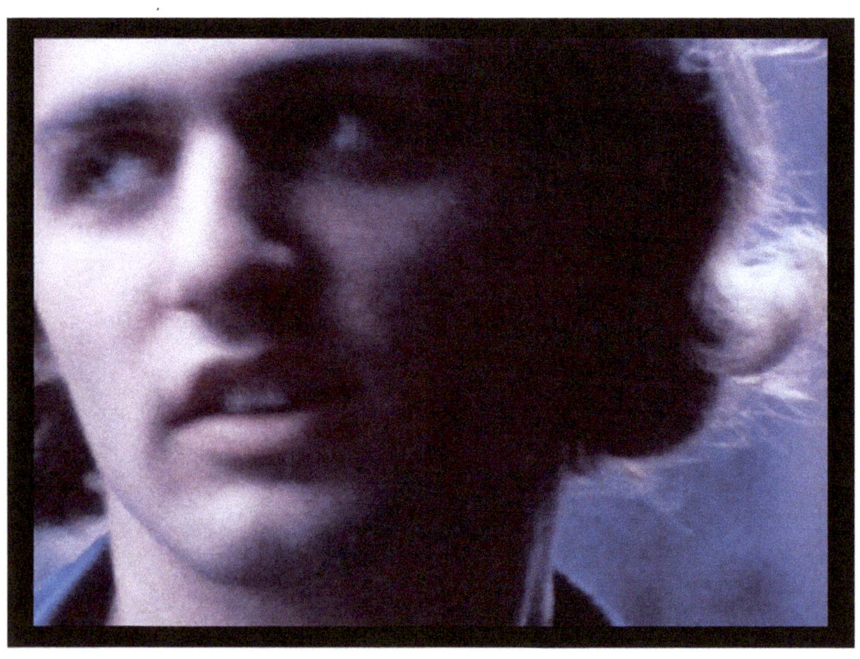

Reel 2 15:36

When he appeared at the Kreeping Kreplach press conference on June 7, 1966, Gerard Malanga seemed to be as close to the center of Andy Warhol's world as Warhol was.

He had met Warhol through the film artist Marie Menken and her husband the poet Willard Maas. Maas had been his English professor at Wagner College on Staten Island. He became an assistant in Warhol's studio in 1963 working first on his silkscreens but eventually on virtually all of Warhol's multiple activities.

Befitting the multiplicity of his activities, his appearances in *Walden* are also diverse - on the panel of Kreplachs at their press conference, animating a small "UPTOWN PARTY" in the apartment of photographer Stephen Shore, and then performing with the Velvet Underground in a hotel ballroom as part of Warhol's Exploding Plastic Inevitable multimedia performance event.

Malanga was clearly ready to inject life into whatever occasion required. In addition to his dancing and acting, he recited his poetry in Warhol's films *Camp* (1965) and *Bufferin* (1966) and was one of the four original editors of Warhol's *Interview* magazine when it published its first issue in November 1969.

After *Lonesome Cowboys* (1968), Warhol's film production came under the more commercially ambitious management of director Paul Morrissey and Malanga left the Warhol entourage to continue to write poetry and, increasingly, to make photographs.

His book of still photographs *Screen Tests Portraits Nudes 1964-1996* grew out of the series *Screen Tests*, the nearly 500 3-minute film portraits on notable personalities on the New York scene that he and Warhol made between 1964 and 1965.

47 STORM DE HIRSCH

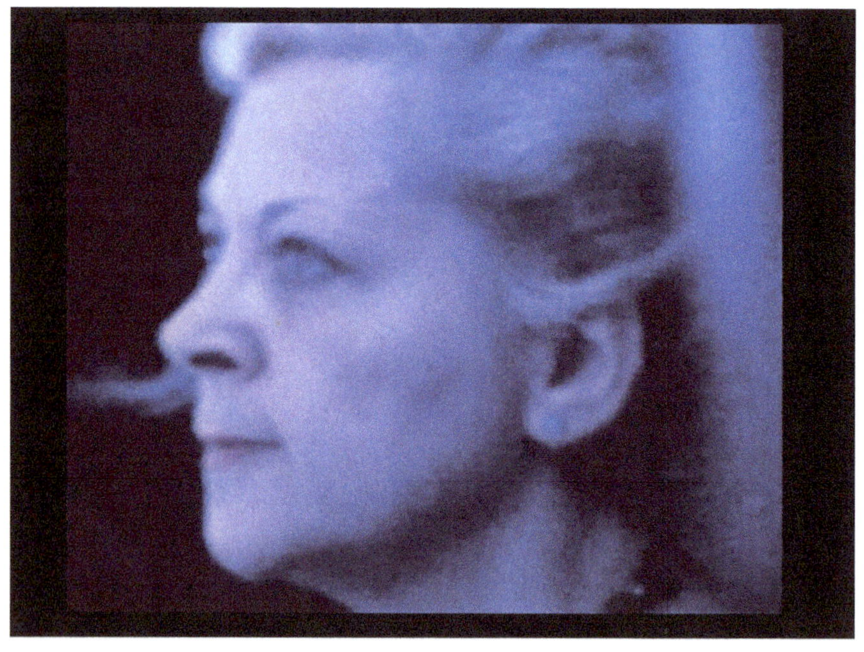

Reel 2 15;41

Storm de Hirsch had known Mekas practically since his arrival in the U.S. Her husband Louis Brigante (see Chapter 34) was on the editorial board of *Film Culture* at its founding in 1954. And while Brigante was assisting Mekas in other production tasks on *The Brig* (1964), de Hirsch filmed *Newsreel: Jonas in the Brig* (1964), a record of the shooting on the set of the Living Theatre production.

The Brig was Mekas's second feature-length film. Like his first, *Guns of the Trees* (1962), its format corresponded to the norm of commercial film distribution. And de Hirsch too was finishing a narrative feature film called *Goodbye in the Mirror* (1964).

But neither artist found their true voice in the expensive narrative-based feature film format. Mekas never returned to it and went on to make *Walden*. De Hirsch too had regrets and would recall:

> ...to make a feature film as my first film is the most idiotic and foolish thing anybody would ever conceive of, except that it was in sheer ignorance.[1]

Although it was a lot more interesting than de Hirsch's comments indicated, *Goodbye in the Mirror* had brought her to a critical realization and she turned to making films more closely aligned with her poetry - intense short works, some of which she would call *Cine-Sonnets* (1965).

Her film *Divinations* (1964), premiered at midnight on December 14, 1964 on a Film-Makers' Cinematheque program of short films at the New Yorker Theater. It was an intense abstract study of color shapes and sounds that lasted less than six minutes and it reflected de Hirsch's real gift: to sculpt with the medium of film itself.

In an interview that Mekas published in his *Village Voice* column, she explained:

I wanted badly to make an animated short and had no camera available. I did have some old, unused film stock and several rolls of 16 mm. sound tape. So I used that - plus a variety of discarded surgical instruments and the sharp edge of a screwdriver - by cutting, etching, and painting directly on both film and tape.[2]

Perhaps partly because she was a woman in a milieu dominated by men, appreciation for de Hirsch's work has been long delayed. But Mekas cannot be blamed; seeing her work, he wrote in 1963, "I couldn't believe what beauty struck my eyes, what unseen sensuousness.[3]

48 ABBIE HOFFMAN

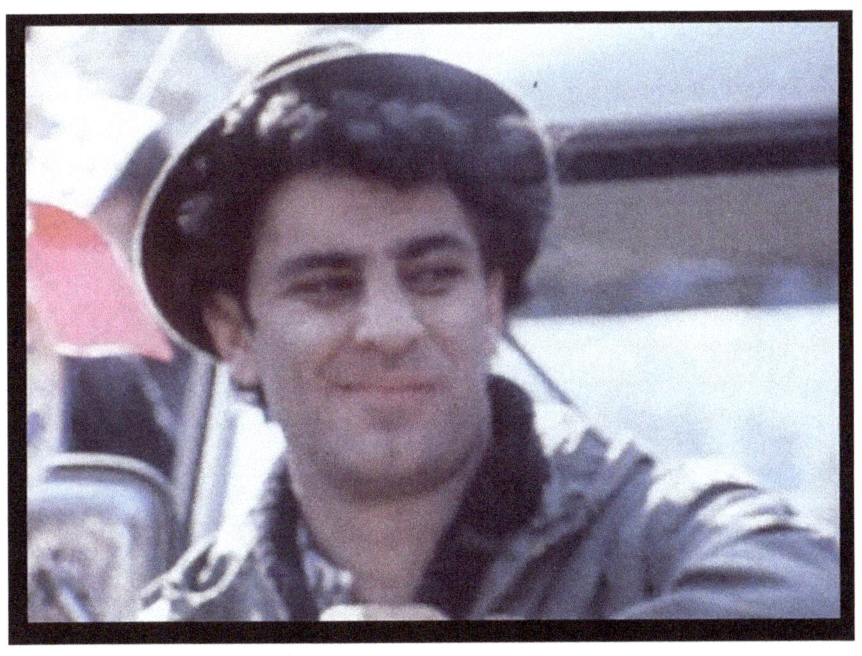

Reel 2 16:56

Political activism was not one of Mekas's main interests in *Walden*. Apart from two melancholy "flashback" scenes of Judith Malina protesting in Times Square earlier in the 1960s, Mekas filmed few overtly political events. But, given the climate of New York in the 1960s, politics were inevitably present at least in the background.

The press conference of the Kreeping Kreplachs in June 1966 was a progenitor of the kind of counter-culture media events that were to become frequent in the following years. Among their primary instigators were two figures who appear briefly in *Walden*, Abby Hoffmann and Paul Krassner. When Mekas glimpses them at the Central Park Be-In in the spring of 1967, they were about to emerge as major actors in the turbulent events soon to follow.

A few months later, Hoffmann and Krassner proclaimed themselves "Yippies," members of the "Youth International Party" and, on August 24, 1967, invaded the New York Stock Exchange and began showering the trading floor with what appeared to be dollar bills. The event was a media sensation, reported on around the world. A few months later, in October 1967, during the massive anti-Vietnam war demonstration in Washington, Hoffman would assist two of the Kreplachs, Ed Sanders and Allen Ginsberg, in their effort to levitate the Pentagon.

The Yippies used another press conference in New York at the Americana Hotel in New York on March 17, 1968 to announce demonstrations at the Democratic National Convention in Chicago that August. Predictably, the publicity they generated guaranteed that the demonstration would be massively attended and the violence that it provoked became a major issue in national political life.

Along with his fellow "Yippies," Hoffman was a defendant in the infamous "Chicago Seven" trial in Chicago, accused of conspiracy and inciting to riot at the Democratic Convention.

As in virtually all of his public appearances, Hoffman's antic behavior in the Chicago courtroom proved irresistible to the national news media who amplified his every outrageous word and action throughout the duration of the trial.

Curiously, since Mekas was not normally reticent about listing the celebrities who appeared in his film, Hoffman was not mentioned on the *Walden* poster. Maybe it was simply because the glimpse of him was so fleeting but it could also have been deliberate. Surely Mekas did not want to link the premiere of *Walden* in December 1969 to the current frenzy surrounding about the Chicago Seven trial.

49 PHILIP CORNER

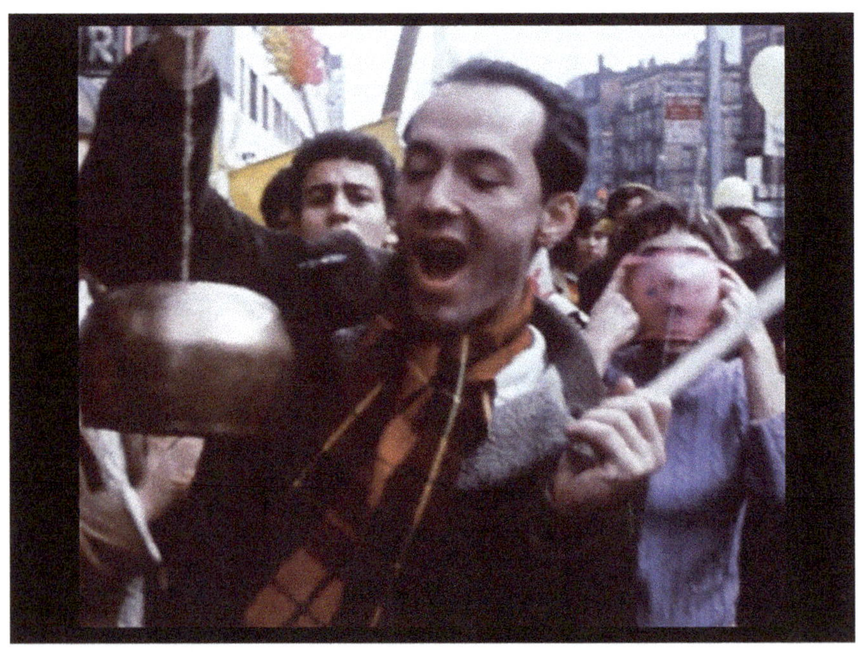

Reel 2 18:23

The spiritual leader Swami Prabhupada had arrived in New York from India in October 1965 to find a burgeoning counter-culture in search of new sources of spiritual guidance. With the encouragement of Allen Ginsberg, he rented a small shop at 26 Second Avenue in the East Village and founded ISKCON, the International Society for Krishna Consciousness.

One of ISKCON's principal practices was to organize street processions chanting the Hare Krishna mantra both as a way to express devotion and to attract converts to the movement. Followers assembled in streets and parks, to sing the mantra accompanied by various percussion instruments. Its first major procession on November 6, 1966 assembled at Tompkins Square Park in the East Village and proceeded, singing and dancing, uptown.

Most of the musicians in the Hare Krishna procession were amateurs but at least one of them, Philip Corner, was actually a major figure in contemporary music.

Corner had studied music at New York's High School of Music & Art in New York City, the City College of NY, and Columbia University, and spent two years in Paris in classes at the Conservatoire National de Musique taught by Olivier Messiaen. Back in New York, he was a composer and musician for the Judson Dance Theater and worked with John Cage whom he would replace as a professor of Modern Music at the New School for Social Research in 1967.

Corner was equally active on the art scene as a founding participant with George Maciunas in the Fluxus Group and collaborator with the Living Theater. His piece "Piano Activities" was one of the most provocative of those performed during a Fluxus tour of Europe in 1962. It consisted of Fluxus artists, including Maciunas, Dick Higgins, and Wolf Vostell gradually dismantling a grand piano and auctioning its pieces to the audience.

50 MARTY GREENBAUM

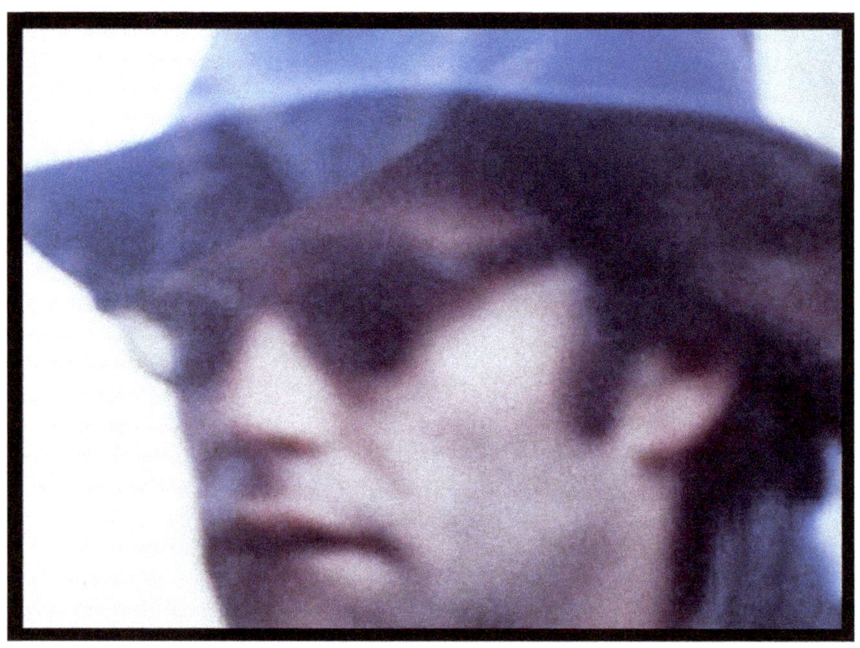

Reel 2 16:44

On April 26, 2020 a memorial service for the artist Marty Greenbaum was held at the place where, almost sixty years earlier, he had shown his art work for the first time. He had been in a group exhibition in 1961 at Judson Memorial Church on Washington Square South.

Briefly visible as a celebrant in Mekas's scenes of the November 1966 Hare Krishna procession, Greenbaum had had a more prominent role in Adolfas Mekas's film *Hallelujah the Hills* (1963) and appears more in earlier diary footage that Mekas was to include in *Lost Lost Lost* (1976). He also played in two films by his friend Robert Frank, *Life Dances On* (1980) and *The Present* (1996).

Greenbaum was an ally of women artists at a time when barriers to female artists in the art world were very high. He was the only male participant in a group show, *Objects,* at the Van Bovenkamp Gallery along with Carolee Schneemann in 1965.

His first solo show was at the Stryke Gallery at 86 E. 10 St. run by the feminist painter Dorothy Iannone and her husband. The gallery was a part of the 10th Street gallery co-op movement which were often artist-run and an avant-garde response to the exclusive galleries uptown on 57th St.

Greenbaum grew up in Brooklyn near Coney Island, working in penny arcades and selling ice cream on the beach. He had been a settlement house counselor on the streets and described himself as:

> a city walker …with photographs, drawing, painting, and collage, I make images that are layered and full of the ephemera of this here and now reality. My work is multi-directional, ricocheting back and forth as if through the strata of time.[1]

He was a pioneer maker of artist's books. The curator Edward Bryant wrote that:

> Greenbaum's books are painterly and tactile transformations of actual books...they do not illustrate; they are their content...like street walls collaged by the violence of time and weather, layered with coats of paint, stuck together and embellished with rhoplex, acrylic, feathers, fur, wax, string, tape, watercolor, ink, clippings...a raw kind of visual poetry...[2]

Greenbaum's last solo exhibition was in 2001 at the Pacifica Fine Art Gallery at 546 Hudson Street. The critic Ed McCormack wrote that the work revealed Greenbaum to be "a refreshingly idiosyncratic visionary whose considerable oeuvre marries the jarring immediacy of outsider art to a consummately sophisticated aesthetic sensibility."[3] He concluded that it was "long overdue for serious reassessment."[4]

51 JEROME HILL

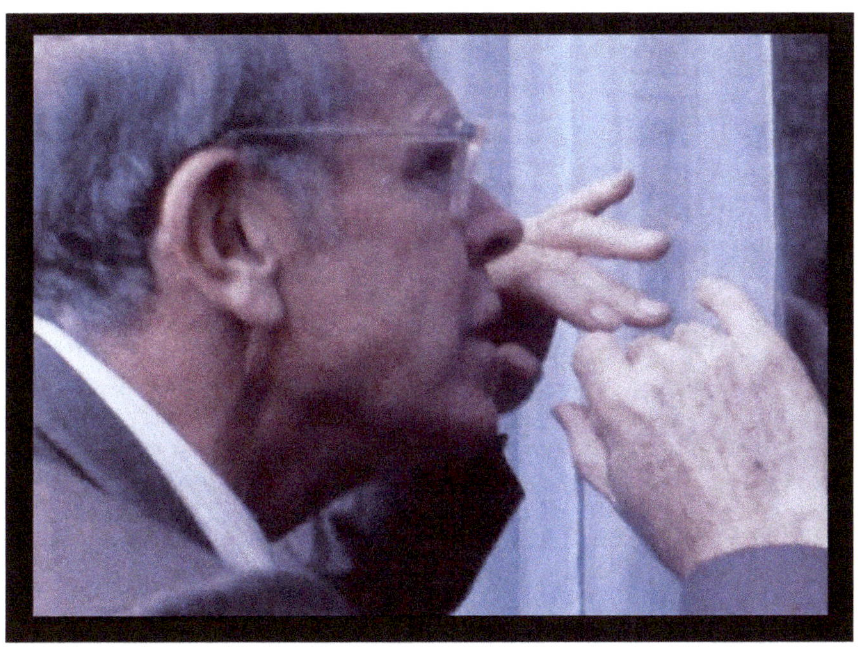

Reel 2 21:13

His brief appearance in *Walden* outside a closed museum trying to get a glimpse of the artwork inside is emblematic of both Jerome Hill's ardent pursuit of the arts and his outsider status as a very wealthy connoisseur peering into a world of, in general, very poor film artists.

An heir to an enormous fortune amassed by his grandfather and namesake, the builder of the Great Northern Railway, James Jerome Hill, he was exceedingly discreet - as much about his extensive philanthropy as about his work as an artist himself. But over forty years after Hill's death, Mekas finally left no doubt about the role of Jerome Hill in the history of American experimental film:

> Without Jerome I do not know how long *Film Culture* magazine would have existed, without Jerome, the Film-Makers' Cooperative would have closed in two or three years, without Jerome, Anthology Film Archives would not even exist, for Film-Makers' Cinematheque, it's the same …So wherever you look there is the presence of Jerome…[1]

In 1956, Mekas had gone to see Hill at the recommendation of MoMA film curator Willard Van Dyke. From its beginning in 1954, *Film Culture* had been in financial difficulty and Van Dyke suggested to Mekas that perhaps Hill could help. Hill not only rescued *Film Culture* but virtually every other Mekas venture and a sizable group of individual film artists as well.

After ensuring the survival of Mekas's magazine, distribution center, and exhibition activity, Hill asked Mekas to provide a list of twelve film artists deserving of help and then provided them with monthly stipends for years. Peter Kubelka, Stan Brakhage, and James Broughton and Mekas himself were among the beneficiaries.

Hill had studied music at Yale, practiced photography with Edward Weston in California, painted in Paris, and mounted theater productions with the Living Theater in a classical Greek-style outdoor theater of his own design overlooking the sea. He was fluent in multiple languages and had homes in the California Sierra Nevada, the Long Island Hamptons, Manhattan, Paris, and the French Côte d'Azur.

The last place appeared to be his favorite. And it was the view from Hill's villa above the small port of Cassis just east of Marseilles that Mekas captured in the short film *Cassis* (1966), later incorporated into *Walden*.

Filmmaking eventually took precedence over Hill's multiple other creative pursuits. He made fairly traditional documentaries (*Grandma Moses*, 1950, *Albert Schweitzer*, 1957), experimented with hand-painted animation (*Death in the Forenoon*, 1966, *Canaries*, 1968) before embarking on his most ambitious work, the autobiographical *Film Portrait* (1972).

In 1967 the Astor Library Building at 425 Lafayette Street, one of the first buildings to be designated a New York City Landmark by the newly formed Landmarks Preservation after the demolition of Penn Station, was being renovated to accommodate the New York Public Theater. Hill discovered there was space available there for a cinema as well.

He commissioned Peter Kubelka's radical design for an "Invisible Cinema," financed its realization, and established Anthology Film Archives with a collection of films that would constitute its "Essential Cinema." The creation of Anthology completed his remarkable legacy as a founding father of American experimental film.

52 KEN KELMAN

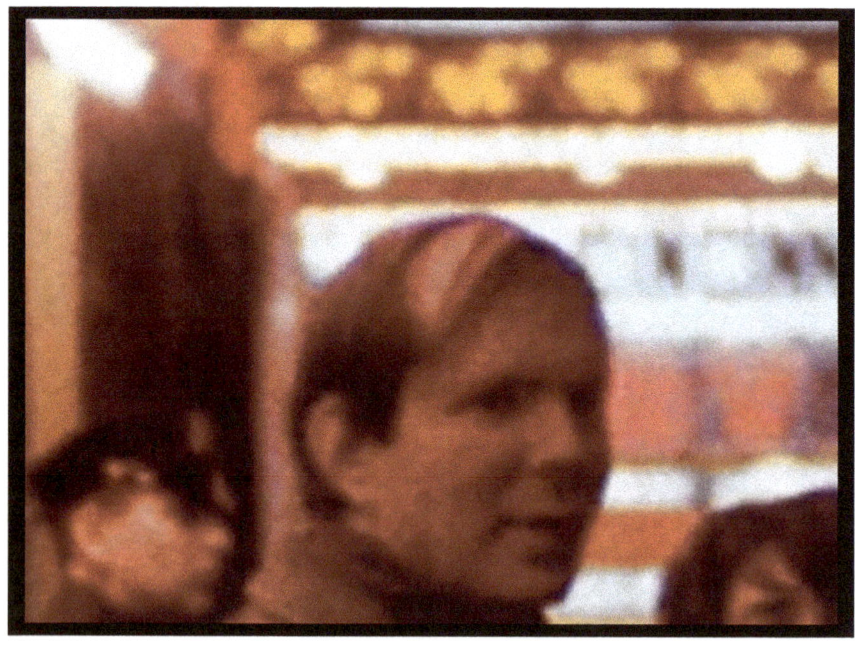

Reel 2 23:00

"Filmmaker Ken Kelman" is cited by Gene Youngblood in his book *Expanded Cinema.*[1] But it is not clear that Kelman made films.

Youngblood identified him as the author of the article "Anticipations of the Light" which was first published in the anthology *The New American Cinema.*[2] But neither that book nor Youngblood's mentioned any of his films by name.

Kelman was sometimes also described as a playwright but any trace of his plays is equally difficult to find. He was apparently involved, as a "cast member"[3] in *Angelface,* the first performance of Richard Foreman's Ontological-Hysteric Theater at the Film-Makers' Cinematheque in 1968, but was not cited as an author.

When Mekas organized his pioneering festival of "expanded" cinema in November of 1965, Kelman was on the list of participating artists. Others on the list would go on to create major works in the domain of multimedia installations, performance art, happenings, and video. But exactly how Kelman participated and what work he did subsequently is not clear.

Kelman was a member of the selection committee for the "Essential Cinema Repertory Collection" of Anthology Film Archives in 1970. With the exception of P. Adams Sitney - who clearly identified himself as a critic not an artist - the other committee members at the time - Peter Kubelka, James Broughton, and Mekas - were filmmakers in the Film-Makers' Cooperative catalogue. Kelman did publish articles in *Film Culture* between 1963 and 1970 but no film of his was listed in the Coop catalogue.

He was clearly important within Mekas's inner circle. As a member of the Anthology selection committee, Kelman held veto power in designating what films were to be considered "essential." But outside that circle, his role remains enigmatic. In a lecture on Carl Dreyer at the Carnegie Museum of Art on November 27, 1973, he was introduced neither as a filmmaker, nor a playwright, nor an artist but simply as a "semi-retired film critic."[4]

53 TIMES SQUARE

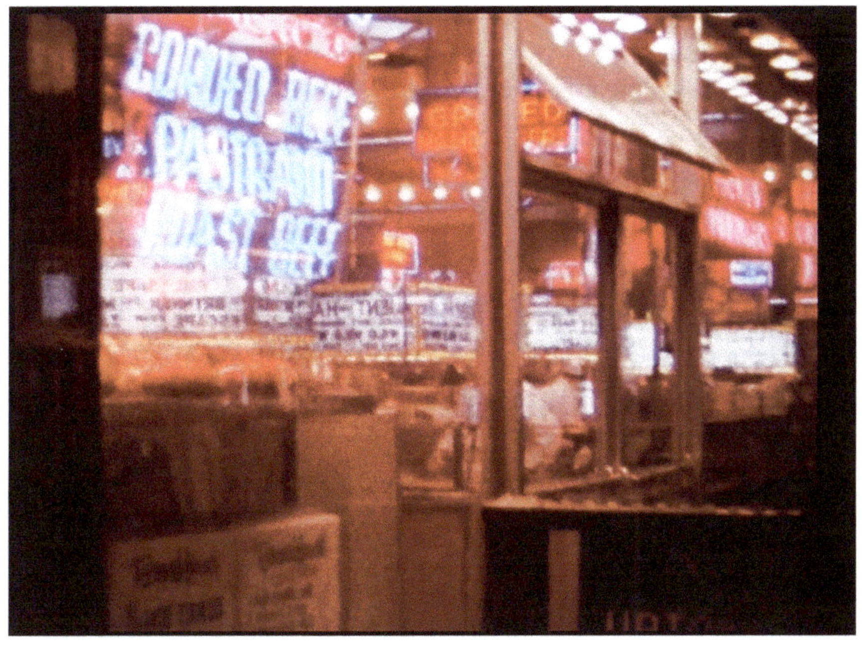

Reel 2 23:21

In November of 1949, the Mekas brothers had sailed from Hamburg on the first stage of a journey to Chicago where the International Refugee Organization had found them jobs. But when their ship docked in New York, their plans changed:

> We went to Times Square that evening. I will never forget the impact which hit us upon emerging from the subway, right smack into the very middle of a sea of neon lights. And in the middle of the sky, there was the moon. But I wasn't sure if it was real or not…The moon no longer a reality of its own; it was a prop in a huge set of New York.[1]

The subway from which the astonished immigrants emerged was below the building that gave the intersection of 42nd St. and Broadway its name, the Times Tower, one of the tallest buildings in New York when completed in 1904.

From the beginning, its exterior was intended to attract attention; the tradition of lowering an illuminated ball from its flagpole at midnight on New Year's Eve was observed by thousands in person and, in the television era, millions around the world. In 1928, "the zipper," a vast panel of 14,800 light bulbs began transmitting breaking news from the site. Four years before Mekas's arrival, it had announced the end of World War II to crowds gathered in Times Square.

The technology of outdoor advertising evolved; in 2019 the individual billboards were replaced by a single 110 meter high LED display. But the role of Times Square as a universally recognized icon for American energy did not change.

The frequent appearances of Times Square in *Walden* were surely also related to its proximity to the Wurlitzer Building at 120 West 42nd St., the home of the Film-Makers' Cinematheque for most of the years covered by the film. And Grant's Cafeteria further down towards Times Square on 42nd St. was a convenient spot to gather between screenings.

The images of mid-town Manhattan are yet another reminder of how different Mekas's *Walden* is from the *Walden* of Henry David Thoreau. Thoreau hated cities but Mekas never forgot the awe he had experienced the evening he had docked in New York for the first time. Thoreau's alternate title had been "Life in the Woods," Mekas's could have been "Life in Times Square."

54 BARBET SCHROEDER

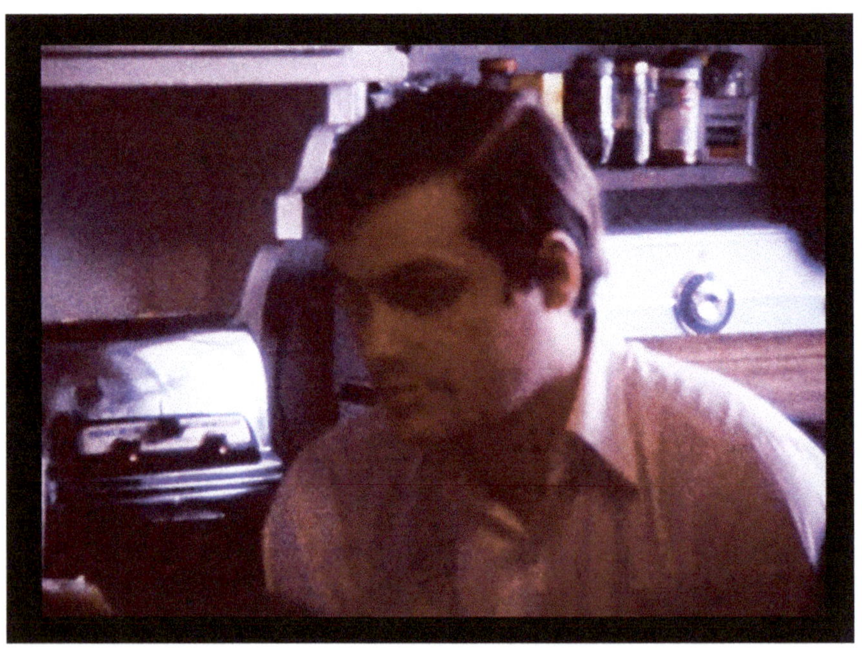

Reel 2 25:16

The 25 year-old Barbet Schroeder glimpsed in *Walden* at breakfast with Barbara and David Stone in early 1966 was, like the Stones, a film producer. He had founded "Les Films du Losange" with Eric Rohmer two years before and had just produced *Paris vu par…* (1965), released in English as *Six in Paris*.

For *Paris vu par…*, Schroeder had commissioned short films from six young directors, Jean-Luc Godard, Eric Rohmer, Claude Chabrol, Jean Douchet, Jean Rouch, and Jean-Daniel Pollet. They would be collectively described as the "Nouvelle Vague" and credited with rejuvenating the French film industry.

Schroeder would go on to a long professional career that had very little to do with avant-garde film. But, at the time, his activity in France seemed to Mekas to be a harbinger of change in the U.S. The first statement of his "New American Cinema Group" declared its ambition to become their American equivalent - a new generation of directors about to take over Hollywood. In 1960 he referred to them as "the American New Wave."[1]

But Mekas's hopes did not last long. A year later, in 1961, he would write in the *Village Voice*, that "the American cinema has different needs and is doing it in a different way, through its independent filmmakers and through its film poets…You just can't transplant styles from country to country, like beans."[2]

By 1964 - shortly before the period covered by *Walden*, Mekas realized that his future was not in "novelistic" cinema of producers like Barbet Schroeder. He wrote:

> I have often been accused of concentrating too much on the new cinema, forgetting Hollywood and Antonioni. I should state here that my actions, most of the time, are calculated (not by my brain but by my intuition). I myself brought Andrew Sarris into the *Voice* to cover the novelistic cinema, which he knows better than anyone else in this

country. Together we are attempting to give as complete an image of the cinema of today as we can...[3]

55 CAFETERIAS

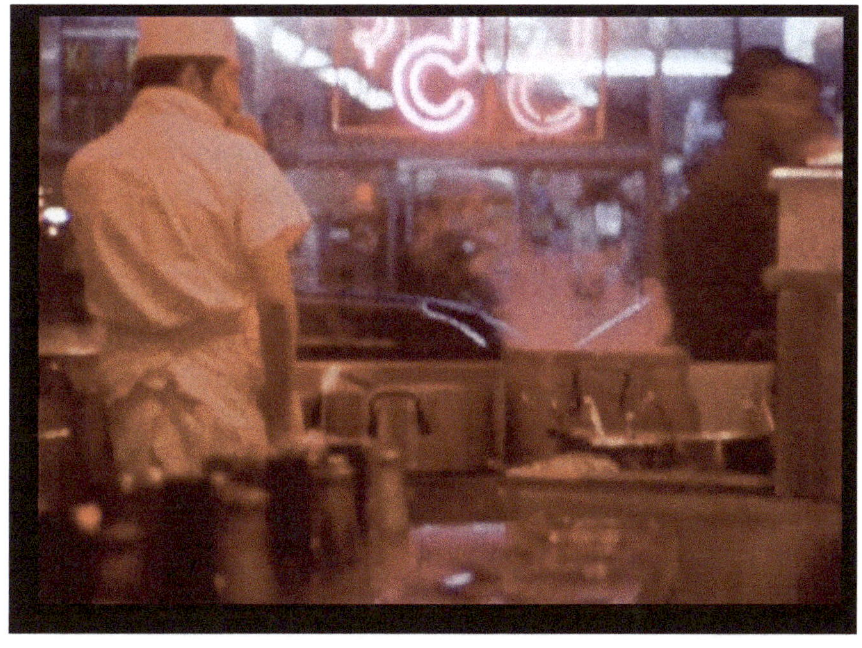

Reel 2 25:16

In *Go*, his 1952 novel about the "beat" world in New York, John Clellon Holmes described Grant's Cafeteria on 42nd Street:

> ...huge, teeming cafeteria on the corner of Broadway, where even steam tables fouled the air with a wild conflict of smells, and servers, presiding over them like unshaven wizards, imprecated the shuffling crowds indifferently, while greasy beardless busboys, like somnambulists, moved among the littered tables mechanically.[1]

What surely attracted Mekas and friends to Grant's fifteen years later was its proximity to the Film-Makers' Cinematheque, in the basement of the Wurlitzer Building just a block down 42nd Street.

Mekas recorded a convivial meal at Grant's which his intertitle describes as GOOFING ON 42ND STREET. It includes, among others, the writer and photographer Gretchen Berg, film artists Jerome Hiler and Nathaniel Dorsky, and the Fluxus artist John Cavanaugh who had his first one-man show at the Cinematheque in February 1967.

In addition to its urban vitality, there were also financial reasons to patronize cafeterias instead of regular restaurants. Customers served themselves so there were no waiters to tip and the duration of meals went unobserved. Long hours could be spent in a warm space at minimal expense.

P. Adams Sitney was later to contend that the ability to survive on very little money was a key element in establishing New York as a center of creative activity. He recalled that:

> My first place in New York City cost me nine dollars a week, and there was a place to eat where the cab drivers used to eat, the Belmore Cafeteria, and you could buy three vegetables for 45 cents - that's 15 cents a vegetable. They had a seltzer tap, and they had lemons, so you could make yourself a lemonade with free lemon, seltzer, and sugar, and then you could sit all afternoon and talk, if you wanted.[2]

The Belmore was as close to the Film-Makers' Coop on Park Avenue South as Grant's was to the Cinematheque. Its neon sign across the street is visible from the Coop's window.

56 JEROME HILER

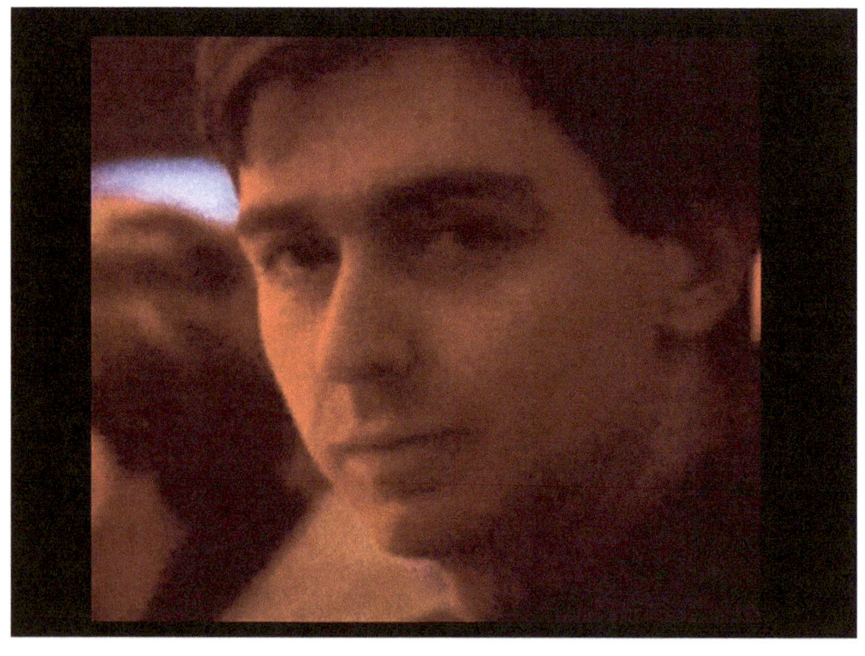

Reel 2 25:24

For decades Jerome Hiler's luminous 16mm films were known only to the few friends for whom he projected them in his San Francisco home. Interviewed in 2014 about his youth at the time of *Walden*, he recalled:

> When I was young, I had the idea that 'someday' I would make a film, have it printed, shown, and distributed - always at some future time. In the meantime, I had a circle of friends who either made films or were enthusiastic viewers. For many years I held regular screenings at home: in New York at my apartment on East Broadway, on Lake Owassa in New Jersey, and in San Francisco. It surprises people to know that I felt satisfied and stimulated with this limited circle, but I was…I admit that I felt irrelevant to the film scene after a while, but I do love people and want to do my best with what time I have left to share my work.[1]

When Hiler did actively begin to exhibit his film work in the 1990s, often along with that of his partner, the better-known film artist Nathaniel Dorsky, it was as if a new talent had been discovered. But, as *Walden* attests, Hiler had been present almost at the birth of the New York film avant-garde.

He first became aware of Mekas's activity when still a teenager in his native Queens:

> I would read Jonas Mekas's column and he would talk about these films that were very new and different from the fare that I had been looking at. I started to go to them. I was only eighteen, living in Queens, but I remember taking the train into Manhattan to the Bleecker Street Cinema at midnight, and a young David Brooks, a filmmaker who at the time was, I believe, the manager of the Bleecker Street, hosted these programs. Stan Brakhage appeared there; I think he presented *The Dead* (1960) there for the first time. He presented *Prelude: Dog Star Man* (1961) for the first time there as well, which

completely blew me away. I think that was one of the things that told me I would love to do this kind of thing, making films.[2]

A friend from Queens introduced him to Gregory Markopoulos:

He was busy shooting *The Illiac Passion* (1967) and, in a matter of weeks, I became his assistant, his location-hunter, and costume designer for nearly half a year. Gregory also let me borrow his Bolex camera, which was an honor beyond imagining. This mutation in my life was so powerful that I took it as a sign that film was my path from then on.[3]

For a while in the summer of 1964 Mekas was showing films at the Washington Square Art Gallery at 530 West Broadway and one of the programs included the first film of Nathaniel Dorsky. The latter recalled: "It was at that show that I met Jerome Hiler and Gregory Markopoulos. In many ways Jerome and I consider Jonas the reason that we met."[4]

In *Walden* Hiler and Dorsky are at the center of a sequence at Grant's Cafeteria (see Chapter 55) at a time when Hiler was a projectionist at the Film-Makers' Cinematheque in the Wurlitzer Building down the street. It was there Warhol told him how to project *The Chelsea Girls* (1966). (See Chapter 60).

But Hiler and Dorsky were never really in tune with the flamboyance of Warhol's entourage. They retreated first to rural New Jersey and eventually, in 1971, to San Francisco where, after a decade-long pause, they began, each in their own style, to pursue a more lyrical approach to film than most of what Hiler had been projecting at the Cinematheque.

But because they were reluctant to make prints of their work, it remained private. Dorsky eventually began distributing his work publicly through Canyon Cinema, including his *Hours for Jerome* (1982) edited from footage shot during their time in New Jersey. But Hiler remained reticent and, for a time, mostly withdrew entirely from film-making to explore, among other passions, medieval stained glass.

Hiler's film artistry only began to be recognized when his 2011 work *Words of Mercury* was shown at the 2012 Whitney Biennial. Describing it, critic Max Goldberg wrote:

> Neon lights and wild grass mingle in spring's amplitude, and when the film comes to rest on a landscape tableau - of falling snow, or two dogs leaping into an inlet - the whole picture trembles with newfound awareness of the world and its frame. Balancing description and being, reflection and volume, intuition and insight. *Words of Mercury* is an extraordinarily poised expression of the old photochemical magic, and a long overdue reminder of Hiler's extraordinary gifts.[5]

57 JOHN CAVANAUGH

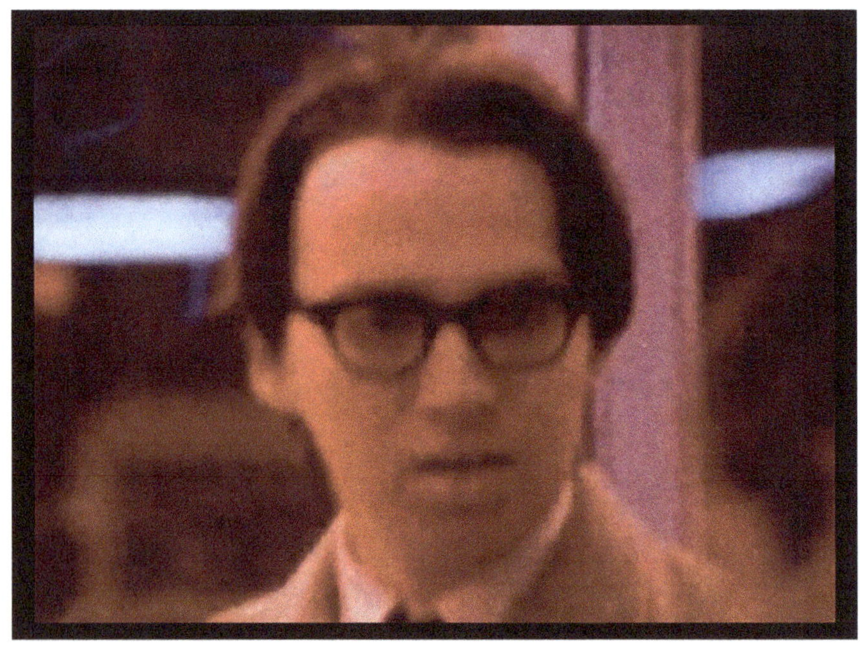

Reel 2 25:25

John Cavanaugh appeared several times in *Walden*, most visibly at Grant's Cafeteria (see Chapter 55). It may have been on the occasion of his first one-man show there in February 1967 or perhaps for the program on April 14 and 15, 1966 which listed *"8mm Studies by John Cavanaugh."*

8mm Studies (1966) would appear to be the same film that P. Adams Sitney describes as *Acid Man* in his 2008 book, *Eyes Upside Down*:

> Around 1966 John Cavanaugh, a part-time employee of the New York Film-makers Cooperative, shot *Acid Man*, inspired by his own LSD experiences. It was an 8 mm film that tried to capture 'states of high energy in the mind' with short, truncated room movements, dramatically shifting colors and trembling foliage, all radically slowed down by projection at six frames per second. Cavanaugh had dropped out of high school to work as a messenger at the Film-makers Cooperative. On a trip to Italy as the guest of the Pesaro Film Festival, he was arrested and spent some months in an Italian jail for drug possession. Eventually released and deported - he was still a teenager - he spent years in a New York mental hospital. His film is now lost.[1]

One film of Cavanaugh's that survived - but with comparable uncertainty about its title - is what is now known as *Fluxfilm n°5: Blink* (1966). In her definitive account of the Fluxus movement Hannah Higgins wrote:

> During a brief encounter with Fluxus in the mid-1960s, John Cavanaugh produced a film called *Flicker* included in the 1966 program of *Fluxfilms* assembled by George Maciunas. *Flicker* consists of alternating frames of black and clear celluloid that, when projected, assault the eye with a battery of flickers in extremely bright white and pure black. After a few seconds of this flickering, the eye becomes fatigued. Vision fades into a temporary blindness characterized by slowly moving, pulsating, colorless blobs that hover over the continuous flash

of film, a response due to the inability of the optic nerve to register the flickering frames.[2]

Cavanaugh's interaction with the Fluxus group may have been brief but *Blink* survived as part of an anthology of Fluxfilms along with works by its better known contributors including Nam June Paik, George Maciunas, Yoko Ono, and Paul Sharits.

In his *Village Voice* columns Mekas rarely connected his own role in the Film-Makers' Cinematheque or Film-Makers' Cooperative with the events that he wrote about and similarly he did not speak about Cavanaugh's employment there in his multiple mentions of him over the years. The last of those mentions was in the issue of December 7, 1967 and obviously referred to the same events described later by Sitney:

> When we talk about the changing eye, we cannot avoid talking about television. I remember John Cavanaugh, who is twenty, one of the most talented of the young film-makers, who went to the Pesaro film festival last June and created there quite a stir with his tactile movies, and who later went to Rome and got busted by the police and who is now in sort of a madhouse. He is so far out they thought he was out of his mind. But he's an artist and more normal than others.[3]

58 GRETCHEN BERG

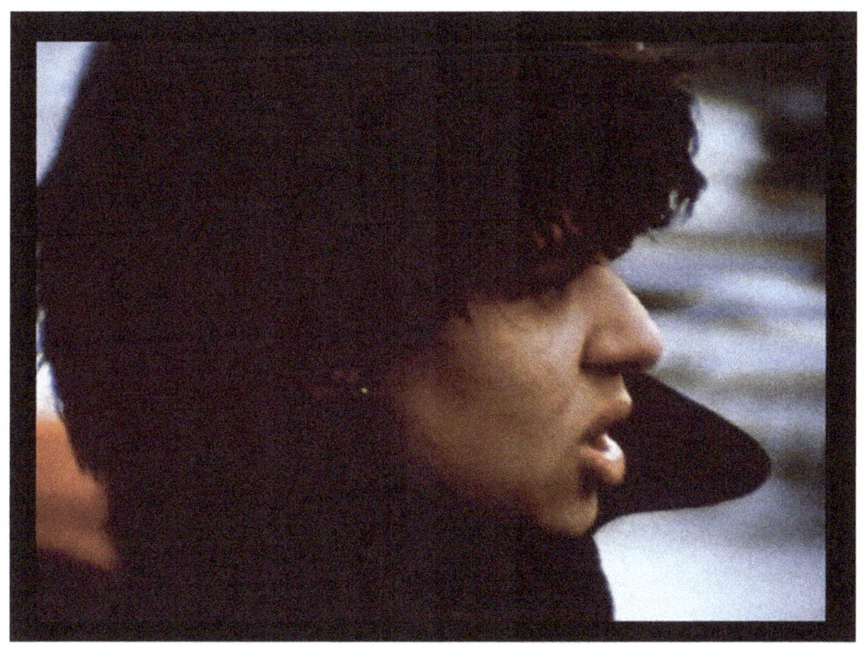

Reel 2 25:26

Gretchen Weinberg (she later shortened her name to Berg) was the daughter of Herman G. Weinberg, a central figure in the New York film world (see Chapter 77). As a child, she often accompanied her father to films and business meetings with such luminaries as Charlie Chaplin, Erich von Stroheim, Orson Welles, Jean Renoir, and Fritz Lang.

Her father contributed to Mekas's *Film Culture* from its inception in 1955, writing a regular column called "Coffee, Brandy and Cigars." And in the issue of Summer 1963, Gretchen made her own first contribution: an interview with film artist Len Lye.

Berg's most notorious interview would be published four years later: "Andy Warhol: My True Story." It appeared in the *East Village Other* in November 1967 and was subsequently reprinted in *Cahiers du Cinéma* and syndicated by the Underground Press Syndicate. Widely considered the definitive Warhol interview, it contained insights such as: "If you want to know all about Andy Warhol, just look at the surface of my paintings and me, and there I am. There's nothing behind it." Or "The artificial fascinates me, the bright and shiny."

The quotes seemingly captured the quintessence of Warhol so they were frequently repeated in other articles about him. But subsequent study of the original recordings by the archivist at the Warhol museum, Matt Wrbican, revealed that the words were not Warhol's but Gretchen Berg's - although Warhol had almost certainly approved her embellishments.

Berg was also an intrepid photographer of the New York scene at the time, including the opening of Anthology Film Archives in 1970. "Troublemakers," a collection of her portrait photographs of children and teenagers protesting in New York between 1967 and 1975, was shown at the Warhol Museum in Pittsburgh in 2007.

59 NATHANIEL DORSKY

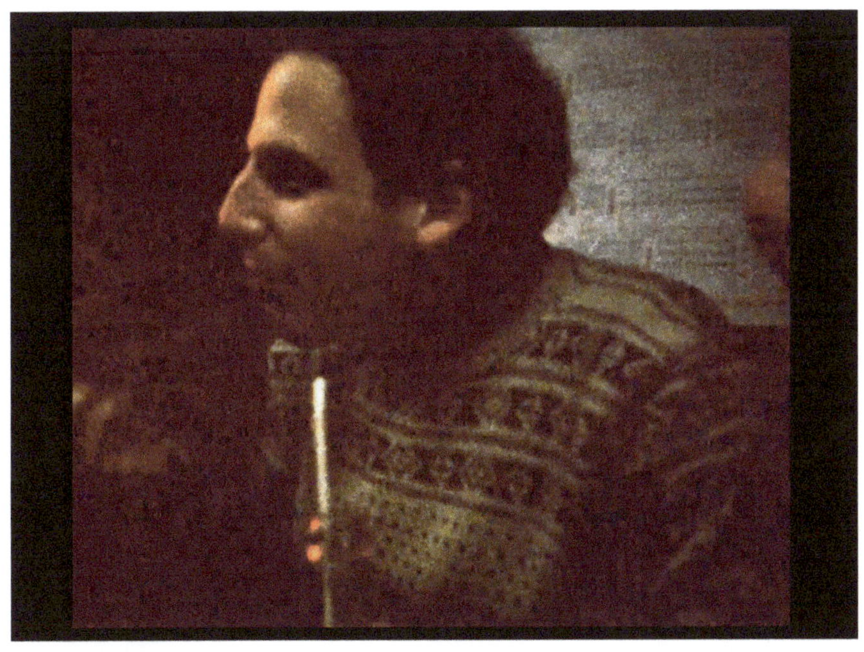

Reel 2 25:29

When Nathaniel Dorsky met Mekas in New York in 2015 on the occasion of his and Jerome Hiler's retrospective at the New York Film Festival, they had not seen each other for half a century. Dorsky recalled their first meeting in 1964:

> I was making 16mm films as a nineteen year old. His weekly column in the *Village Voice* was a beacon that both ignited and confirmed the revolutionary cinema that was beginning to blossom in America. His openness and generosity are largely responsible for the world-wide appreciation of experimental cinema today…when I was twenty and had just finished my first film, *Ingreen* (1964), he came over to my apartment to see it and then scheduled it to be premiered the next week at the Washington Square Gallery.[1]

Dorsky appeared several times in *Walden*, most visibly in the sequence at Grant's Cafeteria (see Chapter 55) and made three more films after *Ingreen* before moving with Hiler to San Francisco. There he made a living as an editor of the films of others before returning to his own work with *Hours for Jerome* (1982). In it, he assembled sequences he had shot while living with Hiler in rural New Jersey between 1966 and 1970. Another master of the medium, film artist Warren Sonbert wrote: *"Hours for Jerome* is simply the most beautifully photographed film that I've ever seen; for once the full achievements of what film can do cinematographically is achieved."[2]

Subsequently, Dorsky devoted himself to film with prodigious energy, producing an extraordinarily rich body of work as well as an inspirational text reflecting on that energy, *Devotional Cinema*, published in book form in 2007.[3]

On the occasion of his retrospective at the New York Film Festival, *New York Times* critic Manohla Dargis wrote:

> For decades, Mr. Dorsky has been on a great search, going out with his 16-millimeter film camera and astonishing eye and bringing back the

kinds of humble, rapturous images that many of us forget to see: a beam of light tracing a man's profile, a crimson flower gently bobbing in the wind, a bit of tape flapping in the wind, a mote of dust, a glimmer, a sparkle, a color, a shape. A mystic of a type, he has found new ways of seeing and thinking not just about film, but also the world.[4]

60 THEATER DISTRICT

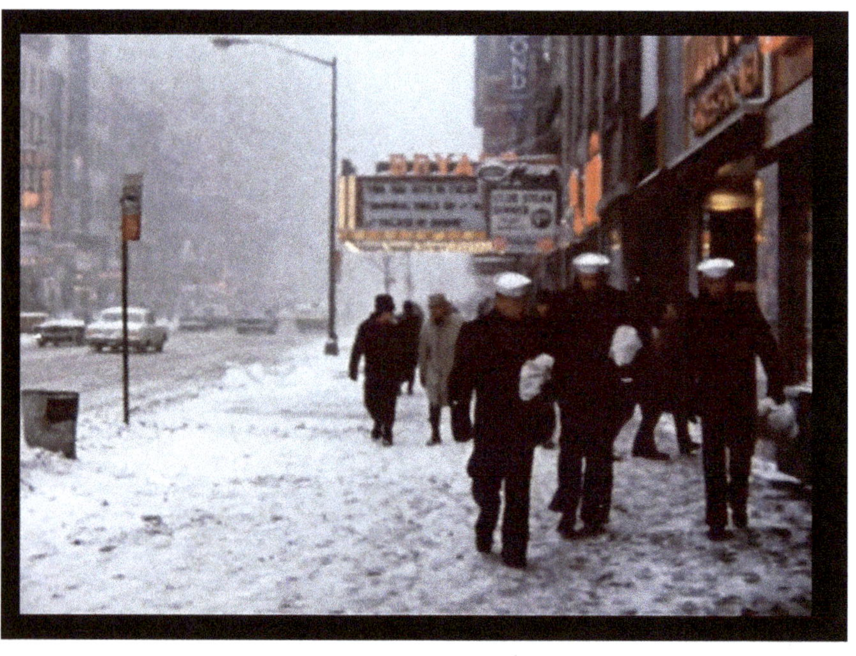

Reel 2 25:38

Mekas's continual struggle to keep film artists' work visible led him from one end of Manhattan Island to another. His programs were held under varied names - Film-Makers Festival, Film-Makers' Showcase, Film-Makers' Cinematheque - and migrated unpredictably over the years from the City Hall Cinema near the East River at 178 Nassau St, in the south to The New Yorker Theater on the Upper West Side near the Hudson in the north.

But between 1965 and 1968, three of the five years in which he was filming the sequences of *Walden*, the name - the Film-Makers' Cinematheque - and location - the Wurlitzer Building just east of Times Square - remained relatively stable.

The stretch of 42nd Street between 6th and 8th Avenues on either side of Broadway and Times Square was the "Theater District," the American capital of live theater for which "Broadway" and "42nd Street" became synonyms. But by the 1960s, as Americans fled city centers for the suburbs, it was also becoming the New York home of pornography, prostitution, and drug dealing.

The Wurlitzer building had been built in 1919 to provide a Times Square showroom for the Rudolph Wurlitzer Company which manufactured the most widely-used organs for theaters showing silent films. But by the mid-1960s, the area was in steep commercial decline and no longer a prestigious address for a national company.

The Wurlitzer Company sold the building in 1964 and the new owners rented its basement theater to the Film-Makers' Cinematheque. "Underground" film was now literally underground.

· · ·

An ad in the November 25th 1965 issue of the *Voice* announced that the Cinematheque would be moving to the theater at "125 West 41st St. or 120 West 42nd St. - in between 6th Avenue and Broadway." But the office building's manager did not want the Cinematheque's audience to be seen using the more respectable entrance to the building on 42nd St. so only the back entrance on 41 St., was permitted to its scruffy patrons. Mekas sometimes listed it in ads as the "41st St. Theater." The first event at the venue was an evening featuring work by Robert Rauschenberg, Claes Oldenburg and Robert Whitman on December 1st, 1965.

For a short period beginning on September 15, 1966, the theater would enjoy genuine commercial success, hosting the world premiere of Warhol's *The Chelsea Girls* (1966). Warhol himself was directly involved as the film artist Jerome Hiler (see Chapter 56), the projectionist at the time, remembered:

Andy told me to play around with the image and the soundtrack as I felt like it. There were two projectors creating two screens, side-by-side. You could have one soundtrack going and then change to the other soundtrack, then you might go back to the first soundtrack. Perhaps even both of them together a little bit. And then you had some gels, some cellophane, and so forth. You would hold the cellophane whenever you felt like it, over one of the projector lenses so that it all went red. And then another one went blue. So he says, 'Be random.'[1]

Because of its popular success, *The Chelsea Girls* eventually moved to a larger theater not connected to the Cinematheque but programming remained lively at the "41st St. Theater." During the summer of 1967, Greg Sharits, brother of filmmaker Paul Sharits, organized a series of expanded cinema events which for seven nights a week combined live music, dance, poetry, film loops, and light shows.

At the end of 1967, the Cinematheque moved on once again. After an unsuccessful effort to obtain authorization to show films in Soho at 80 Wooster Street, screenings resumed at the New Yorker Theater and the Jewish Museum. Soon afterwards, the entire Wurlitzer Building was sold and demolished.

61 STEPHEN SHORE

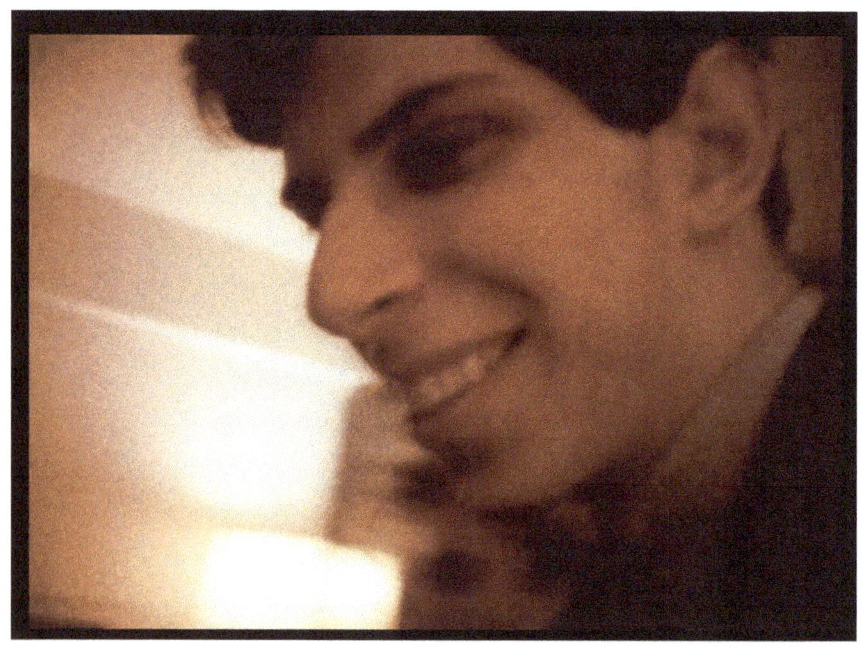

Reel 2 27:30

Walden's intertitle describes a gathering at the Sutton Place apartment of the parents of Stephen Shore as an "Uptown Party." But since geographically the apartment was in midtown, Mekas surely meant "uptown" in a figurative sense: the bourgeois world of the wealthy as opposed to the bohemian one of "downtown" artists.

The Sutton Place neighborhood which begins on East 53rd St may indeed have been home to sedate wealth but it was only a few blocks above a center of very "downtown" activity - Andy Warhol's "Factory" on East 47th St. And its very proximity may have been one reason Warhol's entourage accepted the invitations of Ruth and Fred Shore's teenage son to party at his parents' apartment.

17 year-old Stephen Shore had made a film, *Elevated* (1964) which was shown in early 1965 at Mekas's Cinematheque. There he was introduced to Warhol whose *Life of Juanita Castro* (1964) was also on the program and Shore asked if he could visit the Factory. "I don't remember specifically what I knew about the Factory back then," he recalled, "but within a couple of days of going there I understood I could just stay as long as I wanted."[1] He was to stay for around three years taking photographs which would eventually be published as *The Velvet Years: Warhol's Factory 1965-67.*[2]

Eventually Shore would became one of the most important photographers of his generation as he developed a style of sober color photography that was far removed from the flamboyance of the Factory. But he was to credit Warhol with a lasting influence:

   ...what happened there was that I saw an artist working. I started
   thinking about the kinds of decisions he was making, his use of serial

imagery, and my exposure to him and some of his friends opened a door to a broader aesthetic thinking, which was then what I pursued when I left.[3]

62 NICO

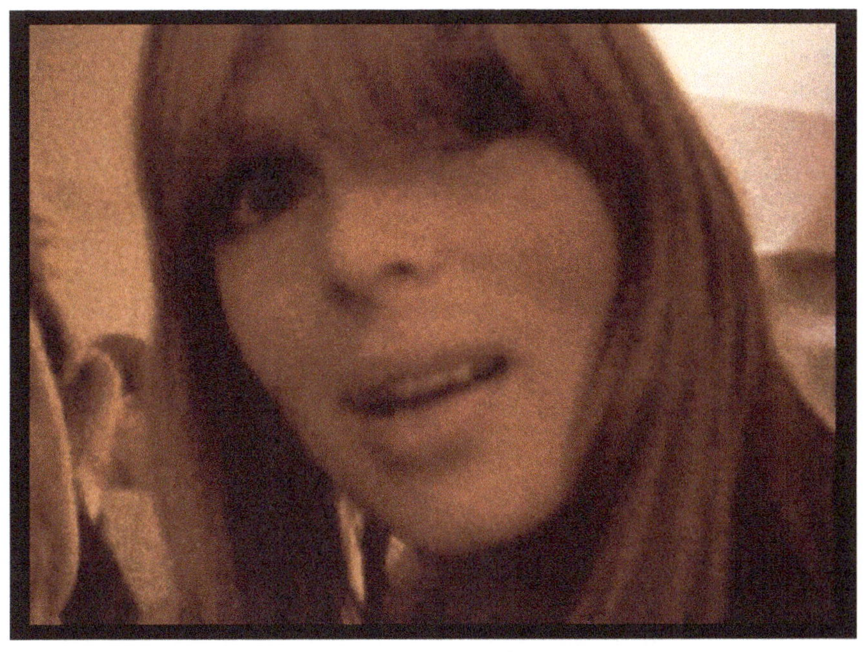

Reel 2 27:01

Glimpsing her at an "Uptown Party," it is easy to see why Nico was invited into the photogenic Warhol entourage.

Born in Germany as Christa Päffgen, she was a fashion model whose striking appearance had attracted the notice of Gerard Malanga in London when Warhol and his associates had been in Europe in May 1965. Malanga told her to get in touch with Warhol's Factory when she came to New York and she did so in late 1966, after signing a contract to work for the Ford Model Agency.

Although her musical experience was slight, she had made a film appearance in Fellini's *La Dolce Vita* (1960) and seemed to suit Warhol's visual requirements for the Velvet Underground rock band and the multimedia spectacle he was developing to accompany its performances, The Exploding Plastic Inevitable.

Paul Morrissey, whom Warhol had recruited to assist in his film-making activity, recalled that:

> I felt that the one thing The Velvets didn't have was a solo singer, because I just didn't think that Lou (Reed) had the personality to stand in front of the group and sing. The group needed something beautiful to counteract the kind of screeching ugliness they were trying to sell, and the combination of a really beautiful girl standing in front of all this decadence was what was needed. That very night, right away I said, 'Nico, you're a singer. You need somebody to play in back of you. You can maybe sing with this group...'[1]

Describing her as a "chanteuse," Warhol accompanied her to the annual dinner of the New York Society for Clinical Psychiatry at the luxurious Delmonico Hotel on Park Avenue to sing at the band's debut performance while Gerard Malanga performed his "whip dance."

The band's other members were purportedly not enthusiastic about Warhol's choice but Nico would record three songs on their first album, "The Velvet Underground & Nico" (1967). She then embarked on a solo career and made her own album whose title exploited the notoriety of Warhol's film in which she had appeared, "Chelsea Girl" (1967).

63 JACK SMITH

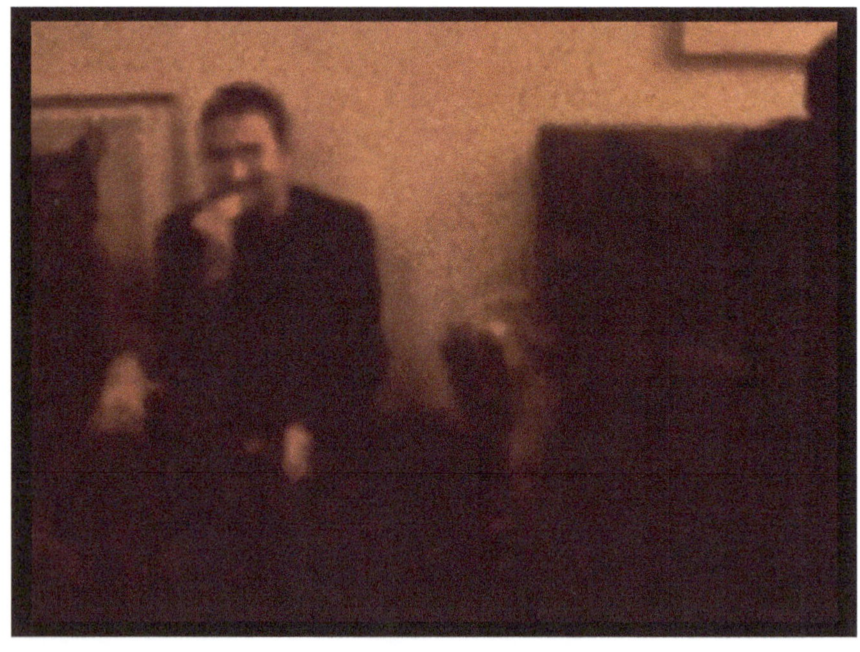

Reel 2 27:43

Sitting on the living room floor in the apartment of the parents of later-to-be-renowned photographer Stephen Shore, he was an unobstrusive figure in *Walden*. But unobtrusive was not a word frequently used to describe Jack Smith.

Smith's *Flaming Creatures* (1963) was the cause of the near-riot when Mekas and Barbara Rubin attempted to project it at the experimental film festival in the Belgian resort of Knokke-le-Zoute in December 1963, and provoked his arrest and jailing in New York afterwards (see Preface). The legal appeal of the conviction of Mekas, along with his accomplices, Flo and Ken Jacobs, eventually reached the U.S. Supreme Court and made Smith an icon of "underground film."

When Abe Fortas, one of the justices upholding the appeal in a lower court, was nominated to the Supreme Court by President Lyndon Johnson, *Flaming Creatures* became a weapon to defeat his nomination in the U.S. Congress. It, along with other purportedly pornographic films, was shown in the offices of the Senate Judiciary Committee in Washington in the summer of 1968 as proof that Fortas's laxity on censorship was a danger to the country.

What was on view in Smith's films - transvestism, sadism, drug use, genitalia - was virtually guaranteed to provoke a violent reaction and attract publicity. And Mekas, whatever his more lofty objectives in combating censorship, also knew that Smith's work would help attract audiences in a way that the quieter, more subtly poetic films he championed could not.

Smith had moved to New York from Texas in 1953 and had performed in Ken Jacobs' first films, his unfinished *Star Spangled to Death* (1959), *Little Stabs at Happiness* (1960) and *Blonde Cobra* (1963), as well as Warhol's *Camp* (1965). The title of the latter would come to be synonymous with the entire aesthetic that Smith's work helped define.

Smith would also be a major figure in the development of performance art, notably working with John Vaccaro, founder of The Playhouse of

the Ridiculous and influencing Richard Foreman's Ontological-
Hysteric Theater.

After Smith's death in 1989, his legacy proved durable and the impact
of his flamboyance undiminished. In 2011, curator Bradford Nordeen
described a screening of Smith's newly restored films at the Museum
of Modern Art:

> A sold-out auditorium, crowded with every age demographic imagin-
> able, though mostly young, in a hushed murmur of anticipation…Pasty
> creatures spewing pearls and peacock witches feasting on pomegran-
> ates in flaming Technicolor,…this postmodern baroque tableau vivant,
> where pandrogynous revelers build heated scenes of whimsy from
> their own body accumulations…piling it high with veils, gauze,
> tapestries and cocks, dirty, wiggling feet and prosthetic noses…danc-
> ing, jiggling, writhing…a flaming playground for debris, glee and
> subversion.[1]

64 MARIO MONTEZ

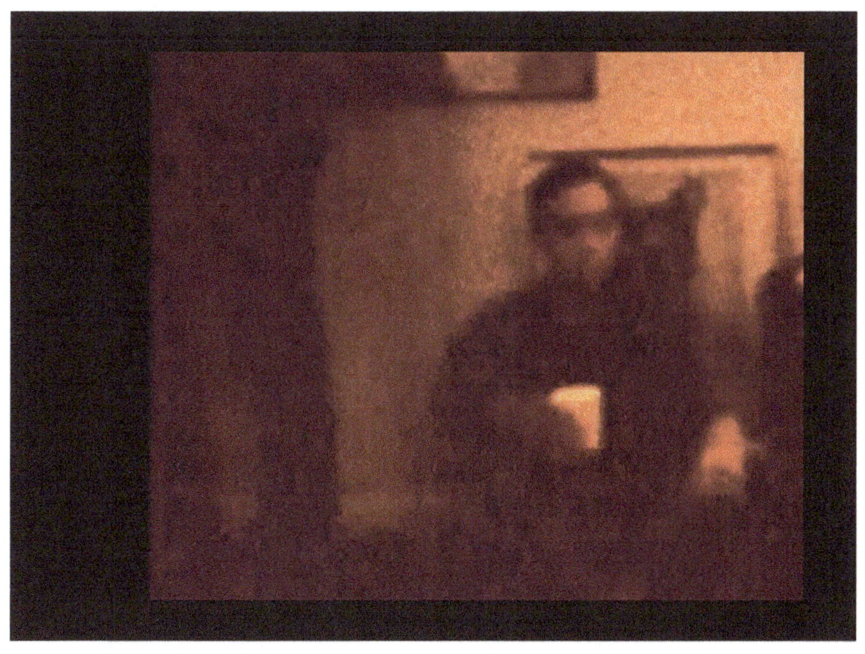

Reel 2 27:43

The actor Mario Montez was born René Rivera in Puerto Rico and was said to "hold the highest position of royalty in the world of underground cinema"[1] by film director John Waters. He starred as Dolores Flores in *Flaming Creatures* (1963).

His name was inspired by the actress Maria Montez who was born Maria Gracia Vidal in the Dominican Republic and was called the "Queen of Technicolor" by Universal Pictures. She starred as Sherazade in *Arabian Nights* (1942).

Maria's namesake Mario arguably became a bigger a star in the realm of "underground" culture than she did in the commercial movie industry. He went on to appear in a number of Warhol films, notably *Harlot* (1965) and *The Chelsea Girls* (1966).

Warhol would write that "Mario had that classic comedy combination of seeming dumb but being able to say the right things with perfect timing; just when you thought you were laughing at him, he'd turn it all around."[2]

A flamboyant presence in his many other films, Montez is difficult to recognize in *Walden*. But thanks to Mekas's description in the poster designed by George Maciunas for the film, he can be glimpsed at the party in the apartment of Stephen Shore's parents sitting on the floor next to the filmmaker who made him famous, Jack Smith.

65 EDIE SEDGWICK

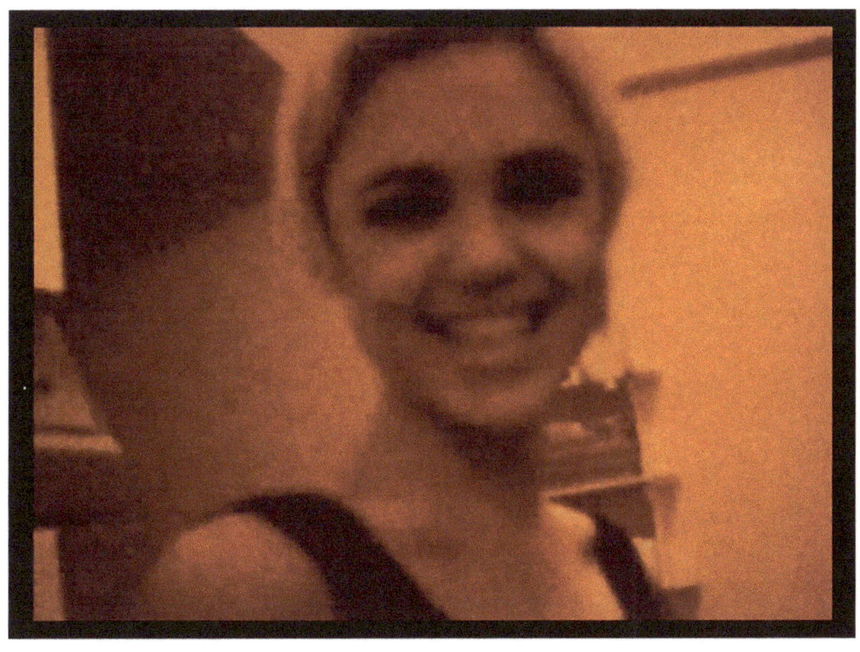

Reel 2 27:58

Edie Sedgwick's presence may have been ephemeral on the 1960s New York art and fashion scene but it was enough to continue to inspire writing and films for decades after her death.

When a film about her life, *Factory Girl*, opened in 2007, the art critic for the *Los Angeles Times* Christopher Knight wrote:

> Warhol transformed Sedgwick into a projection of himself, crafting an idealized feminine persona…Her on-screen presence in *Vinyl* (1965) ignited a quintessential love affair with the camera. She does nothing but sit to one side smoking cigarettes while ogling the sado-masochistic action. But it's hard to take your eyes off her. The 22-year-old is luminous."[1]

The literary critic Rhoda Koenig wrote in her review of the same film:

> 'Edie and Andy,' the non-couple, were the couple of the moment. She took him to parties where everyone else was listed in the Social Register; he stage-managed her appearances, pushing Edie to the cameras and the microphones, where she was white with fear but loved every minute…Edie became an habitué of the Factory, Warhol's loft papered in aluminum foil, where the daytime was spent churning out silkscreen prints and the night on parties that mingled guests who contributed flash, trash and cash with a smorgasbord of illegal stimulants. (Some left the place in limousines, some in ambulances, a regular said.)"[2]

But perhaps the most perceptive observer there at the time was writer and, later, film director Nora Ephron. In one of her first assignments as a reporter for the *New York Post,* she wrote in her "Woman in the News" column of September 5, 1965:

> Edie and Andy have identical hair styles: short-cropped and silver gray. She accompanies him everywhere, to hundreds of parties and publicity

stunts, she in her habit of tights, T-shirt and heels, he in his paint-stained denims.[3]

Sedgwick confirmed Warhol's contention that fame was still fame even if it was only in the eye of the beholder. And he found in Sedgwick an imaginary reflection of himself.

Ephron observed:

> Edie Sedgwick is the girl that everybody is talking about.
>
> No one is quite sure who the everybody is who is talking about her, but no matter. There is too little new that is happening and too many words to write and television talk shows to film to leave a phenomenon like Edie Sedgwick alone. Edie Sedgwick is being talked about because she is here, there, and everywhere.[4]

When Sedgwick died in California in 1971, she had left the city and the decade that gave her her moment of fame but, Warhol's film about her, *Poor Little Rich Girl* (1965), froze her where she always seemed to belong: in the spotlight.

66 LOU REED

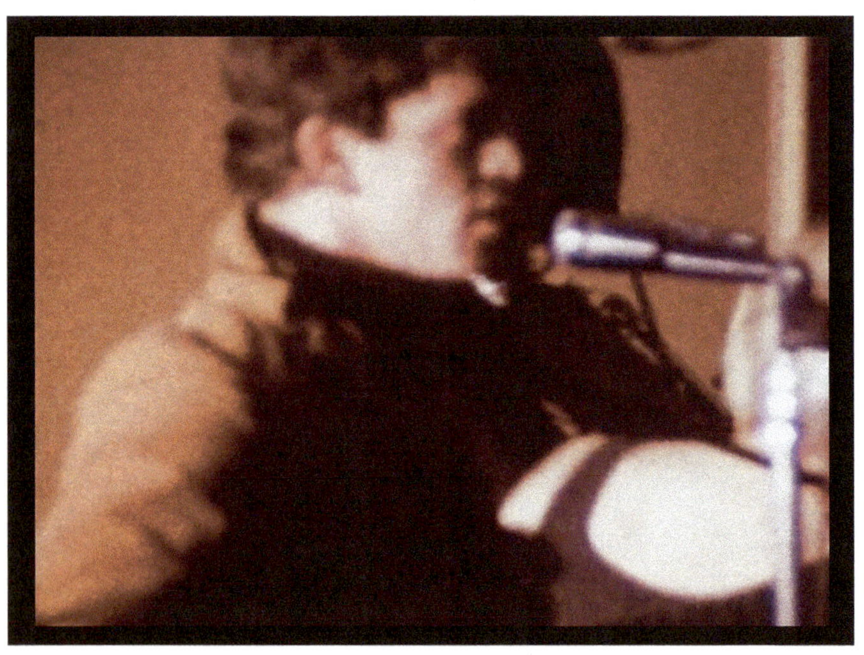

Reel 2 28:23

When Mekas and Barbara Rubin were asked by Warhol to film the first public appearance of the Velvet Underground at the annual dinner of the New York Society for Clinical Psychiatry, they could not have known that they would be documenting the birth of a musical legend.

The group's lead singer, Lou Reed, had been playing in a rock band since he was a teenager in the suburb of Freeport, Long Island. He continued in college at Syracuse University and, when he moved back into his parents' home after graduation, he found work in Tin Pan Alley, as the New York-based pop music business was then popularly known, writing imitations of songs that had already been commercially successful.

Then he met avant-garde artists Tony Conrad and John Cale.

To Tony Conrad the synergy between Cale and Reed was evident immediately:

> Rather than suggesting that there was an influence that flowed one way or another I'm trying to suggest that it seemed like a very powerful encounter in a sense, each of them moving in a direction which was daring and audacious for the other as well as themselves.[1]

Cale remembered:

> When I met Lou, he was a staff writer for some publishing company. He played me the songs he'd written for them, but they were nothing new or terribly exciting. They were just like every other song on the radio. But then he played me several which he claimed they wouldn't publish. He played 'Heroin' first and it totally knocked me out. The words and music were so raunchy and devastating. What's more, his songs fit perfectly with my music concept.[2]

After only one album with the Velvet Underground, Reed, with and without Cale, went on to create music that would make him a giant in the history of rock music. But his debut album "The Velvet Underground & Nico" (1967) remained one of his most revered; it was number thirteen on *Rolling Stone* magazine's list of "the 500 Greatest Albums of All Time," and described as "the most prophetic rock album ever made."[3]

When Reed died in 2013, the poet and singer Patti Smith wrote:

> He was our connection to the infamous air of the Factory. He had made Edie Sedgwick dance. Andy Warhol whispered in his ear. Lou brought the sensibilities of art and literature into his music. He was our generation's New York poet, championing its misfits as Whitman had championed its workingman and Lorca its persecuted.[4]

67 VELVET UNDERGROUND

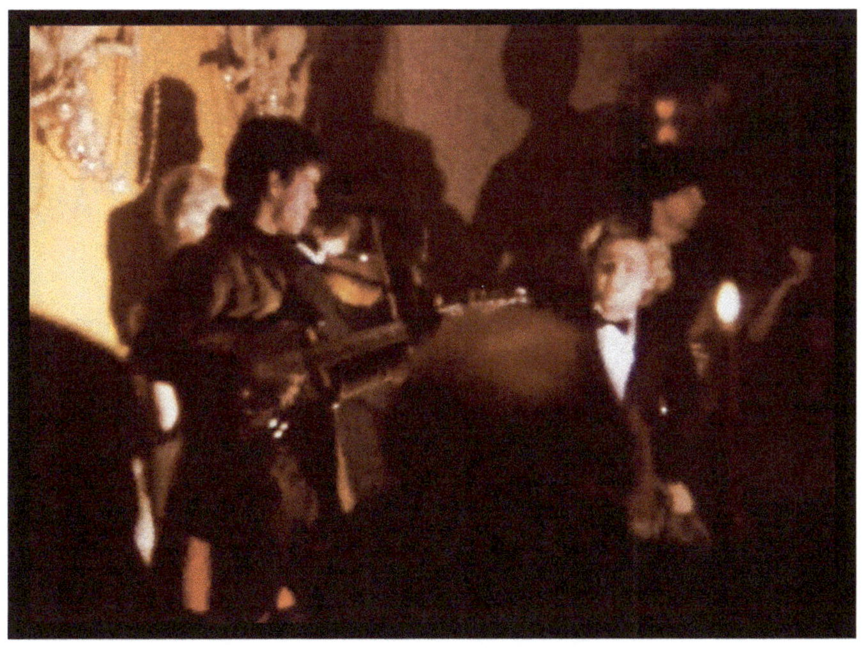

Reel 2 28:34

In June of 1966, Mekas wrote in the *Village Voice*:

> Later this summer the Cinematheque is organizing a huge survey of
> the various new uses of cinema. The leading artists of these new uses
> of cinema (expanded cinema) will take part. As I have said quite often
> before: cinema is only beginning. Don't go to Cannes to look for new
> cinema - come to New York. [1]

The concept of "expanded cinema" was not exactly new; it was a
variant of both the emerging "performance art," as created by Fluxus
artists such as Yoko Ono and Carolee Schneemann, and Allan
Kaprow's "Happenings" of the early 1960s.

But the idea of an "expanded cinema" that overwhelmed the senses by
combining projected film with lighting effects, dancing, and, above all,
rock music, had an impact - and commercial potential - that was
immediately obvious to Andy Warhol.

"Come blow your mind" was the invitation to "The Erupting Plastic
Inevitable with Andy Warhol, The Velvet Underground and Nico" at
the Open Stage on St. Mark's Place that appeared in the *Village Voice* on
March 31, 1966. The next ad for the same nightly event on April 7th
announced it as "The Exploding Plastic Inevitable." But whether
erupting or exploding, the events attracted crowds.

It had begun in December 1965 when Warhol was asked to bring his
entourage to a new discotheque in order to attract publicity. According
to Paul Morrissey (who would direct the later, more commercially
ambitious, Warhol film productions), Warhol agreed on the condition
that he could also provide his own rock band and more.

Morrissey recalled that:

> Behind the group we'll be projecting two or three images of film
> footage, because we were making all these movies that we'd been
> showing at the Cinematheque that had no commercial value, and I

thought this would be a good way to have them generate some money too. This was agreed upon and I was set to go out and find a rock'n'roll group. I didn't know what group it was going to be.[2]

Soon afterwards Barbara Rubin introduced Warhol to a band called the Velvet Underground. As Malanga recalled:

After the set Barbara brought The Velvets over to Andy's table. They were all in their early twenties and dressed from head to foot in black. John Cale's sonorous accent and dreamy deportment bespoke his Welsh background and classical music training. Curly-haired Lou Reed's shy gum-chewing smile identified him most closely with Andy, with whom he shared a similar temperament.[3]

A few weeks later in January 1966 Warhol had the perfect occasion for the launch of his new band: he had been invited to give a lecture at the annual dinner of the New York Society for Clinical Psychiatry in the luxurious Delmonico Hotel on Park Avenue. Instead, he offered to provide them with a multi-sensory extravaganza.

The outlandish occasion was covered by Grace Glueck, the arts reporter for the *New York Times*. She wrote that:

The high-decibel sound, aptly described by Dr. Campbell as 'a short-lived torture of cacophony' was a combination of rock'n'roll and Egyptian belly dance music.[4]

Warhol had invited Mekas and Barbara Rubin to add to the festivities by filming both the band and the audience of psychiatrists. And apparently Mekas was also designated as Warhol's replacement after-dinner speaker. Glueck reported that:

The evening ended with a short talk by Jonas Mekas, film director and critic. But long before that, guests had begun to stream out.[5]

68 JOHN CALE

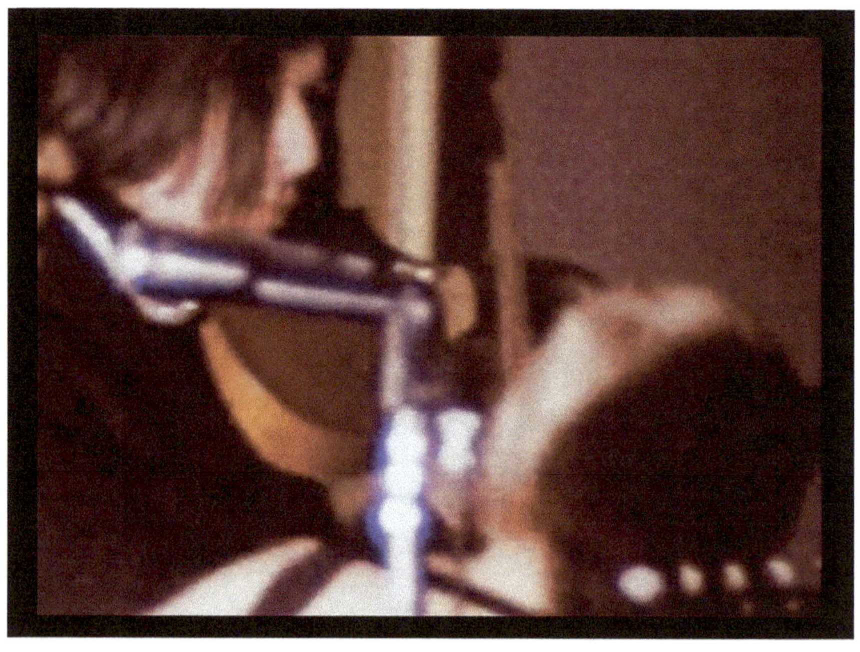

Reel 2 28:42

One of the salient features of *Walden* was the dissociation of its soundtrack from its images. Some sequences had sound that was closely related to the image but it was never completely synchronized in the manner of the "direct cinema" or "cinéma-vérité" of filmmakers such as Richard Leacock or D.A. Pennebaker who were revolutionizing the methods of documentary film in the early 1960s. But in other sections, sound and image are completely independent.

As he had when capturing images, Mekas had a totally personal approach to sound recording:

> By then I was carrying my Nagra or my Sony (tape recorders) and picking up sounds from the situations I filmed. There is a long stretch where I did not have any sounds, so I had John Cale play some background music. It's a very insistent, constant sound that goes on for fifteen or twenty minutes. There is no climax, it's continuous, with some small variations...[1]

John Cale's "background music" was emblematic of his musical practice which extended the boundaries of contemporary music in a way not unlike the way Mekas was challenging the conventions of filmmaking.

Born in Wales, the 21 year-old John Cale had a solid classical music education when he arrived in the U.S. in 1963 on a scholarship to the Tanglewood Music Center in Lenox, Massachusetts. But Cale had already learned about the work of John Cage and La Monte Young while studying in London and was growing impatient with the constraints of classical music.

On John Cage's advice he moved to New York and began working with the minimalist composer La Monte Young and musician/filmmaker Tony Conrad. Cale recalled:

> We formed The Dream Syndicate, which consisted of two amplified
> voices, an amplified violin and my amplified viola. The concept of the
> group was to sustain notes for two hours at a time. La Monte would
> hold the lowest notes, I would hold the next three on my viola, his
> wife Marion would hold the next note and Tony Conrad would hold
> the top note. That was my first group experience ...[2]

Conrad and Cale also discovered a shared interest in popular music
and started to play with a young rock music singer-songwriter, Lou
Reed. Conrad would move on to other things (notably to make the
film *The Flicker*, 1966), but Cale and Reed continued to make music.
Conrad recalled that:

> John was moving at a very, very fast pace away from a classical training
> background through the avant-garde and into performance art and
> then rock...It was phenomenal for Lou considering his interest in what
> would be referred to today as punk - somebody who is really living
> rock and is interested in an extremely aggressive assertive position - to
> discover that classical musicians and avant-garde artists were also
> engaged in that.[3]

Cale and Reed, along with Reed's college friend, guitarist Sterling
Morrison and Cale and Conrad's collaborator from The Dream Syndicate, percussionist Angus MacLise, formed the Velvet Underground
and, when, in December 1965, Barbara Rubin introduced them,
Warhol became their manager and their music became another
product of the Warhol Factory.

True to his contrarian nature, Cale refused to confirm the public image
of the Factory as a haven for indolent pleasure-seeking:

> I'd been working for three hours a day holding a drone, and I'd go to
> the Factory and they had the same work ethic. Andy would be making

films, and Gerard (Malanga) was on the floor making silkscreens. Work was fun and fun was work.[4]

69 WEST SIDE HIGHWAY

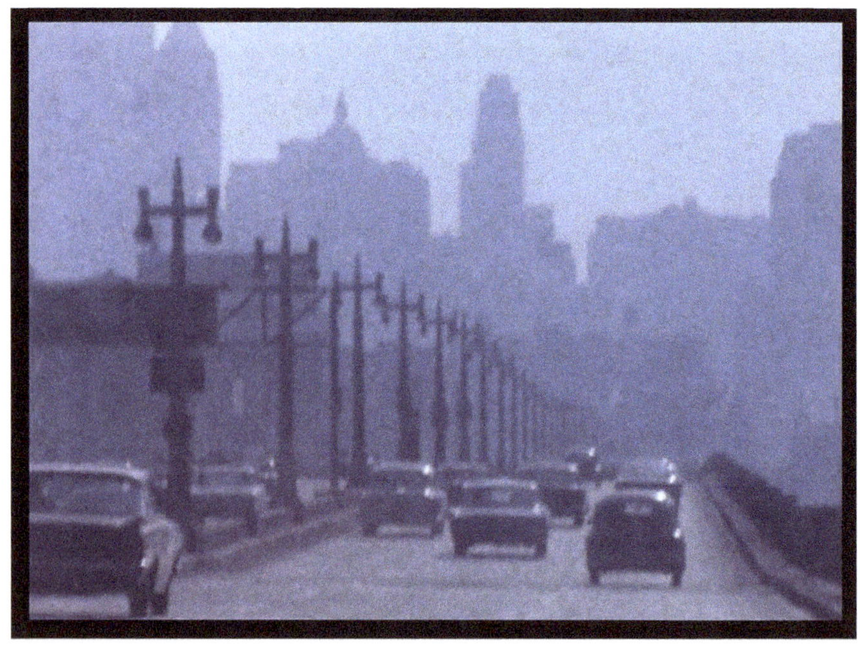

Reel 2 29:31

The brief sequence of an automobile trip down the west side of Manhattan was an anomaly in *Walden*.

Like the bucolic scenes in Central Park which present an imaginary pastoral vision of the city, almost all of the travel Mekas captured in *Walden* presented an imaginary world of train travel. A viewer unaware of mid-20th century America would not guess that passenger rail travel was disappearing in a country fanatically devoted to the private automobile.

The Federal Aid Highway Act of 1956 was instrumental in destroying the passenger railroad system. It also accelerated the white middle class exodus from city centers into suburbia, often leaving inner city African-American neighborhoods as devastated by poverty as the cities in Europe that had been bombarded in the war.

As one of the first urban limited access highways in the world when it was started in 1929, the West Side Highway along the Hudson River was a precursor to and a prototype for this transformation. Progress would be delayed by the Depression in the 1930s but it was finally finished in 1951, in time to serve as a model for how new highways would change America.

But by the time Mekas filmed it in 1966, the flight to suburbia had eroded the city's tax base and road maintenance was being neglected. Though still usable, the highway's condition was deteriorating. There were ambitious plans to replace it but no funding to carry them out. After a number of serious accidents, the West Side Highway was finally closed in 1973 and total demolition was completed by 1989.

New York was one of the rare places in America where one could live without a car and Mekas apparently never owned one. And, in the midst of a national frenzy of highway construction, *Walden* found one that was not under construction but about to be destroyed.

70 NAOMI LEVINE

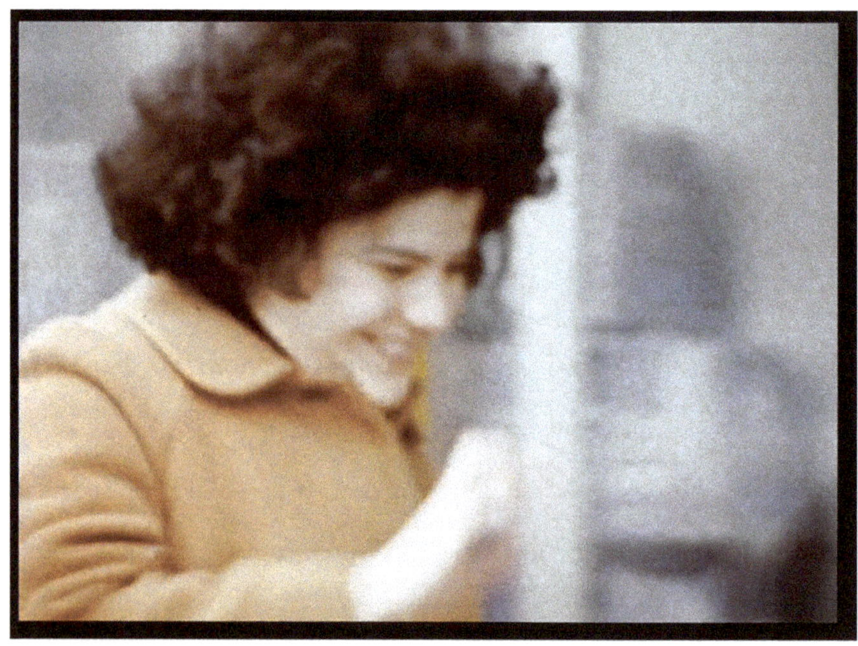

Reel 3 01:00

In the program for *Walden*'s premiere, Mekas identified her as "THE SWEET, MAD NAOMI, OUT OF BELLEVUE," assuming that his audience would understand that "Bellevue" referred to the New York hospital's psychiatric ward. In the sequence that followed, Mekas and Levine approach the loft of Flo and Ken Jacobs along snowy streets. Ken Jacobs tosses an American flag from their window. Levine wraps herself in it and begins rolling in the snow.

It is not clear if the scene was planned or not but, in any case, it recalls both the title of Jacob's unfinished epic *Star Spangled to Death* (1956-60/2001-4) and his film with Levine, *Naomi Is A Dream Of Loveliness*, (1966), shot in the summer 1966 at the Jacobs' Ferry Street loft which Mekas and Levine were about to visit.

Mekas recalled:

I first met Naomi Levine at the evenings I organized at the Film-Makers' Cooperative. Like many others, she sometimes screened unfinished films or just raw footage. One evening she brought one of her first films called *Yes* (1963).

Later she became very emotionally disturbed, difficult to deal with, and spent time in the psychiatric ward of Bellevue Hospital. Once when she was bothering her mother about money, her mother said 'OK, I was saving some jewelry for you when you are more serious, maybe for when you get married, but I will give you the jewelry now… here it is! Now you can sell it.'

So Naomi sold it, and she got like 30,000 dollars and she walked into the street and threw it all away…all the money… into the street…and that was the end of that. And then she ended up in Bellevue. They permitted her occasionally to go out for the day to visit friends but then somebody had to return her to the hospital. And so I took her out to visit Ken Jacobs in a snowstorm one day and then I took her back.

Later, she withdrew all of her films from the Coop and since she died a few years ago, nobody knows what happened to her paintings or her films…Somebody has to look into it. I think her work was quite good and her films *Jeremelu* (1964) and *Yes* (1963) are very important to the period. Later she moved to London and there was kind of a structural period in her work, but the films were never screened. I saw them once but she never distributed them…somebody really has to look into it. I think as an artist she was quite important.[1]

Levine was first visible as one of Warhol's "superstars." From 1963 to 1964, Warhol's prolific first years of production, she appeared in no less than six of his films: *Tarzan and Jane Regained… Sort of* (1963), *Naomi's Birthday Party* (1963), *Kiss* (1963), *Naomi and Rufus Kiss* (1964), *Batman Dracula* (1964), *Couch* (1964). Then she abruptly disappeared from his filmography.

She reappeared as a filmmaker herself with her film *Yes* which Mekas described in his column for the *Village Voice*:

Naomi Levine has just finished her first movie. It is like no other movie you ever saw. The rich sensuousness of her poetry floods the screen. Nobody has ever photographed flowers and children as Naomi did. No man would be able to get her poetry, her movements, her dreams. These are Naomi's dreams, and they reveal to us beauty which we men were not able to rip out of ourselves - Naomi's own beauty.[2]

Shortly afterward, in another column in 1964, Mekas writes that:

There is Naomi, the underground movie star, the 'black lioness,' the 'Egyptian broad;' the voluptuous star of Andy Warhol's Tarzan and Jane, … Now Naomi has become a film-maker herself. Her two movies - *Jaremelu* and *Yes* - were shown on last Monday's program at the Film-Makers' Cinematheque. *Yes* is one of cinema's most beautiful pastorales and a manifesto of a desperately romantic soul.[3]

Levine was invited to present a program at Cineprobe, MoMA's show-case for independent filmmakers on December 11, 1973 and the press release for the event calls her "an important figure in recent American avant-garde cinema" and mentions that *Yes* "was first prize winner at the 1964 Los Angeles Film Festival."

But she apparently made no more films and none are currently available. As Mekas said, "somebody really has to look into it."

71 FERRY STREET

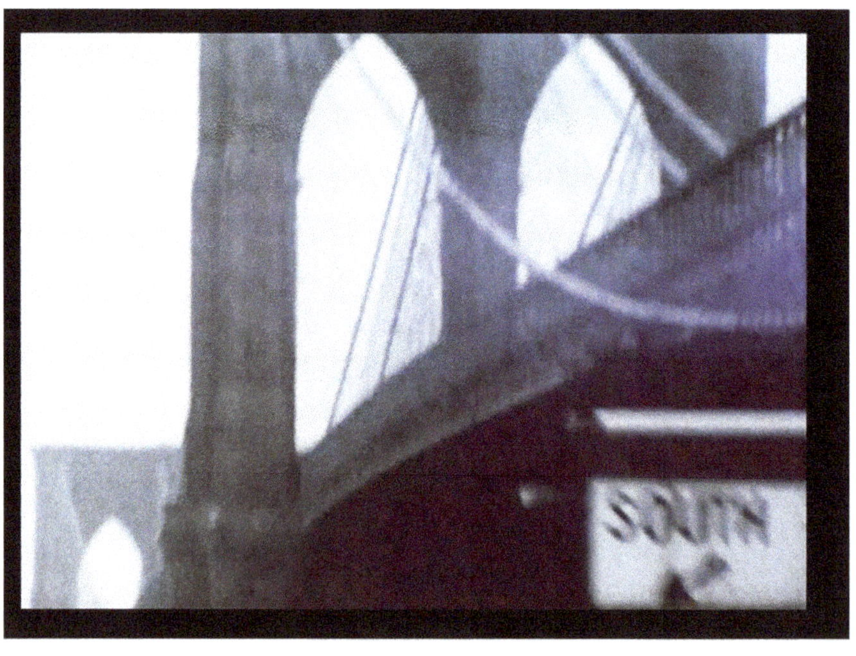

Reel 3 01;47

Ferry Street in Manhattan took its name from the regular steamboat service across the East River established by Robert Fulton in 1814. For over a century, the 12-minute ferry trip provided access to Manhattan from Brooklyn, arriving where the Brooklyn Bridge now stands. It was described by Walt Whitman in his poem "Crossing Brooklyn Ferry," published in 1856.

Ken Jacobs' loft at 25 Ferry Street was in the shadow of the Brooklyn Bridge in Manhattan just across the river from his childhood home in the shadow of the Williamsburg Bridge in Brooklyn. He grew up in a neighborhood of poor immigrants many of whom spoke only Yiddish. Now he lived in a neighborhood which, for a period in the 1950s and 1960s, was home to some of the most important figures in 20th century American art, including the painters Ellsworth Kelly, Jasper Johns, Agnes Martin, and Cy Twombly, and the composer John Cage.

Art Student Florence Karpf had crossed the river too. She moved out of her parents' home in the Astoria neighborhood in Queens to live with Jacobs in Manhattan. They were married in 1965.

Culturally, both Jacobs had travelled to a world quite distant from their origins. But geographically, it was barely two miles from their parents' homes to their loft on Ferry St.

On the roof of the formerly industrial building where he lived, Jacobs shot *The Sky Socialist* in 1963. Completed in 2019, it was, according to critic Amy Taubin:

> …an allegorical narrative of redemption and love…a masterpiece, not only of avant-garde movies, or cityscape movies, or documentary essays, but a movie masterpiece, no modifiers needed.[1]

When Mekas and Naomi Levine visited the Jacobs' loft, it had already been condemned by the city planning commission. Their building and the rest of the street were soon to be demolished and replaced by a housing development of four 27-story towers and five six-story buildings.

Shortly afterwards the Jacobs would leave Ferry St. for another loft a bit farther uptown and even the street's name would disappear from New York maps.

72 FLORENCE KARPF JACOBS

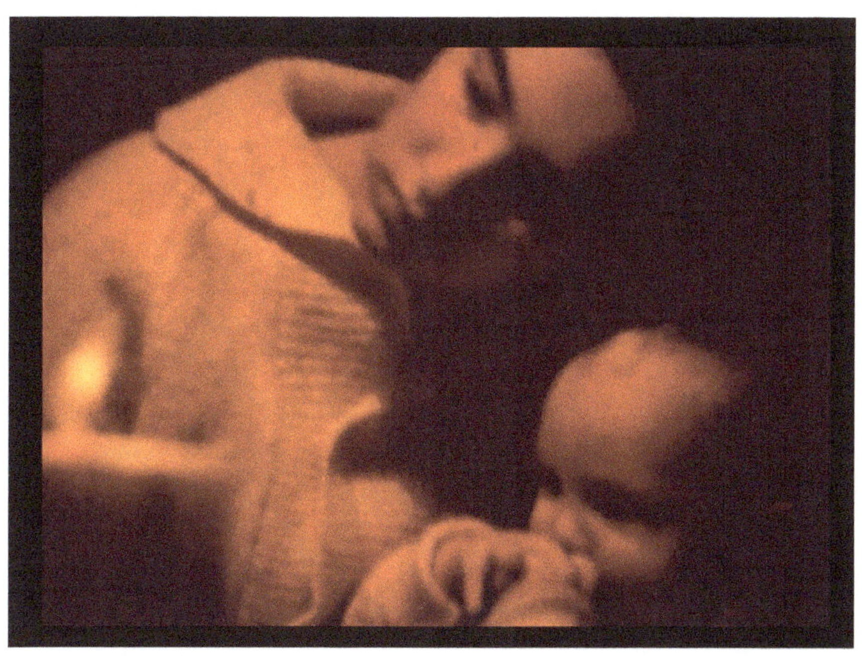

Reel 3 02:55

Florence Karpf was an art student at RISD (Rhode Island School of Design) when she and a friend decided to spend the summer on the ocean in Provincetown, Massachusetts and cover their living costs by drawing portraits for tourists.

The town at the end of Cape Cod was known as an artists' colony where the pioneer abstract painter Hans Hoffman ran a school. There, in the summer of 1961, Karpf met two aspiring New York artists who had come to study with Hoffman, Ken Jacobs and Jack Smith.

Karpf had not liked the traditional approach to painting imposed by her teachers at RISD and, to her parents' relief, abandoned her art studies. She returned to New York resigned to learn stenography. But back in New York in 1963, she reunited with Ken Jacobs and, escaping the confinement of her parents' home in Queens, moved into his loft on Ferry Street in Manhattan.

When Jacobs introduced her to Mekas, Karpf quit her office job at IBM and brought her stenography skills to the Film-Makers Coop. Both she and Jacobs were at work at the Cinematheque, when, on March 2, 1964, police interrupted a screening of Jack Smith's *Flaming Creatures* (1963) and arrested them both along with Mekas.

Karpf married Jacobs in 1965 and, for the next half century, helped her husband create one of the most important bodies of work in the history of experimental film. But she neither sought nor received any recognition and still considered herself primarily a painter. Her husband stated:

> I acknowledge Flo as a collaborator, regardless of what she says. At the
> talk the other night, I tried to induce Flo to stand so people could
> know how important she's been to me. But she wouldn't face the audi-
> ence. It has to do with her particular personality, and I'd be abusing
> her, forcing her away from her character, if I said, 'Flo, you must stand
> up. You must be acknowledged!'

As much as possible I'll have Flo look at what I'm doing. I'm always asking, 'What do you think of this? Do you like this?' I don't know how I could have continued without her ability to see and value what I'm doing through long stretches when nobody else was supportive… I'm very dependent on her.[1]

Critic Amy Taubin confirmed this in an essay on the Jacobs' work:

From the first days of our friendship, I was aware that Flo functioned as the 'reality principle' in relation to Ken, who often envisions and desires the impossible. She is also the most trusted other pair of eyes for his work, bringing to this task an aesthetic that is highly compatible with his own, but - and this is important - which was formed before she met him. It was not, however, until I transcribed this interview that I realized that Flo Jacobs is nothing less than the producer of Ken Jacobs' cinema."[2]

73 KEN JACOBS

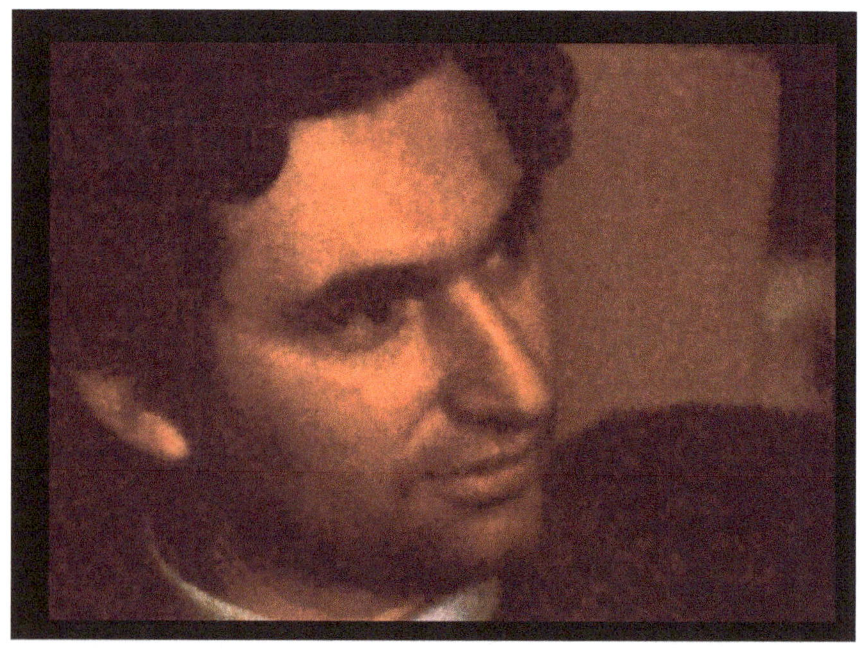

Reel 3 03:07

The introduction to an interview with Ken Jacobs, in a series called "Conversations with History" conducted at the University of California at Berkeley in 1999, reads:

> For more than 35 years, drawing on his skill as an imaginative illusionist, a workman-like tinkerer, and a worshipper of film frame by frame, Ken Jacobs has confronted reality and unmasked established powers.[1]

While it is not acknowledged, Ken Jacobs almost certainly wrote the description himself. A more objective writer would have mentioned his fundamental role in the development of the New York avant-garde of the 1960s and that he was one of the major artists to emerge from it.

From a working class Yiddish-speaking family in Brooklyn, Jacobs dreamed of crossing the river:

> New York was the Emerald City from where I was. I was on the other side of the East River and I could see it. So I stepped out and there was the Williamsburg Bridge that went right to New York. But it really was an enormous cultural, psychological distance. And at some point I had to leave Williamsburg and take my chances in New York.[2]

He studied painting with the pioneer of Abstract Expressionism Hans Hofmann in 1956-57, and although he ultimately chose filmmaking over painting, he always regarded Hofmann as a major influence on his work.

Mekas recalled their first meeting:

> Ken Jacobs used to come to poetry readings and I first did not even know that he made films or that he was interested in making films. I thought he was a writer, wanted to be a writer...because he came to these readings. During one of these evenings, he projected his footage of *Orchard Street*...and that's how we met.[3]

Orchard Street (1955) was Jacobs' first film, a portrait of a Lower East Side street inspired by his viewing of *In the Street* (1948) by Helen Levitt and James Agee. But it was somehow appropriate that Mekas was first confused about exactly what medium Jacobs worked in. He was not, as Mekas first thought, a poet, but the exact definition of Ken Jacobs' work has always been elusive - expanded cinema, performance art, theater, 3D experiments, happenings, multimedia.

And his influence as a teacher and advocate has been profound as well; in 1964 he defended the work of others against censorship, getting arrested with his wife Flo and Mekas for showing Jack Smith's *Flaming Creatures* (1963). In 1965 he founded the Millennium Film Workshop which offered practical instruction to aspiring filmmakers and provided a forum for established filmmakers to show and discuss their work.

He had an even greater impact as a teacher after another important filmmaker, Larry Gottheim, invited him to help start the first regular undergraduate degree program in the U.S. devoted to personal experimental film and video at Harpur College in Binghampton, N.Y. in 1969. For thirty years he inspired students there, including some who would go on to become important critics such as J. Hoberman and Scott McDonald.

Michele Pierson, co-editor of a collection of essays on Jacobs, *Optic Antics*, concluded in it that he "is one of the most innovative artists in the history of cinema and the most productive, accomplished, and influential American avant-garde filmmaker working today."[4]

74 JUDITH MALINA

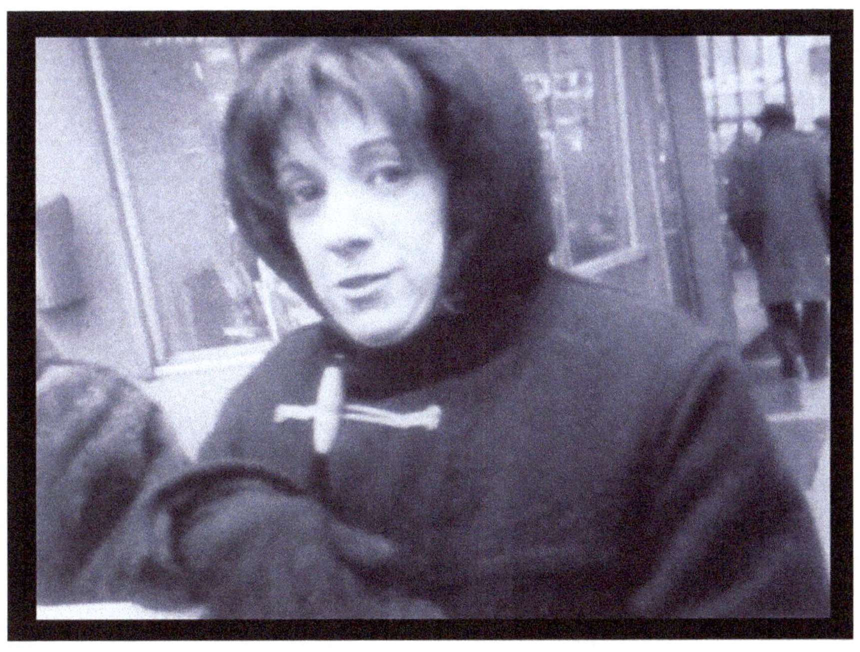

Reel 3 04:19

In general *Walden* contained scenes in color shot between 1965 and 1969, in approximate chronological order. But there was a striking exception - a "flashback" in black and white of Judith Malina in Times Square around 1961.

She was part of the Women's Direct Action Vigil against the resumption of nuclear testing. It was clearly a fringe activity at the time and there was no indication that, a few years later, peace demonstrations would be common on every college campus in America and thousands of anti-war protesters would gather on New York streets.

A second flashback was inserted into the last reel of *Walden* that also included Malina's husband Julian Beck in front of the United Nations. The two sequences are unusual for their abandonment of chronology and color but not in their emotional tone. They took place in winter - the season that seemed to trigger Mekas's nostalgia for the past and remind him of the pain of exile. On the soundtrack his voice commented "It was snowing, it was freezing…no one was there. But the Becks were there, marching for peace."

Like Mekas, Malina had arrived in the U.S. as a refugee from Germany, but as a young child not as an adult. She grew up in a very American tradition of political protest, attending her first anti-Nazi rally in New York at age seven. Unlike Mekas, her art was always overtly political; the Living Theater which she had founded with her husband Julian Beck in 1947 was both avant-garde in form and explicit in its anti-authoritarian political content.

In 1963 the Living Theater presented a scathing portrayal of life in a U.S. Marine Corps military prison written by Kenneth H. Brown who had served a sentence in one while a Marine. The production was abruptly curtailed and its producers, the Becks, charged with tax law violations. But before the Becks could be evicted, Mekas arrived with his camera:

The theatre was already locked up by the owner. We got the cast and the equipment into the theatre through the sidewalk coal chute, late at night…there was no time for reshooting, no time for mistakes: I was a circus man on a tightrope high in the air. All my senses were stretched to the point of breaking…I threw myself into it, and I used it as raw material, as it happened, as if it were a real event which, in truth, it was…And there I lay, that morning, on the floor, exhausted,… everyone was gone. The theatre was empty and dead now. This was the last time the Becks gave a performance in New York. It was suddenly so sad. I thought I was completely alone.[1]

After his fictional narrative feature, *Guns of the Trees* (1961), *The Brig* (1964) seemed to indicate that Mekas was adopting a "cinéma-vérité" style. But he did not continue in the style of *The Brig*, turning instead to a unique and far more personal form of expression - the film diary - whose quintessential mood is expressed in the wintry black and white "flashback" scenes of Judith Malina in Times Square.

75 COLUMBUS CIRCLE

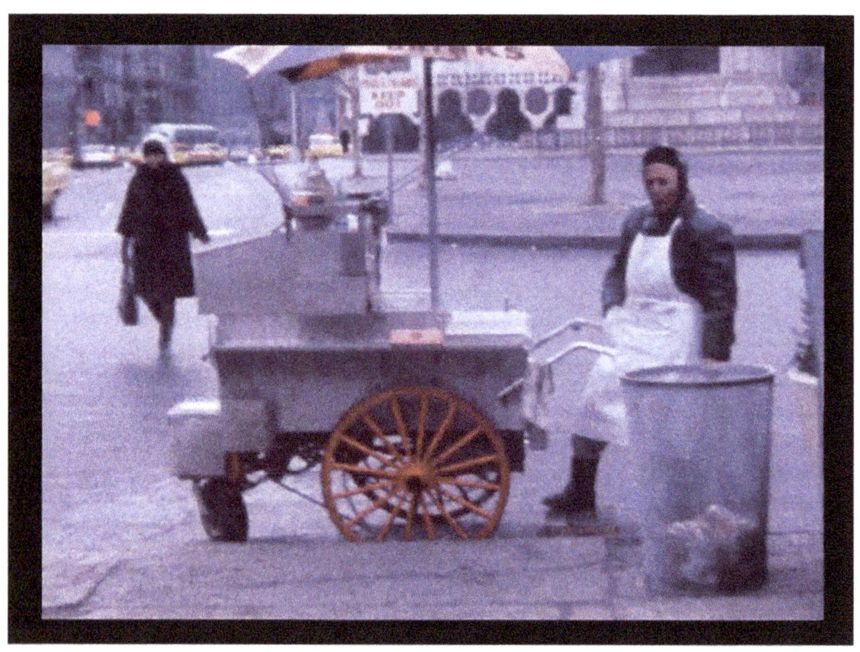

Reel 3 06:42

Columbus Circle, at the southwest corner of Central Park, was one of the most frequently seen places in all of *Walden*. It was immediately recognizable by the "lollipop" shapes at the bottom of the facade of the building facing it. Designed by the architect Edward Durell Stone to exhibit the art collection of the supermarket magnate, Huntington Hartford, it was called the Gallery of Modern Art.

"The new museum resembles a die-cut Venetian palazzo on lollipops,"[1] wrote Ada Louise Huxtable, the architecture critic of the *New York Times* when it opened in 1964. From then on, the structure's detractors referred to it as "the lollipop building."

The design reflected Hartford's opposition to Modernism and his opposition extended to the work that the museum exhibited. Huxtable explained that "In spite of its name, the Gallery of Modern Art is primarily a museum for a collector who does not admire modern art."[2] Abstract expressionism was nowhere to be found on the museum's walls.

Curiously, the short life of the Gallery of Modern Art corresponded almost precisely to the period when Mekas was filming *Walden*: it opened in the winter in 1964 and closed in the spring of 1969.

For a brief period beginning in March 1969, it was also the home of the "Film-Makers' Cinematheque in Exile." The Cinematheque's programs had been nomadic since Mekas had been prohibited by city authorities from holding public events at 80 Wooster Street. But, given the museum's conservatism, the relationship was unlikely to end well and it did not.

A Cinematheque announcement in the *Village Voice* read:

> To the People of New York: Last Friday, the Gallery of Modern Art stopped the premiere screening on new works by Stan Brakhage, under a pretext that the films were obscene. We take this space to express our disgust with the Gallery's action; How does a gallery dare call

itself a gallery 'of modern art' when in reality it's the ENEMY of modern art?[3]

The enemy was soon vanquished. Little more than a month later, the Gallery of Modern Art closed and the building was given to the city of New York to be used as a cultural center.

But it continued to be a source of conflict over decades, remaining vacant much of the time. Closed to the public, it continued to be used for press screenings, organized for precisely the group who held it in the most contempt: professional critics.

A 2004 plan to renovate its facade (and disguise Edward Durell Stone's "lollipops") prompted Huxtable's successor as *New York Times* architecture critic, Nicolai Ouroussoff, to recommend its complete demolition: "You can make a convincing argument that there is not much worth saving here."[4]

76 FILM-MAKERS' COOP

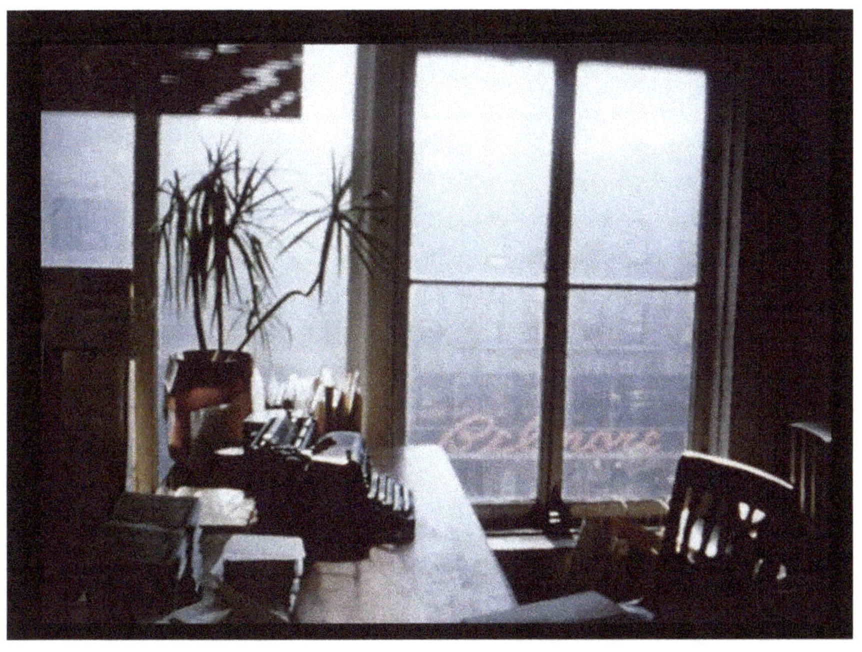

Reel 3 12:51

When in the summer of 1961 Mekas published in *Film Culture* "The First Statement of The New American Cinema Group," he was clear: "we know what needs to be destroyed."[1]

> The official cinema all over the world is running out of breath. It is morally corrupt, aesthetically obsolete, thematically superficial, temperamentally boring. Even the seemingly worthwhile films, those that lay claim to high moral and aesthetic standards and have been accepted as such by critics and the public alike, reveal the decay of the Product Film.[2]

Less clear was what was to replace it. At first, it appeared to be sort of an American version of a worldwide phenomenon - the Nouvelle Vague in France, the British New Wave, Cinema Novo in Brazil - young film directors ready to challenge their elders in the commercial film industry.

An American conduit for this energy already existed in Cinema 16 - the exhibition and distribution company founded by Amos Vogel in 1947. And Vogel was an articulate advocate for alternative, non-commercial forms of film as well as feature films. But he saw his role as a critical arbiter and refused films that he considered uninteresting even if made by filmmakers he already distributed.

Mekas, on the other hand, was a tenacious defender of total artistic license and found any critical barriers to distribution unacceptable. When Cinema 16 refused to distribute Stan Brakhage's *Anticipation of the Night* (1958), Mekas formed the Film-Makers' Cooperative as a division of the New American Cinema Group with no restrictions on the source or number of films accepted.

He was living at the time at 414 Park Ave. South and made it the Cooperative's headquarters.

I slept under my editing table. The rest of the place was taken over by filmmakers, who were almost always there, screening their films to each other and friends.[3]

The public exhibition activities of the Film-Makers' Cinematheque were nomadic over the years, but the Cooperative never moved and, even if no longer his home, the Park Ave. South loft continued as both a workplace and meeting point for Mekas and his many friends and allies over the years. Plans were made and strategies devised in its front room and in the Belmore Cafeteria across the street whose neon sign could be seen from the Coop's front window.

Although in retrospect Amos Vogel's curatorial approach might seem more like common sense than authoritarian censorship, it was not the one that survived. Cinema 16 closed the next year.

Mekas's cooperative model - perhaps in part based on the agricultural cooperatives he remembered from his Lithuanian childhood - proved more durable, not only surviving but serving as a model for other experimental film cooperatives around the world.

77 HERMAN G. WEINBERG

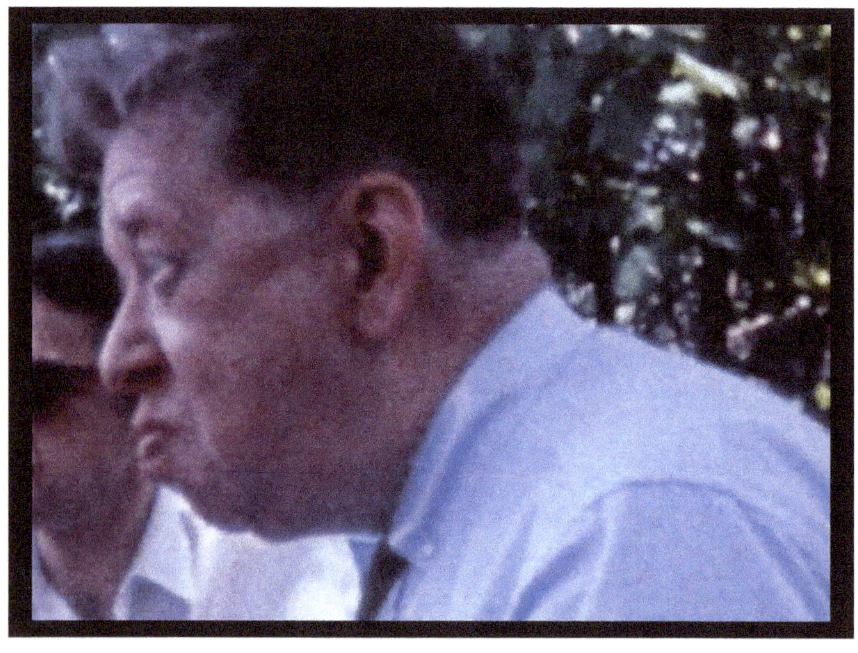

Reel 3 14:14

Herman G. Weinberg seemed to live and breathe cinema. He made films himself, managed movie theaters, adapted foreign films to English, wrote criticism for numerous film publications, taught film history at the City College of New York, and published books on the film directors he most admired. When the Mekas brothers founded *Film Culture* magazine in 1954, Weinberg wrote an article for their first issue.

A native New Yorker, Weinberg had begun in the film industry working on the musical scores of silent German films. When the sound era arrived, he pioneered the process of translating the dialogue of imported films into sub-titles audiences could read quickly enough to follow the film's story. He soon extended his linguistic skills beyond German to French, Spanish, and Italian so he could write sub-titles for films in those languages as well.

In the vernacular of the film industry at the time, a theater that showed foreign films was an "art house" and Weinberg ran one, the 55th Street Playhouse in Manhattan. It premiered the anti-fascist documentary *The Spanish Earth* (1937) by Joris Ivens as well as prestigious "art" films by other European directors, such as Jean Renoir and Luis Buñuel.

Weinberg's alliance with Mekas was curious given their highly divergent notions of what constituted film "art." The former's heroes were not iconoclasts like Jack Smith and Stan Brakhage but Hollywood icons such as Ernst Lubitsch and Josef von Sternberg.

But Mekas's affection was unfailing. He wrote in a column entitled "On H. G. Weinberg, The True Lover of Cinema:"

> …My special tribute of the year goes to Herman G. Weinberg…he writes with so much love for the movies that you read and you go crazy thinking about where are you going to see those movies, and when.[1]

Shortly before Weinberg's death in 1983, Anthology Film Archives published his autobiography *A Manhattan Odyssey: A Memoir*. Containing Weinberg's personal reminiscences, it was a somewhat unusual choice for Anthology since it was not, like its other publications, focussed on the theory and practice of experimental film. Publishing it was more likely Mekas's personal homage to its author and their shared devotion to, as the title of Weinberg's collected writings was titled, *Saint Cinema*.

78 RIVERSIDE PARK

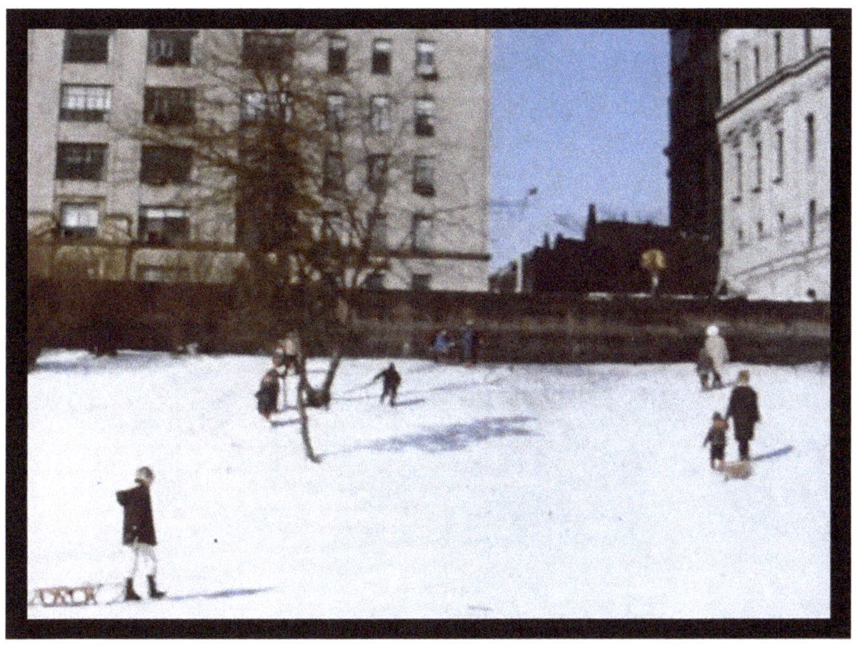

Reel 3 14:56

While Central Park was clearly Mekas's favorite urban oasis, he occasionally filmed another one just to its west along the Hudson River. Riverside Park was less convenient to his travels up and down Manhattan but, at least in the period he was living on the Upper West Side, it still attracted him - particularly after snowfalls when its slopes descending towards the river brought out enthusiastic sledders.

Like Central Park, Riverside Park was originally designed by landscape architect Frederick Law Olmsted. But Olmsted's vision of bucolic river views had disappeared in the coal smoke of locomotives pulling cars full of livestock down to the meatpacking district of lower Manhattan. The train tracks also cut off pedestrian access to the river.

In the 1930s, Robert Moses, the master builder of so much of 20th century New York's automobile-centric infrastructure, decided to streamline the road system circling Manhattan and cover the railroad tracks for his parkway. The park embellished the roadway with recreation areas and green space for the neighborhood.

When the green space turned white with snow and children careened down its slopes on sleds, its appeal to Mekas's camera was irresistible.

79 OLMSTED HIKE

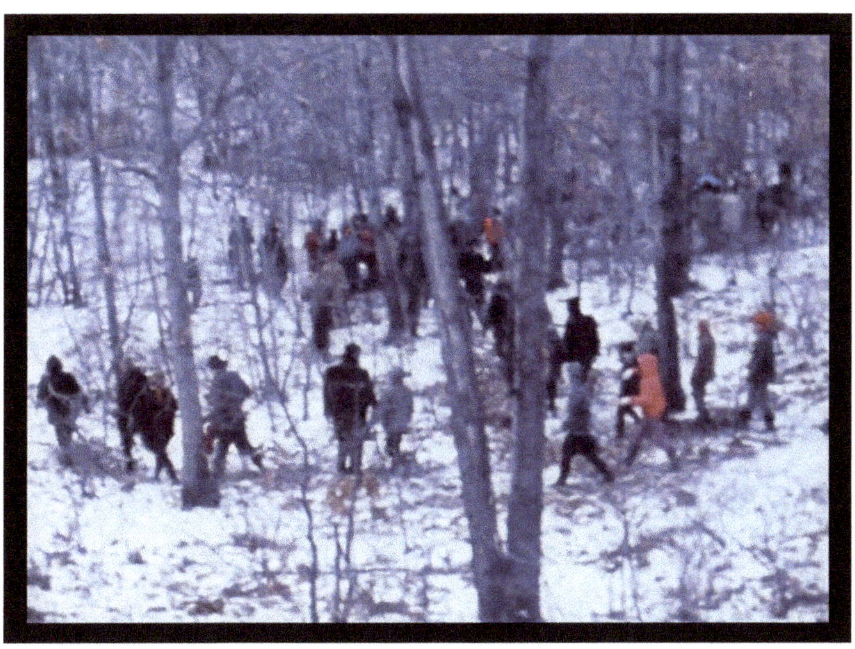

Reel 3 19:11

Whether Be-Ins, Kreeping Kreplach press conferences, or Hare Krishna parades, the public events Mekas filmed in *Walden* were more likely to involve artists, poets or musicians than commissioners, mayors, and senators. An exception was the winter day on Staten Island when he filmed an "Olmsted Hike."

Robert Moses, chairman of the New York's Triborough Bridge and Tunnel Authority, wanted to build a highway to speed motorists from New Jersey to Long Island across his newly completed Verrazzano Narrows Bridge connecting Staten Island to Brooklyn. The path of the planned highway cut through a wooded area that the great landscape architect and designer of Central Park, Frederick Law Olmsted, had envisioned as part of a "greenbelt" around New York City.

To oppose Moses's plan, environmental groups organized annual "Olmsted Hikes" that followed the proposed highway route through the endangered forest and invited celebrities, politicians and the press to follow.

An historian of the environment movement, Charles E. Little wrote:

> The greenbelters, for some perverse reason, liked to organize them in
> the winter, and yet, despite the season, hundreds of people would
> show up - strung out along the Olmsted Trail for a half-mile or more,
> feeling noble and healthy in mind and body.[1]

Among the noble and healthy that Mekas and numerous journalists followed over the icy woodland slopes were New York City Mayor, John Lindsay, his ebullient Parks Commissioner Thomas Hoving, and New York Senator Jacob Javits.

Given the political weight of the participants, it was not surprising that a compromise was eventually negotiated that rerouted Moses's highway. In 1970, the "Olmsted Trailway" was designated one of two "Special Natural Features Districts in the City of New York."

And Mekas was not indifferent to the power of political celebrity either. When an ad in the *Village Voice* announced *Walden*'s premiere at the Elgin Theater on December 20, 1969, its list of stars began with two Olmsted Hike participants: "Mayor Lindsay, Senator Javits."

80 JOHN LINDSAY

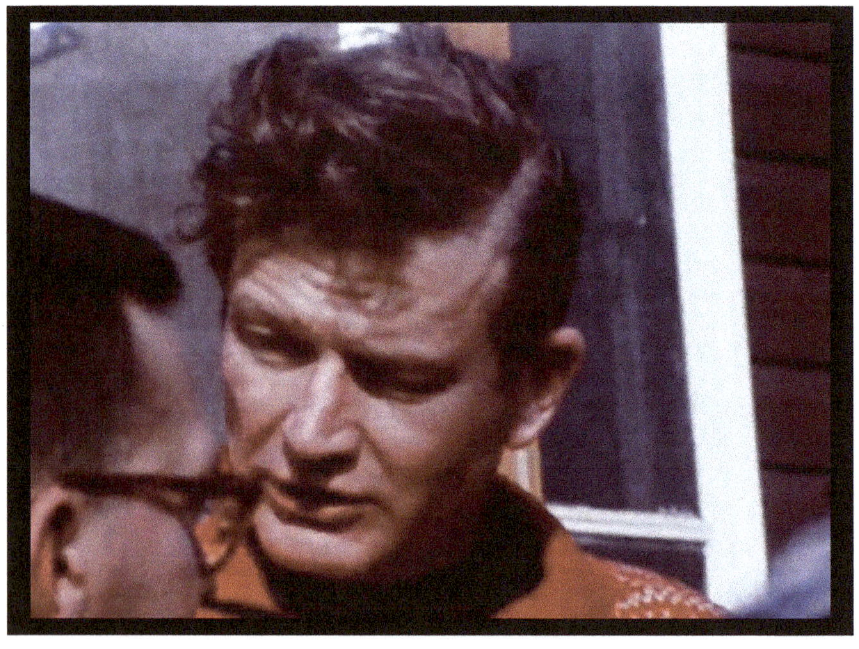

Reel 3 19:11

"He is fresh and everyone else is tired."

It was the slogan for John Lindsay's successful campaign for mayor of New York in 1966, borrowed from an admiring description of him by the newspaper columnist Murray Kempton.

Several months after the election, Mekas, to whom the slogan applied perhaps better than it did to Lindsay, offered the new mayor advice in his *Village Voice* column. In April 1966, he wrote:

> Mayor Lindsay: Please put your ear to the windows, and to the walls, and to the ground, and listen to the new vibrations in the air - and it's not only because it's April! It's a different kind of April that's in the air…Dear Mayor Lindsay: Don't let yourself be dragged down by the ghosts of the past![1]

Curiously, the years covered by the ever-optimistic Mekas in *Walden* correspond almost exactly to those of the charismatic Lindsay's first term as mayor. And in age the two were only thirteen months apart. (Lindsay was born on November 24, 1921, Mekas on December 24, 1922.)

But they came from very different places.

In 1949, when Mekas had arrived in the U.S. as a displaced person, Lindsay had already passed his bar exam to practice law in New York. By the time Mekas started *Film Culture* with almost no money in 1955, Lindsay was an assistant to the U.S. Attorney General in Washington and preparing to win election as a U.S. Congressman representing the "Silk-Stocking" district of the Upper East Side of Manhattan.

On May 13, 1965, a few months after Mekas started filming *Walden*, declaring "The Wind Was Full of Spring," Lindsay announced his candidacy for mayor of New York. Lindsay won election in November and took office in January 1966 but by the time Mekas wrote his open letter to the mayor in April, the "ghosts of the past" were indeed trying to drag him down.

On the new mayor's first day in office, a transit workers strike shut down all bus and subway service. Later in his first term, he was confronted with a teachers' strike that resulted in the closure of all schools, a sanitation strike that left garbage uncollected for weeks, and a job slowdown by police and fireman. For a few weeks even Broadway theaters were closed by a strike. In the last months of his first term, a huge unpredicted blizzard struck and Lindsay was blamed for the fact that, for several weeks, city snow ploughs were unable to clear all of the city's streets. Critics promptly dubbed it "the Lindsay snowstorm" (see Chapter 108).

In June of 1969, as Mekas was filming the last of the sequences which he would incorporate into *Walden*, Lindsay was running for reelection. He won by a narrow margin in October but even more troubles awaited him in his second term. Near the end of his life he reflected that his new campaign slogan could have been:

"He is tired and everyone else is dead."

81 THOMAS HOVING

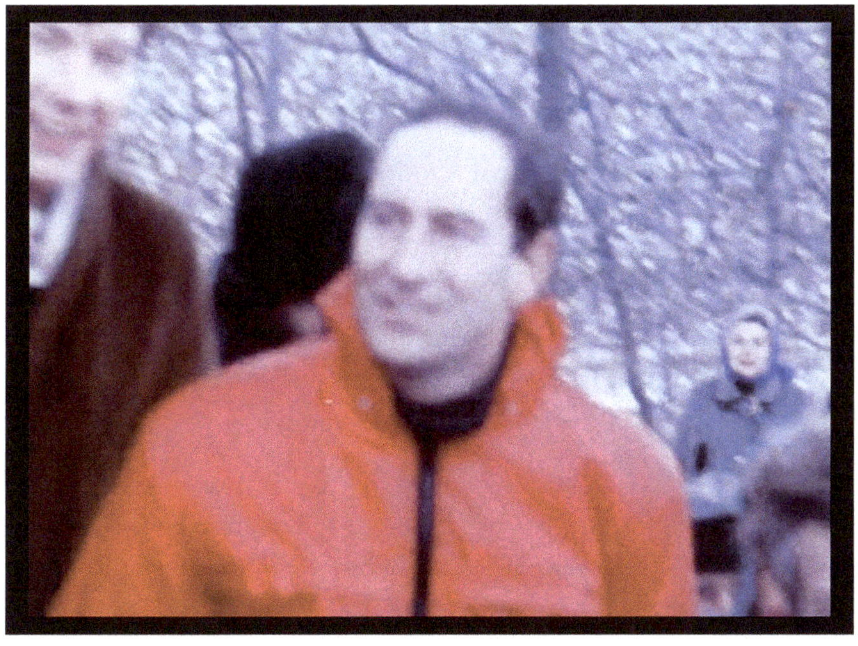

Reel 3 19:11

At first glance Thomas Hoving could not have been farther from the "underground" culture documented in *Walden*. A traditional academic, he was a specialist in medieval art with a PhD from Princeton. Starting at the Metropolitan Museum of Art as a curatorial assistant, he was subsequently promoted to curator of medieval art.

He had worked as a campaign volunteer for John Lindsay's congressional campaigns and the newly-elected Lindsay asked him to become his Parks Commissioner, a post that had been held by the powerful highway builder Robert Moses from 1934 to 1960. As Lindsay surely intended, Hoving's approach would be radically different from his predecessor's: he argued that "parks are works of art just as a painting or sculpture is and they need to be cared for as an artistic entity."[1]

But it must have surprised everyone, including perhaps his employer, when the staid academic proposed a series of "happenings." The term had originally been coined by the artist Allan Kaprow for spontaneous mixed media performances and had attracted greater attention with Warhol's "Exploding Plastic Inevitable" which Mekas had filmed in 1966.

"Hoving's Happenings" mixed high and low culture - dance contests, magic shows, barbershop quartets, a recital of Goethe's *Faust*. From kite-flying to costume parties, these official events drew inspiration from the avant-garde and culminated in the March 1967 "Be-In," a mass celebration in Central Park that, in retrospect, proved to be a landmark event in the late 1960s counter-culture.

The former Parks Commissioner Robert Moses was reported to be filled with horror at the "misuse, disorder and freakish behavior" that took place there. But, for Mekas, the events combined two of his great passions - celebratory gatherings and Central Park.

Hoving himself served only six months as Lindsay's Park Commissioner before being named the new director of the Metropolitan

Museum and returning to the more rarefied museum world. Meanwhile the mass gatherings which had begun as relatively apolitical "Hoving's Happenings" would take on a less festive tone as they evolved into increasingly angry protests against the escalating war in Vietnam.

82 JACOB JAVITS

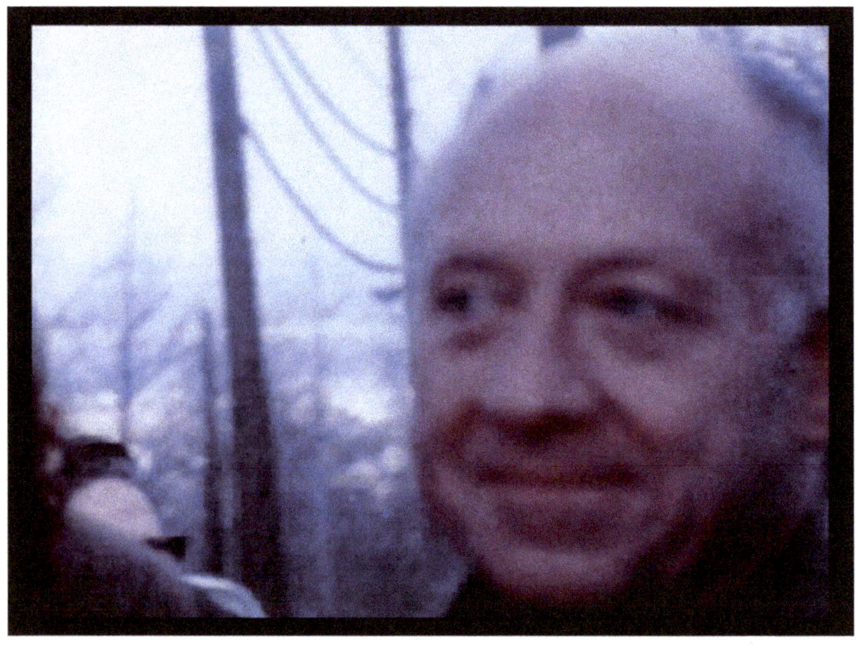

Reel 3 19:11

When Senator Jacob Javits appeared to hike through the snowy woods in defense of the Olmsted Trailway, he seemed to be dressed for a business meeting. Unlike his fellow political celebrities, the athletic Mayor Lindsay and Park Commissioner Hoving, Javits did not seem ready for a rambunctious snowball fight.

It was not only because Javits was their elder by several decades but also that, unlike his youthful colleagues, he had not grown up playing sports at private schools in New England. Instead he had helped his mother sell dry goods on the streets of the Lower East Side.

Javits had become a Republican to eradicate the corruption of the Democratic organization referred to as Tammany Hall which dominated New York City politics in the early 20th century. But by mid-century, his own breed, the "liberal Republican," was dying too.

His career representing the city in the U.S. Congress had begun in 1946 at a time when northern Republicans were to the left of conservative Southern Democrats. But as the two parties eventually realigned along a stricter right/left axis after World War II, Javits found himself increasingly at odds with the mainstream of his party.

But he remained popular in New York for his support of progressive positions - such as saving the Olmsted Trailway from highway builders - and, no doubt thanks in part to his visibility on such occasions as the Olmsted Hike (see Chapter 79), he easily won his next election for a third term in the U.S. Senate in 1968 and went on to a fourth in 1974.

Javits was a key Congressional supporter of the National Endowment for the Arts, which funded projects such as the one by the Albright-Knox Gallery in 1968 which commissioned Mekas to create the first version of *Walden*.

83 JANE WODENING

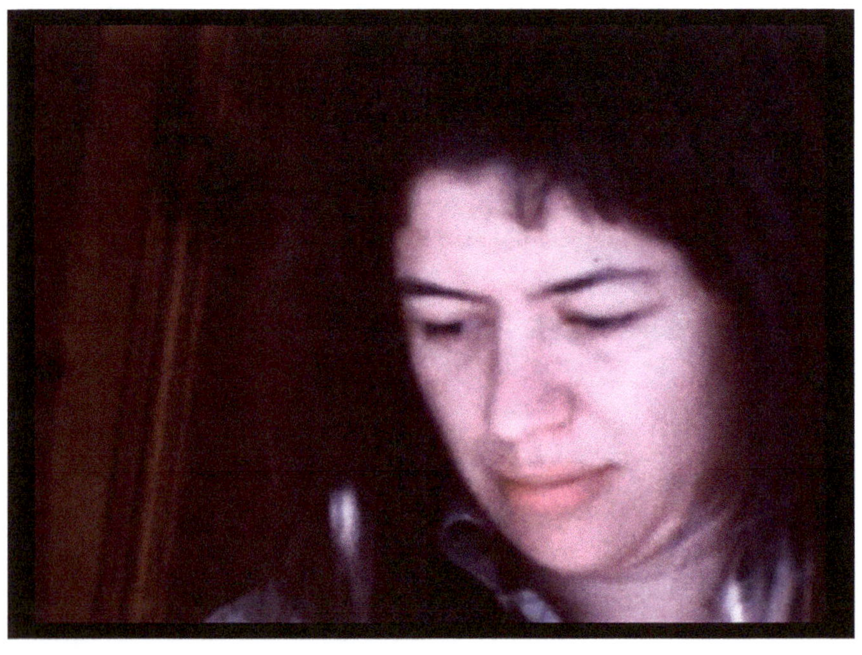

Reel 4 09:02

Mekas's visit to the home of Jane Wodening and Stan Brakhage was the longest single episode of *Walden*. And it was unique in more than its length: geographically, it was the farthest west - the Rocky Mountains - and it contained the most footage of Mekas himself shot by others.

In a small cabin at an altitude of 9000 feet, Wodening wrote, "we lived for twenty-three years with five children and a yard full of animals, my sanity and my delight."[1] Her delight was evident in *Walden* as she helped (and sometimes filmed) the city dweller Mekas as he learned about mountain life. Mekas noted on the *Walden* poster: "Jane and the Author ride the donkey, which isn't that easy to do…"

Although Jane Brakhage's name (Wodening after her divorce) was not explicitly visible on her husband's films, he was to contend that the signature, "By Brakhage" that he scratched by hand on all of his films did not refer to him alone but "by way of Stan and Jane and all the children Brakhage."[2]

Brakhage stated that he had been profoundly influenced by three women, Gertrude Stein, Marie Menken, and Jane; the first for her writing, the second for her films, and the third for her direct impact on his life. Brakhage said that before meeting her he was suicidal and had decided to kill himself upon completion of what was later to be seen as his first important film, *Anticipation of the Night* (1958).

While her psychological influence is impossible to quantify, there is no question about Jane Wodening's centrality as a subject of Brakhage's camera. The best-known example is *Window Water Baby Moving* (1959). The film's frank depiction of her giving birth to their first child also included images filmed by Jane to capture her husband's reactions.[3] Its impact was enormous. Critic Archer Winsten described the film as being "so forthright, so full of primitive wonder and love, so far beyond civilization in its acceptance that it becomes an experience like few in the history of movies."[4]

Another collaborative work was *Wedlock House: An Intercourse* (1959) which portrayed a marital quarrel during which the Brakhages filmed each other by passing the camera back and forth.

During her marriage to Brakhage, Wodening kept a scrapbook of letters, photographs, and notes which documented a critical period of the filmmaker's life. After their divorce in 1987, she began to publish her own writing and in 2015, she published a series of stories based on interviews with her husband she had recorded in 1983. She described her book *Brakhage's Childhood* as:

> a biography of a child, taken from the memory of that child grown up…Stan and I worked together a lot in his medium; this time, we worked together in my medium.[5]

84 RICHARD FOREMAN

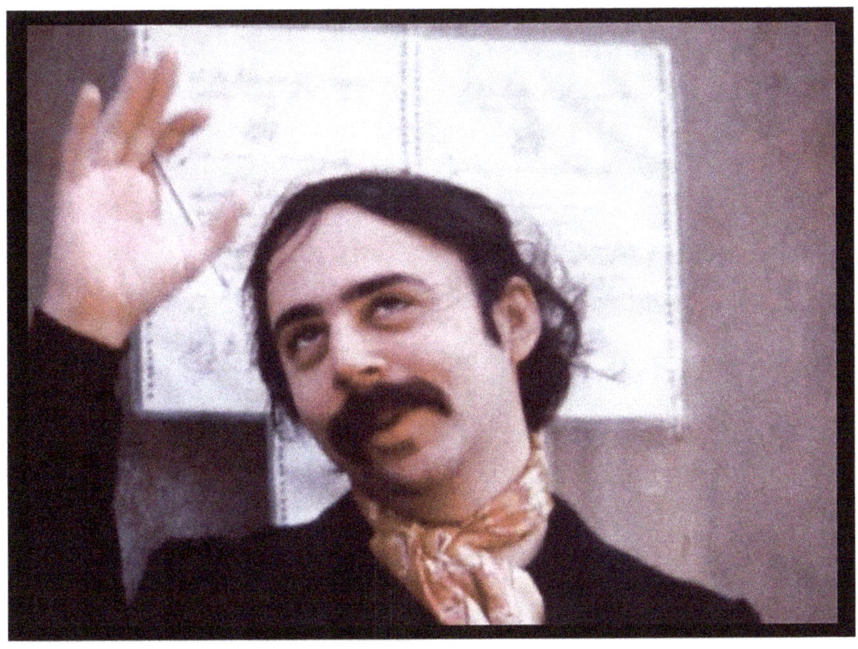

Reel 5 00:43

Mekas remembered:

> When we were still screening at the Gramercy Arts Theater, this guy
> Richard Foreman always used to come in with a young woman, Amy
> Taubin. He was always in a very heavy fur coat, like a bearskin coat,
> and they came to almost every screening. That's how I met them and
> that's how we became friends.

Later when I bought part of 80 Wooster Street and joined George
Maciunas's cooperative building, the floor which I purchased was full
of junk from floor to ceiling, covered with all kinds of rotten stuff and
I asked myself what in the world I was going to do with it all. And
somehow Richard showed up and said 'I will move everything out if
you let me use it occasionally for some plays.' I said 'Sure, sure do it!'
So he emptied it, he got some worker friends, so he helped me there
during the first stage and then he staged his first three plays there.[1]

In Richard Foreman's third appearance in *Walden* he can be seen on
Wooster Street near the building he had helped clean out for his
theater. But before that, he had also appeared briefly at two other of
Mekas's preferred locations for filming: Riverside Park with his wife
Amy Taubin and the Columbus Circle entrance to Central Park with
artists Michael Snow and Joyce Wieland.

Foreman had moved to New York after graduation from the Yale
School of Drama and was drawn to the radicalism of Judith Malina and
Julian Beck's Living Theater as well as Mekas's defiance of official
censorship with the screenings of *Flaming Creatures* (1962). He
founded his Ontological-Hysteric Theater in 1968 with a vision of
what he called "total theater" and he declared his intention of:

> stripping the theater bare of everything but the singular and essential
> impulse to stage the static tension of interpersonal relations in
> space...[2]

He shared with Mekas a commitment to challenging assumptions about how their respective media should behave. And the radicality of his approach linked Foreman to filmmakers with similar inclinations; his form of live theater was closely related to the film-as-performance art of filmmakers such as Jack Smith and Ken Jacobs.

Foreman's cleaning work for Mekas had earned him the right to use the Filmmakers Cinematheque at 80 Wooster Street for the first production of the "Ontological-Hysteric Theater," *Angelface*. But it was just a few months before city authorities denied Mekas permission to continue holding public events in the space.

Foreman and his company were forced to move on to other spaces, but they would continue performing and promoting radical theater around the world over the next five decades. He made a feature film, *Strong Medicine*, in 1978 and, starting in 2012, declared that he had lost interest in theater and was concentrating on film. He went on to make three more features.

85 HANS RICHTER

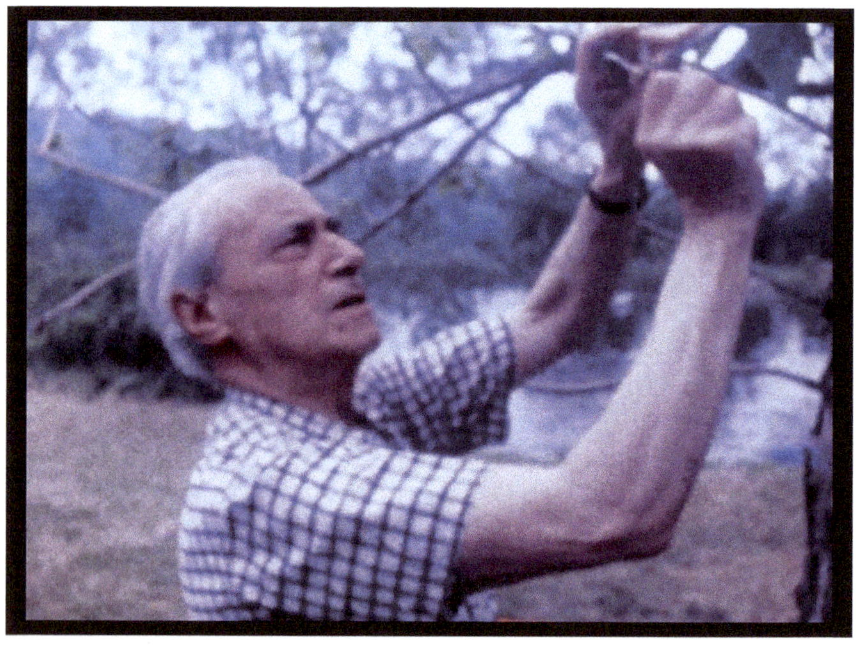

Reel 5 02:48

Almost seven decades later, Mekas recalled their first meeting:

> I met Hans Richter in 1951 about a year after I came to New York. I
> had already read about him in Frank Stauffacher's book on "Art in
> Cinema," to which he had contributed and he was running the Insti-
> tute of Film Techniques that he had founded at the City College of
> New York. I wrote to him that I had no money, but would like to know
> if I could sit in on his classes for free. A few days later I received an
> answer in two words: "Just come!"[1]

Hans Richter had been one of major figures in modern art to flee Nazi Europe, helping to shift its center of gravity from Paris and Berlin to New York.

In the 1920s, Richter, along with other artists in Berlin, (Viking Eggeling, Walter Ruttmann, Oskar Fischinger...) and colleagues in Paris (Man Ray, Marcel Duchamp, Fernand Léger...) had demon-strated that moving images, in addition to entertaining audiences with theatrical narratives, could also be used to extend the reach of visual art. On May 3, 1925, his first abstract works *Rythmus 21* (1921-4) and *Rythmus 23* (1923) were shown in a program entitled "Der absolute Film" to a sold-out audience in a 900-seat theater in Berlin.

As an exile in New York Hans Richter re-engaged with film and enlisted some of his fellow refugees, among them Max Ernst, Marcel Duchamp, Fernand Léger and Man Ray, to contribute episodes to *Dreams That Money Can Buy* (1947).

But his influence was even greater as an educator; he founded the Institute of Film Techniques at the City College of New York. His meeting with Mekas there can be seen as the moment when the pre-war European period of the history of experimental film connected to its post-war American chapter.

Almost a half century after Richter's first experiments in abstract animation in Berlin and almost two decades after their first meeting in

New York, Mekas visited him at his summer home in rural Connecticut. By the summer of 1968, Mekas had already shown a first version of *Walden* at the museum that commissioned it, the Albright-Knox Gallery. But he was still trying to decide on its final form.

On Walden's soundtrack the eternally curious Richter can be heard asking Mekas: "So what are you doing?" And Mekas begins to explain:

> I have been shooting for the last four years every day or so...I have been like keeping a film diary and now I'm beginning to edit and structure it and and so I have like twenty hours of film which I'm...

Then they are both distracted, apparently by some sort of insect. The subject changes and no more is audible of a unique exchange between the pioneer of the first chapter of the history of experimental film and the pioneer of its second.

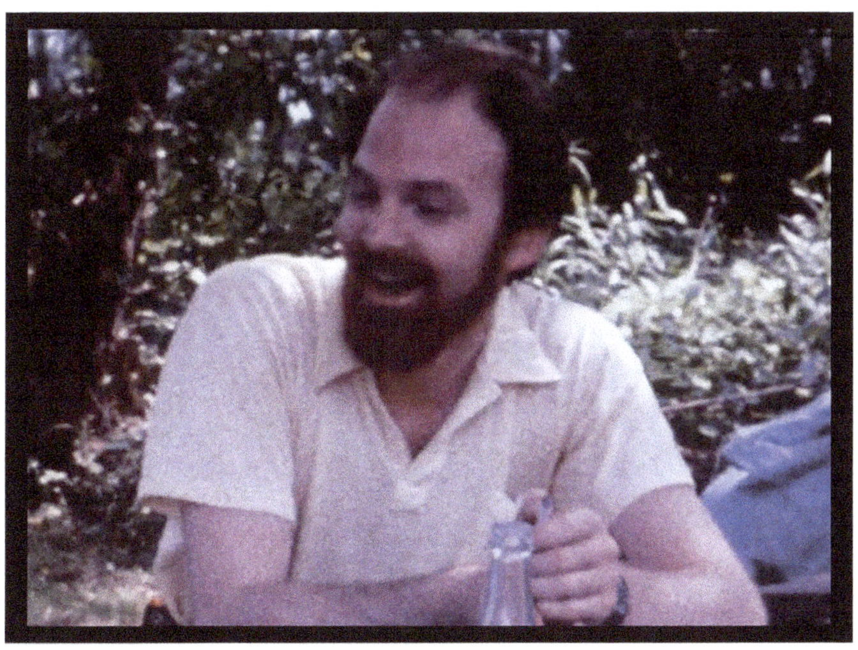

Reel 5 03:02

Mekas recalled:

> Standish Lawder was married to Hans Richter's daughter but I had
> met him before he was married. In 1965 I organized an expanded cine-
> ma/expanded arts festival, and I showed his work. It was a survey of
> what was happening in that area of art and featured about 30 different
> artists. I included him because I knew he was working with projecting
> slides that he burned and painted. He would put various color
> substances on slides, and then when the heat touched them, they
> began to melt producing this melting, moving, sliding action on the
> screen. So I included him as a practitioner of expanded cinema.[1]

The films that Standish Lawder would go on to make in the late 1960s
and early 1970s are still compelling but it was not his first career - his
training was as an art historian.

Lawder's PhD thesis at Yale was an exploration of the intersection of
film and modern art. Expanded and published as a book in 1975 (and
republished by Eyewash Books in 2019), *The Cubist Cinema* cogently
articulated the central role of film in the major currents of modern art,
Dadaism, Surrealism, and Cubism, as exemplified by the work of
Richter, Viking Eggeling, Walter Ruttmann and, most importantly,
Fernand Léger and his *Ballet mécanique* (1924).

But as he was completing his PhD thesis, Lawder also embarked on a
series of enthralling films of his own - notable among them *Necrology*
(1968), *Runaway* (1969), *Dangling Particle* (1970), and *Corridor* (1970).
They can be seen as examples of the structuralist/materialist movement in experimental film of that period but, unlike much other work
in that category, they were also visually lively and irresistibly funny.

Less typical of his films at the time was the one he can be seen making
in *Walden* and released four years later, *Sunday in Southbury* (1972). It
was Lawder's view of the same occasion and he described it in the
Film-Makers Coop catalogue:

I had long wanted to make a film on Hans Richter who has been an important figure in my life, and this is the result. Almost unedited, it was shot one summer Sunday afternoon in 1968 at a picnic with friends and relatives. Jonas Mekas was also shooting the event, and his version is included in his recent film *Diaries, Notes and Sketches.*[2]

87 RAY JOHNSON

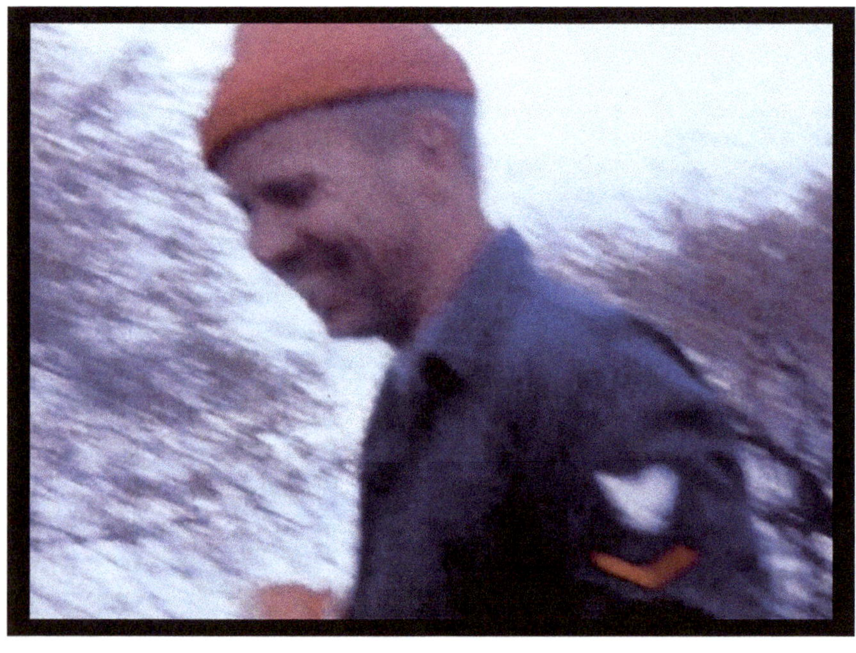

Reel 5 09:15

The happy stilt-walker Mekas captured at the 1967 Central Park Be-In, Ray Johnson, was "New York's most famous unknown artist,"[1] the founder of the little-known movement, the New York Correspondence School, also called Mail Art. While artist Allan Kaprow and the Fluxus Group were attracting attention to their "Happenings," Johnson was deliberately not attracting attention to events he called "Nothings."

When curator Sevim Fesci attempted to interview Johnson for the Smithsonian Archives of American Art, he elicited mostly unintelligible non-sequiturs but Johnson did admit that:

> There's never been in New York an exhibition of correspondence art. I don't know how it could be organized because just to do it would kill it…it's all very, very personal. I have my own secret about the whole thing. I mean I have my own very private jokes.[2]

Johnson contended that reacting to art in public, unavoidable in a gallery or museum, was far less interesting than reacting in private such as when opening personal mail. Accordingly, much of his art took the form of poems on postcards, small collages, drawings, and objects sent to his friends and fellow artists through the mail. In his lifetime few were exhibited and sold through established art market channels.

But his work was no secret to those inside the art world and glimpses of it came out through the admiring accounts of critics. One of those who understood him best was Grace Glueck, the arts reporter for the *New York Times*, who in 1965 had labeled him "the most famous unknown artist" and twenty years later was still attuned to his work, calling him "A Witty Master of the Deadpan Spoof" and reporting Johnson's description of one of the more unusual pieces of mail art that he had received:

> 'Once someone sent me an elephant dropping from the Sacramento Zoo,' reported the egg-bald artist the other day, clad in a holey blue sweater with the red of a T-shirt showing through. 'It was beautiful,

almost a religious object. I put it on a Victorian table and made drawings of it.'[3]

And in an imaginary letter to Johnson after his suicide in 1995, critic
David Bourdon wrote:

The major museum retrospectives and million-dollar auction sales
never happened for you. If the international art world had agreed to
historicize you as the one and only father of mail art, would you have
been any happier? If you had been granted a greater share in the enormous reputation and fortune that inundated your Pop-Art pals, how
would you have handled it? You gave away so much NYCS[4] mail art
over the decades, bedeviled most of the dealers and collectors who
were interested in you, and found so many ways to sabotage whatever
market remained for your 'serious' collages, is it any wonder that the
art world's money-changers and reputation-launderers avoided you?[5]

88 PAUL KRASSNER

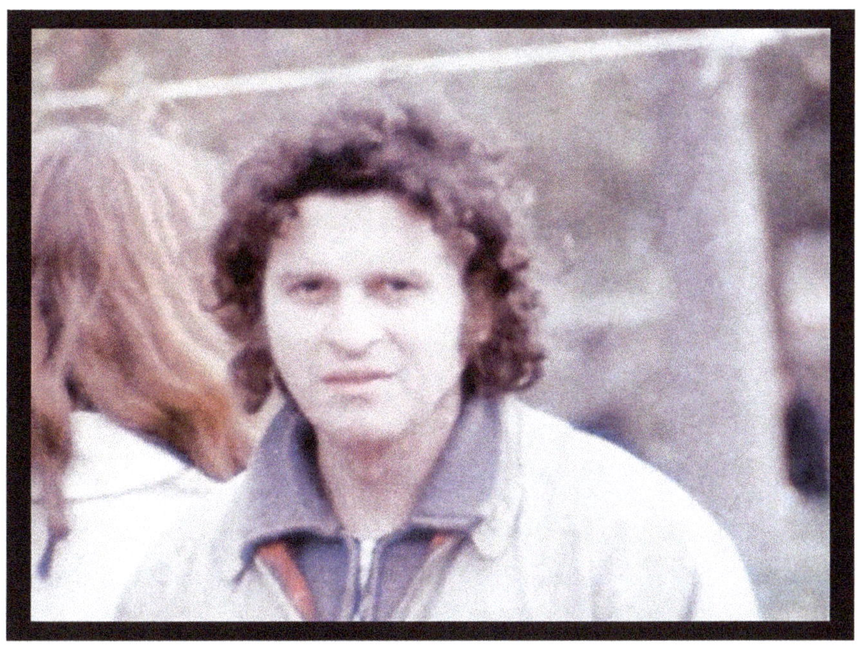

Reel 5 09:42

He appeared to be just a bystander to the celebrations at the Central Park Be-In in the spring of 1967, seemingly wary of Mekas's camera and the more boisterous celebrants who were happy to clown for it. But in fact Paul Krassner was a key figure in the event and the counter-cultural ferment swirling around it.

Krassner had started a magazine called *The Realist* in 1958 which was at first just an off-shoot to the main 1950s source of satire, *Mad Magazine*. But in the 1960s, *The Realist* touched a nerve in a new generation and eclipsed its parent publication. Its young readers were eager for humor and commentary that would offend their parents' sense of propriety. They were not disappointed when, shortly after the Central Park Be-In, *The Realist* published the "Disneyland Memorial Orgy" poster showing iconic Disney cartoon personalities engaged in a variety of sexual activities and drug use.

Later in 1967, Krassner would join Abbie Hoffman and Jerry Rubin in the founding of the "Youth International Party," the "Yippies" and begin plotting the demonstration at the Democratic National Convention that would change American social and political history.

In retrospect, it is tempting to interpret Krassner's skeptical expression when caught by Mekas's camera as evidence that he already realized that the festive mood of the Be-In would not last long. Its next incarnation, less than a month later, would not be a celebration but a protest. It became the "Spring Mobilization to End the War in Vietnam" and drew hundreds of thousands of less cheerful participants who, after assembling in Central Park, marched to the United Nations, in the first of what were to become increasingly angry protests against the war.

89 PETER BEARD

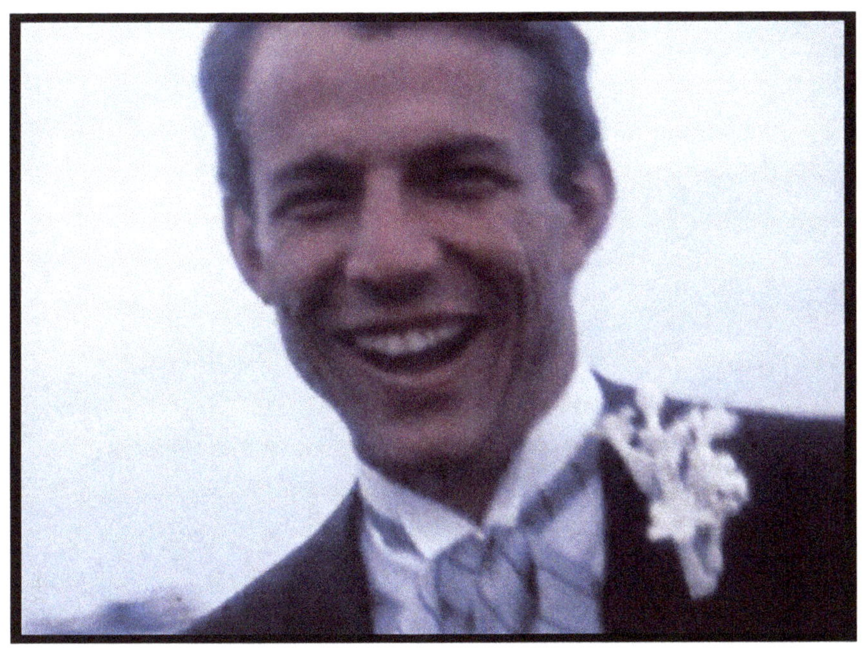

Reel 5 10:20

Mekas recalled:

> When Adolfas told Jerome Hill that he was looking for someone who could play the lead in *Hallelujah the Hills* (1963) and the lead had to be a person who could climb trees, jump over rocks, and be full of the spirit of adventure and physically capable, Jerome, without thinking at all, said 'I know the person! It's my nephew!'

> And he pointed to a magazine right in front of us on the table and said 'Look! There he is!' It was *Life Magazine* with a full page picture captioned, 'Peter Beard: Young Man of the Year.' He had already been in Africa doing research on crocodiles on one of those big dangerous lakes. So we met him and it was immediately clear that he was the guy.[1]

Peter Beard and his cousin, Mekas's friend and benefactor, Jerome Hill (see Chapter 51), were heirs to a great 19th century fortune. James J. Hill, Beard's great-grandfather and Jerome Hill's grandfather, was nicknamed the "Empire Builder" for his role in building and operating the Great Northern Railway which established the first trans-continental rail link to the Pacific Northwest in 1893.

A profile of Beard published in Vanity Fair in 2007 began:

> Whether he's at a New York nightclub or deep in the African wilderness, world-famous photographer and artist Peter Beard is surrounded by drugs, debts, and beautiful women. On the eve of a major retrospective of Beard's work in Paris, the author finds the man described as "half Tarzan, half Byron" weighing his future at his Kenyan Shangri-la.[2]

It was Mekas's friendship with Beard that resulted in his invitation to film Beard's high society wedding at the bride's Newport estate, The Ledges. And, in later years, Beard would also be visible in Mekas's visits with Jacqueline Kennedy Onassis who asked Mekas to give filmmaking lessons to her children. It was an unlikely realm for a

Lithuanian refugee who less than 20 years earlier had been living in a German displaced persons camp.

Beard seemed to move effortlessly between very different worlds. His membership in American high society made him a natural choice of husband for the Newport heiress Minnie Cushing. But Beard was equally if not more comfortable in rural Africa and he insisted on returning there shortly after his wedding. His marriage to Cushing lasted only three years.

Beard was also at home with fashion models, movie stars, business tycoons, rock musicians and anyone else who would pay his expenses and provide him with recreational drugs. Interviewing him was a happy task for journalists; his repertoire of outlandish stories was inexhaustible.

If the traditional Newport society wedding was an anomaly in Mekas's diaries, it turned out to be just as unusual for Beard. His relatively sedate role as the tuxedoed groom in *Walden* might have been the most conventional one he ever played.

90 NEWPORT

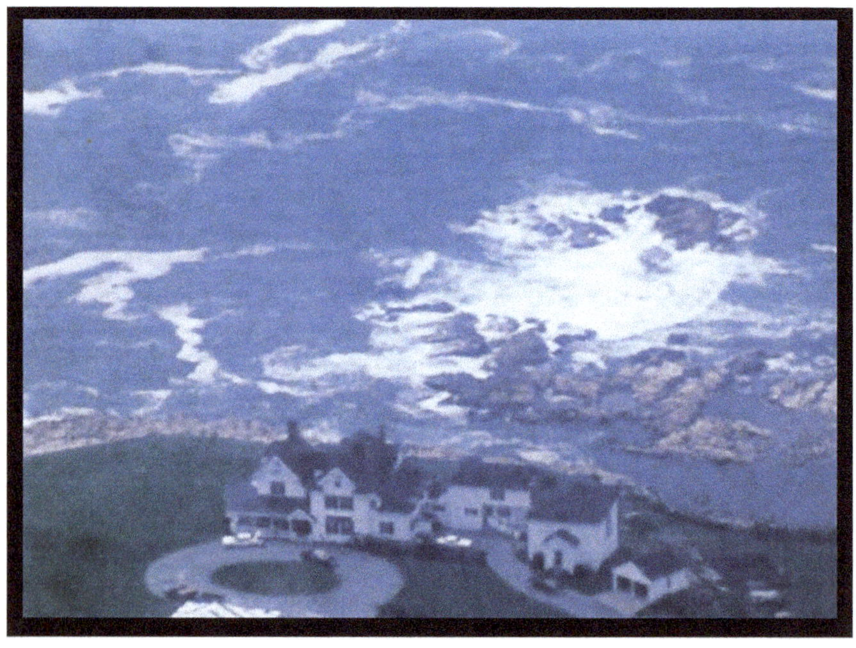

Reel 5 10:40

If some of *Walden*'s street scenes of New York City - such as those of black workers toiling in the rubble of a demolished building or unloading a coal truck - were reminders of the existence of an urban underclass, the sequence labelled "One Day in Newport," showed "the Author," at the other extreme, boating at sunset in front of oceanfront mansions.

Mekas was not strictly apolitical; he was clearly a champion of artistic freedom when he felt it was under threat from institutional authority. He was willing to go to jail to defend his right to show *Flaming Creatures* (1963). And in *Walden*'s two "flashbacks," he paid homage to Judith Malina in her lonely Times Square vigil for peace. There is no ambiguity in the intertitle he inserted into a 1966 sequence: "Police violence erupts in Times Square, marchers jailed."

But there is little indication that Mekas was troubled by economic inequality. And he was a grateful beneficiary of the great wealth of his friend Jerome Hill which financed many of his activities.

Peter Beard, who had appeared in Adolfas Mekas's *Hallelujah the Hills* (1963) was Jerome Hill's cousin and an heir to the same fortune. When Beard planned to marry the equally wealthy Minnie Cushing at her majestic seafront property in Newport, Rhode Island, he invited Mekas to document the occasion.

The wedding was at the ancestral home of the Cushings built by the bride's great-grandfather who had made a massive fortune in trade with China. The Cushings' estate, The Ledges, was among the many grandiose mansions built during the "Gilded Age" in Newport where the wealthiest Americans came in the summer and displayed their unlimited means.

Mekas's wedding sequence shot at The Ledges begins with sweeping aerial views of the Cushing estate and ends with a helicopter departure of the bridal couple.

The event was dutifully described in the next day's *New York Times*:

The bride wore a long white organdy dress with appliqués of organdy flowers, crystals and chalk beads on the hem and long sleeves. On her head was an arrangement of white organdy flowers and a full-length tuile veil, which she later removed for the reception.[1]

In a few minutes *Walden* shifts from rural Colorado ("I FIND RABBIT SHIT!") to the grounds of a Newport mansion ("Wedding feast"). No moral or political distinction is evident.

91 ROXBURY

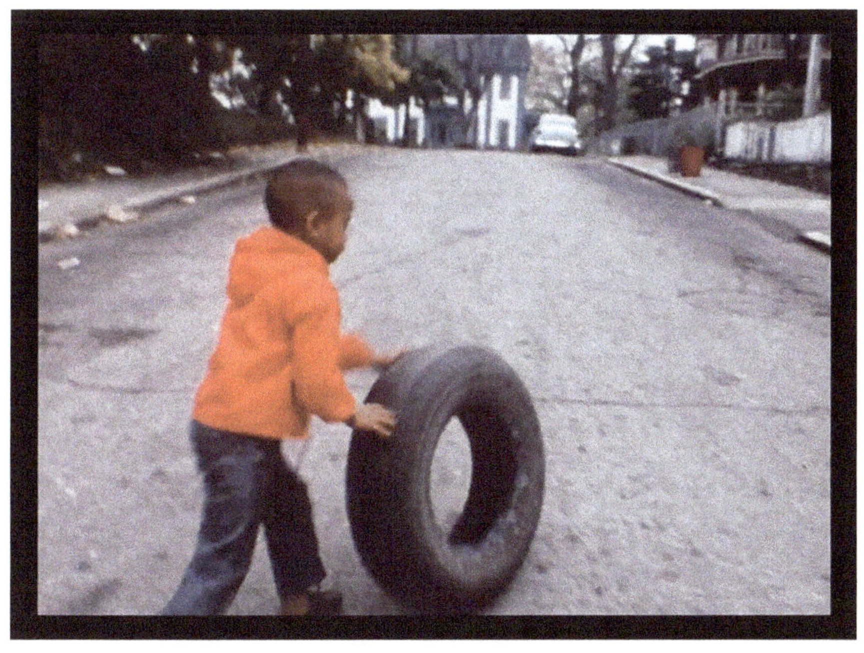

Reel 5 25:16

Soon after the heiress Minnie Cushing departs her oceanfront mansion in Newport by helicopter, *Walden* shows a black child pushing an old tire up the street in the poor Boston neighborhood of Roxbury. Mekas changed the order of certain sequences in the different versions of *Walden*, so the contrast may have been intentional but it was more likely purely chronological - just the record of two trips to visit two very different friends - Peter Beard in Newport and Mel Lyman in Boston.

The latter was a musician who played harmonica and banjo in a popular folk music group called the Jim Kweskin Jug Band. Mekas had used their music as the soundtrack for his *Notes on the Circus* (1966) which he had put into distribution as a separate film before incorporating it into *Walden*.

Lyman had lived in Mekas's apartment in New York for a while, writing a book whose publication Mekas funded. It was not clear if its title was intended ironically: *Autobiography of a World Savior*. Later in 1966 Lyman moved to Boston and founded what became known as The Fort Hill Community in the poor neighborhood of Roxbury. In February 1967, a headline in the *Bay State Banner*, a local black community newspaper, announced:

White Revolutionaries Settle in Roxbury

The article went on to explain:

A large white family lives high on Fort Hill in Roxbury. Like the black community around it, it is committed to changing the American social system. The family is actually a community of families. Boston's young people call them the leaders of the Hippies, but to themselves they are simply "The Hill People." Their goal is to find freedom for themselves, and to set a model for young white Americans. A year and a half ago the first settlers moved to the hill and began to restore dilapidated homes for their families. Now there are almost a dozen couples with a total of 19 children, as well as a number of single men and women. The Hill People have restored a half dozen houses at little expense by doing the work themselves.[1]

Among the Fort Hill Community's activities was the publication of an "underground" newspaper, *The Avatar,* and, as the *Bay State Banner* reported, "a movie house for experimental films (Cinematheque)." The former had a major impact on Boston's exploding counter-cultural scene but the latter project, which was certainly connected to Mekas's visit, never materialized.

Apprehension about the cult-like nature of the "Mel Lyman family," was high after the murders committed by the "Charles Manson family" dominated headlines in 1969. And it did not help that excerpts from the *Autobiography of a World Savior* had been published regularly in *The Avatar*.

But suspicions about a darker side to the group were never confirmed and its members eventually founded a highly profitable construction company and moved to Los Angeles. Its web site in 2020 stated simply: "The founders began learning to build while renovating their own personal homes in Boston."[2]

92 MEL LYMAN

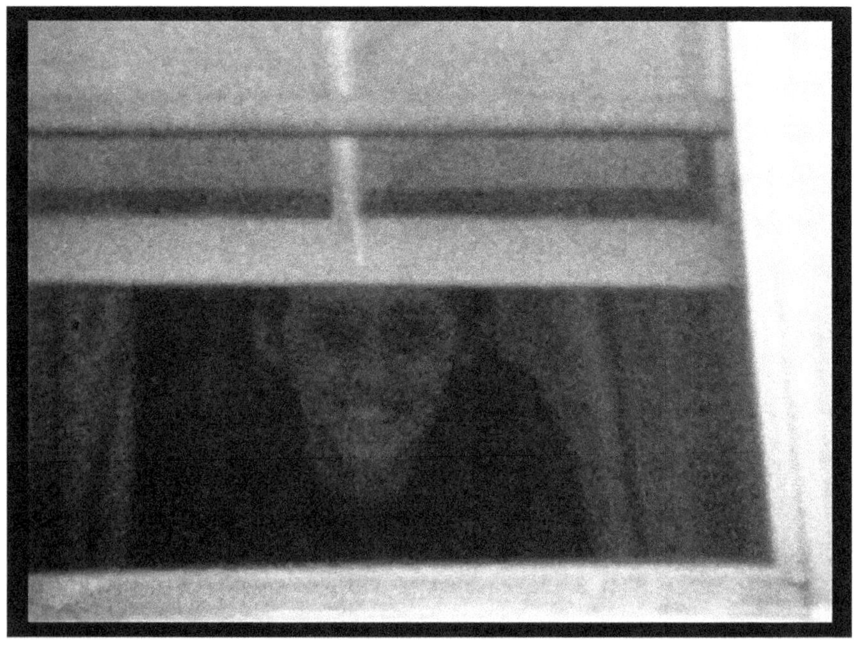

Reel 5 26:30

Mel Lyman's ghost-like face behind a screen window in the predominntly African-American Boston neighborhood of Roxbury is as hazy as his relationship to Mekas. It was his only appearance in the final version of *Walden* but he had appeared in a previous version.

The soundtrack of Mekas's short film *Notes on the Circus* (1966) which he later incorporated into *Walden*, had been provided by the Jim Kweskin Jug Band, one of whose members, Mel Lyman, was sharing Mekas's apartment on Third Avenue. In the first version of *Walden*, the sequence immediately following the circus scenes was described on Mekas's poster as:

MEL (GOD) MAKES COFFEE;

Mel makes coffee pot, demonstrates it, makes coffee

we all enjoy the coffee, the children

Mel drives uptown

According to Mekas, Lyman was homeless when he offered him a place to stay. While there, Lyman reportedly wrote *The Autobiography of a World Savior* in a single sitting and Mekas funded its publication. Its title page read: "Copyright by Jonas Press, 1966."

Shortly afterward, Lyman moved to Boston with plans to set up a Boston branch of the New York Film-Makers' Cinematheque. He and a "family" of young followers established the Fort Hill Community in Roxbury. Along with the renovation of a number of houses on Fort Hill, Lyman and his community started a new "underground" newspaper, *The Avatar*.

The Cinematheque project never materialized and, after his visit to Roxbury, Mekas and Lyman do not seem to have crossed paths again. By the time Mekas was editing the final version of *Walden* that would premier in December 1969, public perceptions about communes led by god-like gurus had changed enormously.

The artist-filmmaker Bruce Conner recalled talking regularly with Lyman at the time:

> And I told Mel one of my private theories. I said that mostly what people do when they talk about God is a projection of what they think God is, and it always comes down to a projection from a person. So the best way to find out what God is is to say you're God yourself...It was just an idea - I wasn't gonna use it myself. But in retrospect, I figure Mel must have used it.[1]

Then, in August of 1969, a series of brutal murders by another cult led by a self-proclaimed messiah shocked the world. The young women who had committed the murders were followers of Charles Manson, a mysterious misfit who, like Lyman, saw himself as a world savior. When Jim Kweskin, Lyman's former band leader who had become one of his followers, was asked about the comparison, he replied, that while "the Manson Family preached peace and love and went around killing people," the Lyman family, "don't preach peace and love. And we haven't killed anybody - yet."[2]

Suddenly the reference to "God" as an alternative name for Lyman and the title of the autobiography Mekas had helped publish did not seem so funny. The MEL (GOD) MAKES COFFEE sequence was not included in the final version of *Walden*.

93 JESSE BENTON

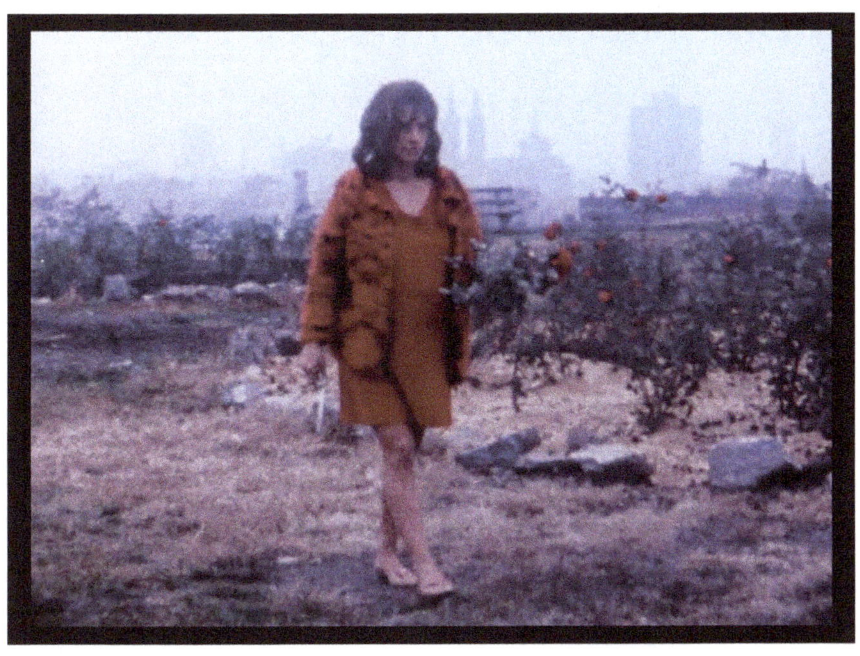

Reel 5 26:33

If Mel Lyman, the founder of the Fort Hill Community in Boston, was glimpsed only through a second floor window during Mekas's visit recorded in *Walden*, Jessie Benton, his partner at the time, was more visible. She was the community's matriarch and had made possible the acquisition of the various houses on Fort Hill.

Benton surely met Lyman as a fellow musician but if the couple had the means to buy real estate it was probably less because of their musical talents than because Benton's father was one of the best known painters in the history of American art.

Thomas Hart Benton became famous as a "regionalist," a painter in an original indigenous style that, since the 1930s, had attracted attention by its very distance from the prevailing trends of modernism. He had been featured on one of the first color covers of *Time* magazine in 1934 as a painter of "The U.S. Scene." Through his daughter, Benton would become the Fort Hill Community's most important benefactor.

In addition to financing the purchase of the Roxbury houses, Jesse Benton contributed a large house and property on the island of Martha's Vineyard which became a pastoral retreat for the urban commune. And the sale of paintings by her father was another reliable source of funds.

In later years, after Lyman's disappearance and presumed death in 1978, Benton remained the matriarch of the Fort Hill Community which survived and prospered as a home construction company. She was also an articulate defender of her father's artistic legacy.

94 GIDEON BACHMANN

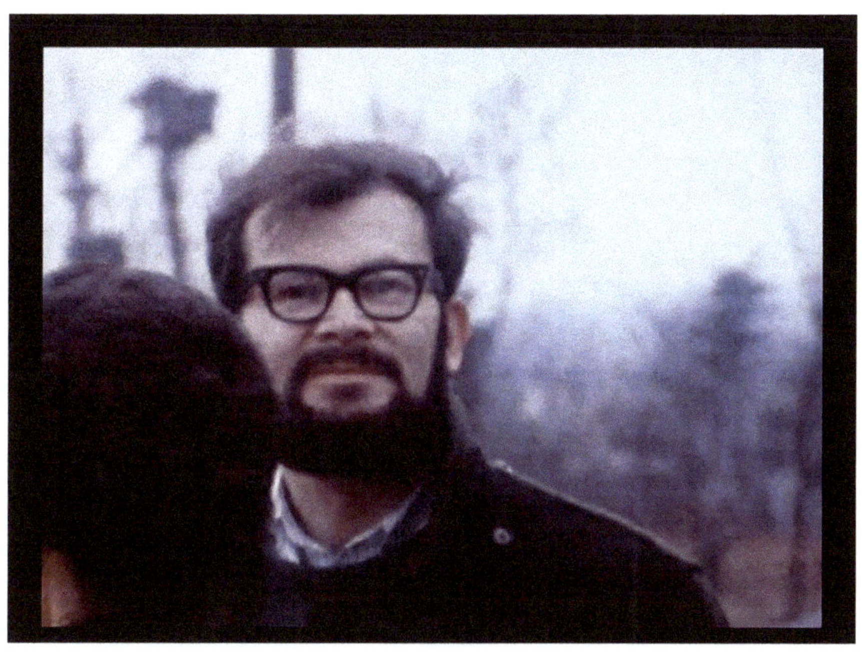

Reel 5 27:01

Mekas recalled on the *Walden* soundtrack:

> It all looks very foolish now, when I'm looking back but that fall, one
> Sunday morning, we packed up, Gideon, Willard, Adolfas, and myself,
> Gideon's TV crew from Germany….and we went to New Jersey.

The German public television group ZDF had commissioned Gideon Bachmann to reveal the inside story of the scandalous "New York underground." So, with a professional German crew and surely a budget to match, Bachmann reunited some old friends to simulate the making of an "underground" film.

Bachmann was a filmmaker, journalist, and radio commentator born in 1927 near Stuttgart, Germany. He had emigrated with his family in 1936 to what was then Palestine, lived briefly in Prague, and landed in the U.S. in 1948, the year before Mekas arrived. In New York in 1952 he and Mekas met in Hans Richter's class at the City College of New York.

Bachmann produced a weekly radio program called "The Film Art" which received wide syndication on public radio in the U.S. and he went on to a long career as president of the American Federation of Film Societies, founding editor and publisher of *Cinemages* magazine, and host at major international film festivals.

During the television production, Bachmann kept a written diary. The entry for December 9, 1967 read:

> Jonas is the genesis of everything. Back then, fourteen years ago, my
> friend Jonas and I learned how to make films together, when we were
> studying under Hans Richter at the City College of New York…. At
> that time we had founded the Group for Film Study together, had
> begun publishing *Cinemages,* together we were Amos Vogel's Cinema
> 16's sole competitors. Then we went our separate ways - due to our

different ideas - and Jonas began *Film Culture* and I, step by step, moved to Rome...now Jonas works on his diaries.[1]

Bachmann eventually settled in Rome where he played small roles in Federico Fellini's *8 1/2* (1963) and *Juliet of the Spirits* (1965) and, while Fellini was making *Satyricon* (1969), he directed a widely acclaimed television documentary portrait of the director at work, *Ciao Federico* (1970).

95 WILLARD VAN DYKE

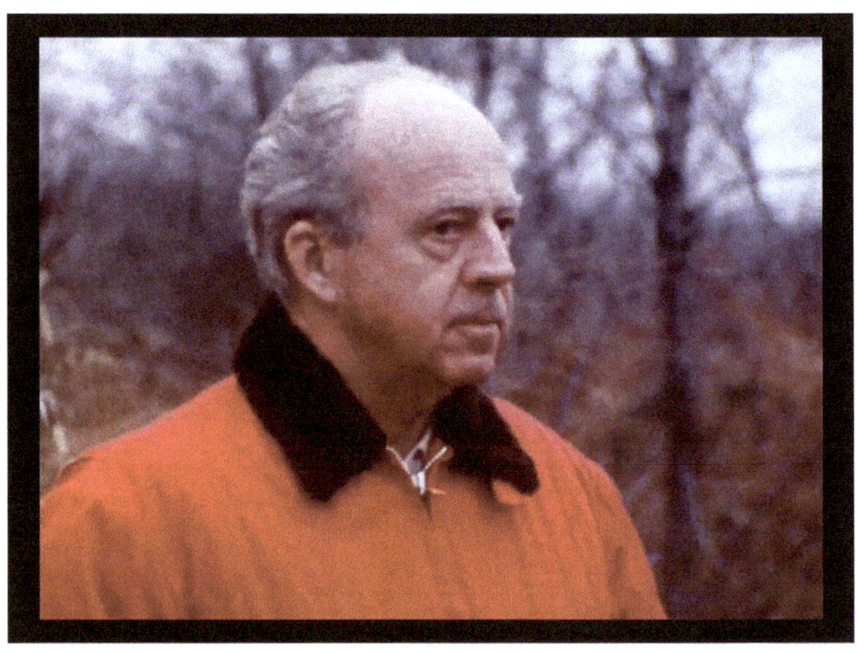

Reel 5 27:11

When the German journalist Gideon Bachmann was commissioned to produce the television documentary *Underground New York* (1968), it was an occasion for him to see old friends from his days at the City College Institute of Film Techniques in the early 1950s: Adolfas and Jonas Mekas, and Willard Van Dyke, then the director of the Department of Film at the Museum of Modern Art.

Van Dyke can be seen in *Walden* pretending to be serious as he oversees the staged shooting of an "underground" film, but his real role in the support of experimental film was not a joke. Mekas recalled that when he first arrived in New York:

The MoMA Film Department was not open to new independent filmmakers at the time and we had many sessions trying to change their thinking. Before Willard, the director was Richard Griffith who recognized the early French avant-garde, the classics so to speak, but was not open to the current generation.

Willard became more and more open and ended up being very supportive. He had made some very important documentaries, *The City* (1939) for example, and three or four other classic documentary films from the 30s into the 40s.[1]

MoMA's first film curator, Iris Barry, was appointed in 1935, only six years after the museum's founding. She was active in the preservation of notable Hollywood films, as was her successor Richard Griffith when he succeeded her in 1951. They did important work as scholars and curators but remained more focussed on products of the film industry than on the work of individual artists who worked in film.

Things started to change when Griffith retired in 1965 and was replaced by Willard Van Dyke, an actual filmmaker and photographer. Van Dyke had been part of the NYKINO group within the militant Film and Photo League in the 1930s, committed to bringing the Russian revolutionary Dziga Vertov's theory of the "Kino Eye" to

America. *The City* (1939), the film to which Mekas refers, was made with photographer/filmmaker Ralph Steiner and was among a number of Van Dyke's documentaries with strong ties to the European tradition of avant-garde documentary film.

Although Van Dyke's school of documentary seldom intersected with Mekas's avant-garde, they were allies. It was Van Dyke who originally suggested that Mekas contact Jerome Hill whose philanthropy underwrote much of Mekas's activity. He had also volunteered to testify on Mekas's behalf as an expert witnesses to the artistic merit of *Flaming Creatures* (1963) at its obscenity trial in June 1964. The court eventually declined to accept his testimony on the grounds that artistic merit was irrelevant to obscenity.

Less than three years after his appointment in 1965, Van Dyke announced a new film series at MoMA. Its first press release on December 17, 1968 read:

CINEPROBE: A CONFRONTATION BETWEEN FILM-MAKER AND FILM-VIEWER

To curate the series, Van Dyke hired Larry Kardish who had been working at Mekas's Film-makers Coop. With Cineprobe's first program in January 1969 featuring Stan VanDerBeek, personal film artists finally had a regular showcase at a major New York art museum. Its press release read:

> The series, according to Willard Van Dyke, head of the Film Department, is designed to provide the Museum audience with an informal encounter with young film-makers. Much of Cineprobe's value will be in the exchange that follows each showing. 'It is seldom that an audience has the occasion to receive firsthand information from the filmmaker,' Mr. Van Dyke declared.[2]

Van Dyke was no longer at MoMA by the time Mekas himself was the object of a Cineprobe in 1976 but he had proved a loyal friend when it mattered most.

96 HELLA HEYMAN

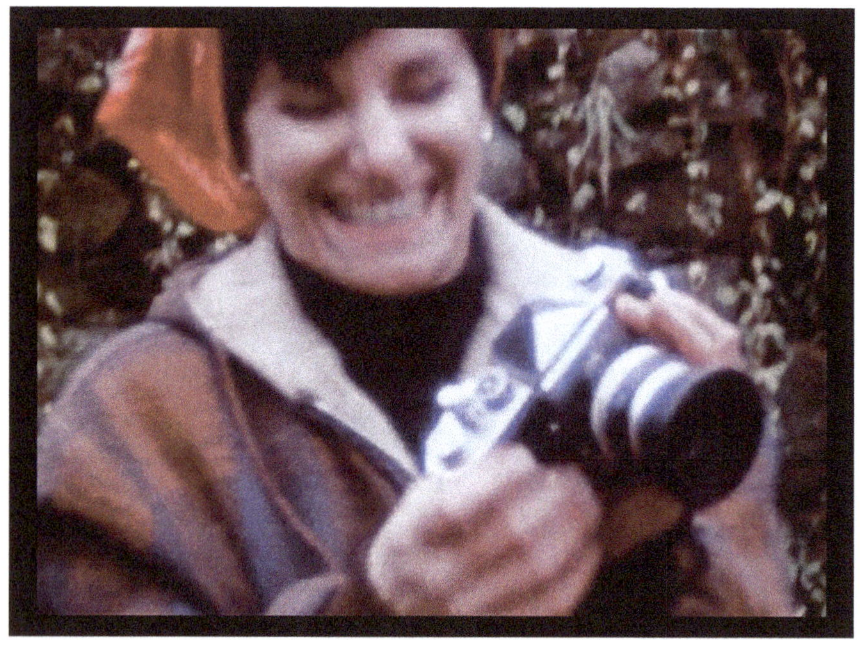

Reel 5 29:44

The ostensible purpose of the small group who travelled to rural New Jersey in the autumn of 1967 was to give German television audiences a view of the making of an American "underground" film. Two members of the group, Adolfas Mekas and Willard Van Dyke, were filmmakers who had been instructed by the German director Gideon Bachmann to pretend to be filmmakers. But it was not clear if a third member, the photographer Hella Heyman, was one of the actors or part of the crew.

She could have been there as a friend to pretend to photograph the making of the simulated "underground" film. But she was also a photographer who could have been hired to photograph the real television documentary.

As a professional, she was well-qualified. She worked for the Rapho Agency which represented many of the greatest photographers of the 20th century and was particularly associated with the school of "Humanist Photography." Heyman had contributed to the most important exhibition of this group - and probably the best-known exhibition of photography ever held in the U.S. - *The Family of Man* - organized by Edward Steichen at the Museum of Modern Art in 1955.

Born in Germany, she had emigrated with her family to the U.S., and worked as an assistant to the painter and art dealer Galka E. Scheyer who recommended her to Josef Albers for admission to Black Mountain College in 1940. After a semester, she moved on to New York where she met Maya Deren and became the cinematographer for Deren's two landmarks of the American avant-garde: *Ritual in Transfigured Time* (1946) and *At Land* (1947).

She eventually married Deren's former husband, the pioneering documentary and experimental filmmaker Alexander Hammid who had worked closely with Van Dyke at the Office of War Information during the 1940s.

Perhaps Van Dyke had arranged for Bachmann to hire her to take photographs of the production. But then Adolfas Mekas, pretending to direct his "underground movie," instructs her to climb a tree as if she was acting in his simulated film.

In any case, they were all, as Mekas explains on the soundtrack, "having a good time in New Jersey on an autumn day."

97 WENDY CLARKE

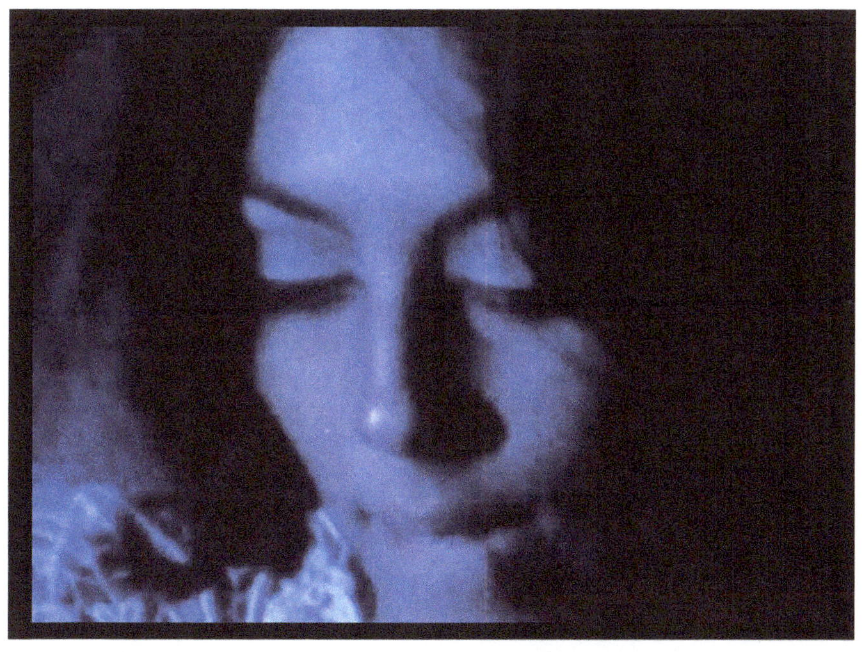

Reel 6 00:54

As he had for his brother Adolfas and his collaborator P. Adams Sitney, Mekas arrived with his camera for Wendy Clarke's wedding. She later recalled:

> Jonas was very quiet so you didn't know he was there a lot. He was the perfect person to do this because he never took over and his presence was always somewhat removed. Very nice, but not active, not in front of your face…My mother sort of did it all. It was her doing, I have to say. The strobe light and all the bands. My grandmother had to leave and a couple friends couldn't take the strobe light…Barbara Rubin did all the decorations. I just remember thinking that it looked like a whorehouse in heaven. It was blue and pink tulle. There were all these streamers - it was just billowing tulle.[1]

In retrospect, the fact that the bride, her mother and another guest who was fleetingly visible, Ed Emshwiller, were all soon to be recognized as pioneer artists in the emerging medium of video art, seems to call attention to the particularities of the medium of *Walden*: 16mm color film.

Mekas was filming in his habitual style, in short bursts of frames, many of them unavoidably over or under-exposed because of the extreme variations in lighting conditions. If he had been shooting in video, the medium that Shirley and Wendy Clarke as well as Emshwiller had begun to explore and that he himself would eventually adopt, the visual result would have been completely different.

Shirley and Wendy Clarke had embraced video simultaneously. Shirley Clarke's film career was at a low ebb, following her failure to find backing for film projects in Hollywood. She would recollect that:

> By 1970 I was lying on my back staring out the window, saying things like, "If it weren't for my daughter, I wouldn't bother staying alive."[2]

She got a new lease on life when she and Wendy established the "The Tee Pee Video Space Troupe" in their studio space atop the Chelsea Hotel. Based loosely on the idea of an improvisatory jazz ensemble of different musicians, the videographers celebrated a diversity of approaches to the medium. As Wendy put it "…video was so exciting. It was so new. There was no history, which was very freeing."[3]

Wendy Clarke would go on to produce an important body of video work on her own beginning around 1977. Mekas himself continued to shoot film until around 2000 when, like so many filmmakers at the time, he migrated to video himself.

98 SHIRLEY CLARKE

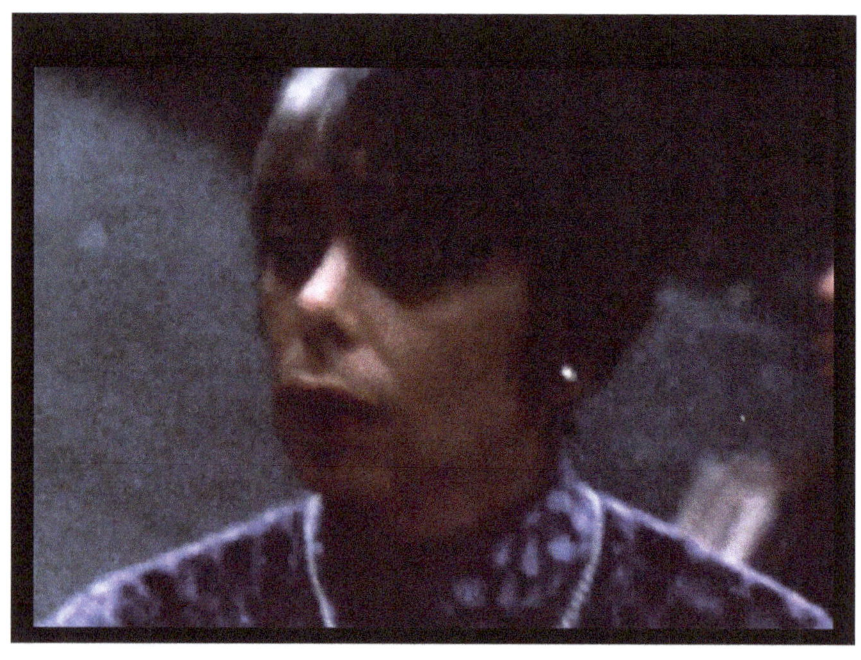

Reel 6 01:15

Shirley Clarke was one of Mekas's oldest friends in New York; they had first met in Hans Richter's film class at City University of New York in 1952 at a time when Clarke, a dancer, was looking for ways to expand her means of expression:

> I got tired of rehearsing for six months for one performance and wanted to preserve forever what everyone had worked so hard to achieve. [1]

Her early experiments with film were exhilarating and brought her to a realization:

> ...one had to destroy one art to be true to the other; dance as it existed had to be transformed into good film. Dance was not only a human being whirling in space, but also someone walking down the street, or your hair waving in the breeze.[2]

Clarke's early films alone such as *In Paris Parks* (1954), *Bullfight* (1955) and *A Moment in Love* (1957) would have secured her recognition as an important film artist. But she was still restless with the restrictions of the medium and frustrated with the limited audience for short poetic works.

She moved on to more ambitious feature-length films with provocative subjects: heroin addicts (*The Connection*, 1961), Harlem gangs (*The Cool World*, 1963) and *Portrait of Jason*, 1967) – about a black gay prostitute and aspiring cabaret singer. She planned to distribute the latter through the Film-Makers' Distribution Center that she had formed with Mekas and Louis Brigante in the hopes of creating a profitable structure for commercially viable films.

But the distribution venture was a financial failure and led Clarke to believe that she could only achieve her aims in Hollywood. The results there were no better; her daughter Wendy recalled:

> It was very horrible for her when she went to California. There she
> was in Hollywood. I don't think it ever would have really worked.... It
> was horrible for someone who thinks of the piece you're making as a
> creative work of art...I just remember the struggle that my mother
> had. She wasn't 'regular;' she wasn't commercial.[3]

At the time of her daughter's wedding recorded in *Walden*, Clarke had
reached the same conclusion as she had when she moved from dance
to film, "one had to destroy one art to be true to the other." Through
her daughter Wendy, she discovered a new "other" - the rapidly developing
medium of portable video.

When Mekas interviewed her about *Portrait of Jason*, she seemed
already to realize that film did not meet her needs:

> The underground has been exploring poetic cinema and the changing
> vision. Cinéma vérité has called to our attention that people are the
> most interesting subject. Yet we have rarely allowed anyone to really
> speak for himself for more than a few minutes at a time. Just imagine
> what might happen if someone was given his head and allowed to let
> go for many consecutive hours. I was curious, and wow! did I find
> out.[4]

Clarke needed a medium free of the time and money constraints of
film and in the rapidly developing technology of portable video, with
the help of her daughter, she found it. Working from her top floor
studio in the Chelsea Hotel, she would found the Tee Pee Video Space
Troupe, and become a pioneer of the new medium of video art.

99 JUD YALKUT

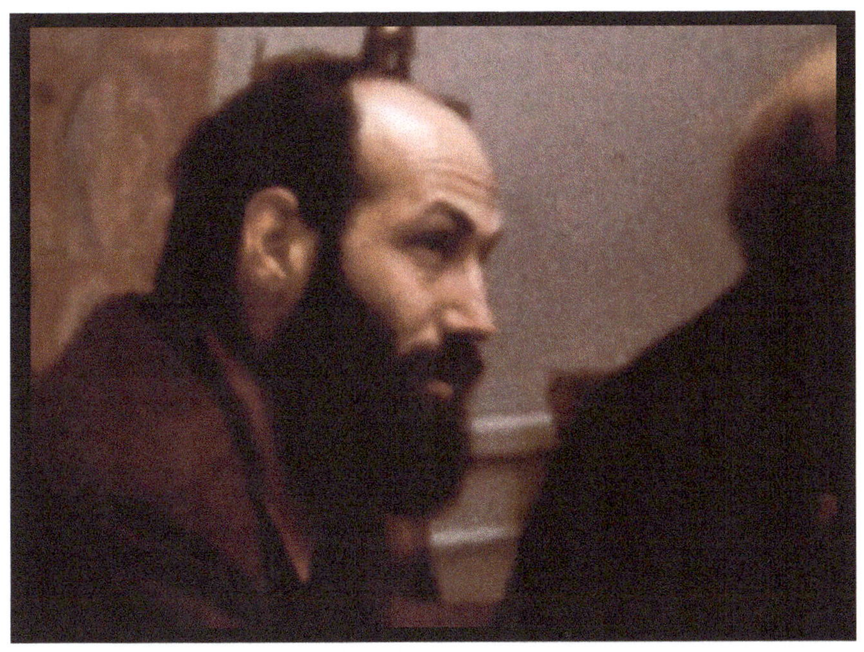

Reel 6 09:22

When Mekas filmed Shirley Clarke and Jud Yalkut sitting on the floor of her Chelsea Hotel loft eating bagels, he joked in his narration that it was because Gideon Bachmann wanted some "real underground footage" for his German TV documentary. What Bachmann probably meant was that he wanted some unusual effects not usually seen on film and Mekas, by shooting himself in a mirror, tried to comply.

But what Yalkut and Clarke were actually planning in late 1967 was a real "underground" development in moving image-making which did not involve film at all.

Fifteen years later, Yalkut would write of his own role at the time:

> New York City became from the beginning a magnetic center for many of the explorers in the new video realm. As an early practitioner of the electronic visual arts himself, the author seemed also to be one of the few concerned with periodically recording and publishing aspects of the history of this new medium and its adherents...*Electronic Zen* is an attempt to enumerate the probings of the first Cybernauts using the tools of new video technology.[1]

The first major public presentation of the work of these "cybernauts" was in May of 1969, a ground-breaking exhibition called "TV As A Creative Medium" at the Howard Wise Gallery on 57th St. The show was a catalyst for a new generation of moving image artists exploring electronic rather than film-based imagery and Yalkut was at its center both as practitioner and chronicler.

As a practitioner, Yalkut moved freely between film and electronic media. In a 2004 interview he explained how:

> You take the film and put it back into video and do things that can't be done in film. You make use of the imperfections of the medium and you become more aware of what the limits of the medium are.[2]

He staged live performances which combined the projection of 8mm, 16mm and 35mm film, audio tape recorders, and the emergent technology of video.

In the early 1960s, Yalkut was a resident film-maker for USCO, "The Company of Us," a pioneering mixed-media arts collective. In November 1965 USCO was part of Mekas's "New Cinema Festival I," his ground-breaking festival of expanded cinema which also showed the work of Nam June Paik, Aldo Tambellini and other precursors of the digital era.

In 1966 Yalkut started collaborating with Nam June Paik. It was a working partnership that would continue into the 1970s. Together, they produced hybrid film-video works that mixed moving image technologies, electronic manipulations, performance and installation.

But Yalkut's roles as a chronicler and teacher were equally important. In 1984 he compiled an account of the origins of electronic moving image art, *Electronic Zen*, which sadly never found a publisher in his lifetime. But the "cyber" world that he and Shirley Clarke were surely imagining on her floor in 1967 now recognizes his legacy.

100 CHELSEA HOTEL

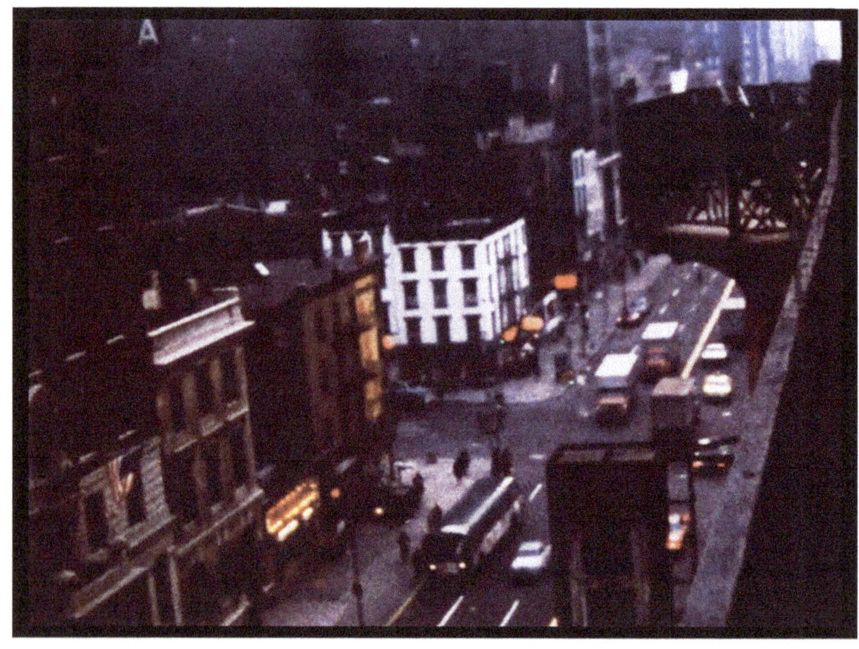

Reel 6 13:22

> Many strange lives open before our eyes…Lovers, dope addicts,
> pretenders, homosexuals, lesbians, and heterosexuals, sad, fragile
> girls, and hard, tough girls - quiet conversations, doing nothing, tele-
> phone conversations, passing the time…social games, drug games, sex
> games. …We don't always understand what they are talking about,
> only short fragments of conversations really reach us clearly. As the
> time goes, this gallery of people and lives grows into a complex human
> hive.

In his *Village Voice* column of September 29, 1966, Mekas was
describing a new Warhol film, *The Chelsea Girls* (1966) but it was also a
description of the place that gave the film its name and where some of
Warhols "superstars" (Viva, Edie Sedgwick) lived: the Chelsea Hotel.

Warhol's film alone would have given the hotel a place in 20th century
cultural history but its notoriety was already well established.At its
opening at the beginning of the century, it had mostly housed person-
alities of the Broadway theater world but its clientele would expand to
include celebrity poets - Dylan Thomas, Allen Ginsburg, writers - Jack
Kerouac, William Burroughs, playwrights - Arthur Miller, Tennessee
Williams, and musicians - Patti Smith, Jim Morrison, Virgil Thomson,
John Cale, Édith Piaf, Bob Dylan, Jimi Hendrix, Leonard Cohen, artists
- Jean Tinguely, Jeanne-Claude and Christo, Larry Rivers, Diego
Rivera, Claes Oldenburg, Willem de Kooning, and photographers -
Robert Mapplethorpe, Henri Cartier-Bresson.

Moving image art was no exception - Harry Smith lived and made
films in Room 328, Shirley Clarke had a penthouse apartment on the
roof where she convened the pioneer video artists of her Tee Pee Video
Space Troupe.

From 1967 until 1974, which included a good part of the period
covered by *Walden* (1965-1969), Mekas lived in Room 725. Shortly
after he had moved in, Gideon Bachmann and his German TV crew

filmed him for their report on "underground New York" in front of the hotel and, four decades later, Mekas edited Bachmann's footage into a short film, *I Leave Chelsea Hotel* (2009). It consisted of a short sequence he described as "I exit Chelsea Hotel and proceed towards Seventh Avenue where I catch a taxi."

101 ERNIE GEHR

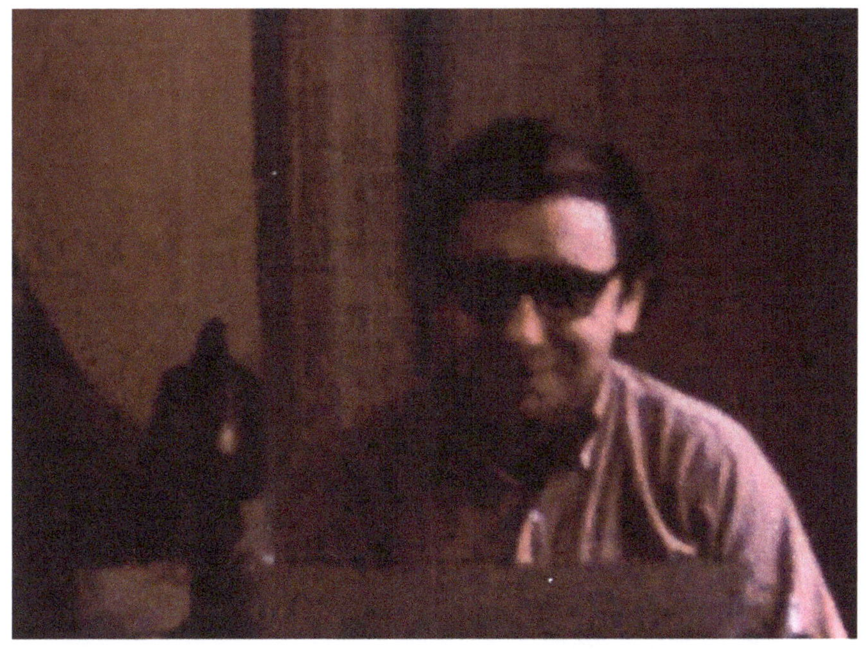

Reel 6 16:03

Mekas recalled:

> I met Ernie Gehr through Richard Foreman. Somehow Richard knew
> him and drafted him in one of his plays. So he was in the early
> Foreman plays, and then I discovered that he was making little films
> and I liked them. And then when we needed somebody to work at the
> Film-Maker's Cooperative, I drafted him... he worked in the Film-
> Makers Cooperative for months...even years... I don't remember now.
> And that's when he made the film *Still* (1969-71), through the window
> of the Film-Maker's Cooperative.[1]

Mekas met Gehr shortly after Gehr had enrolled in the Millennium
Film Workshop that artist Ken Jacobs had just founded to provide
instruction and equipment. But when Gehr was ready to go out into
the street to film, the workshop had no more cameras available; all
that remained was a light meter. So for a week, Gehr walked the
streets of New York just measuring light.

The story is perhaps apocryphal but nevertheless revealing of Gehr's
art. His films at first appear rudimentary - sometimes just recording
subtle changes of light. But his patience opened new avenues of visual
and temporal perception.

Thirty years after Gehr had made *Still* through the Film-Makers' Coop
window, the critic Fred Camper wrote that while viewing it:

> We feel not only how transitory and limited our perception of this
> seemingly eternal street is, but how horrible, almost claustrophobi-
> cally impoverished, is our usual vision. Ironically, that sense sets the
> mind to work in protest, imagining new superimpositions and begin-
> ning to see all objects not as solid things but as accretions of light, just
> as they are on our retinas.[2]

Many film artists of Gehr's generation found the transition of image-
making technology from celluloid film to digital electronics problem-

atic, but for Gehr it was not. Critic Daniel Kasman described *Water-front Follies*, a 2008 digital work by Gehr in terms uncannily similar to descriptions of Gehr's first 16mm films forty years earlier:

> These three shots, despite their utter simplicity and the patience asked for from the audience, are replete with micro-narratives, color, emotion, and the textures of painting, of cinema, and of the movement of life.[3]

102 NEW YORK HARBOR

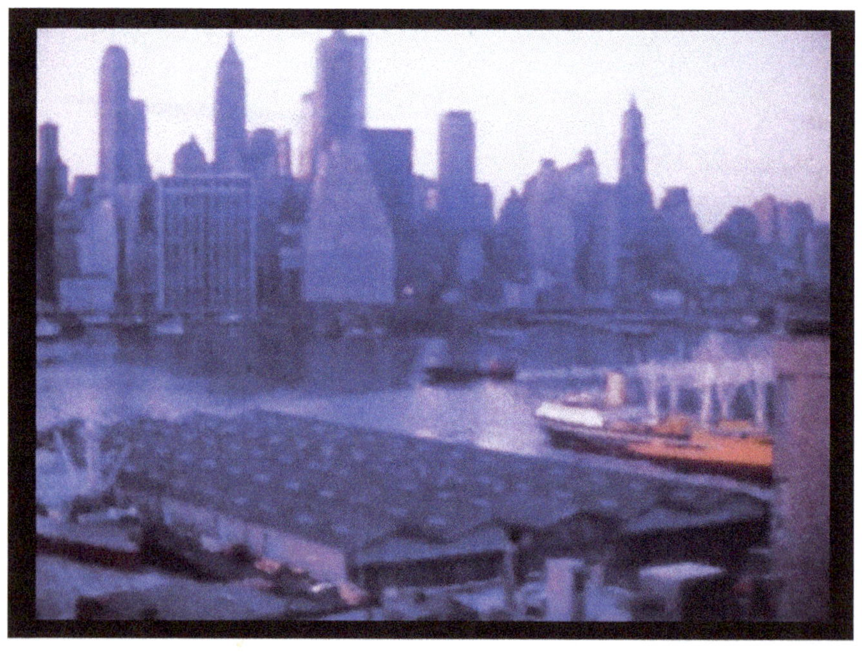

Reel 6 16:24

Marie Menken and her husband Willard Maas lived in an historic 19th century building, the Arlington, at 62 Montague Street in Brooklyn Heights with a spectacular view of New York Harbor. It sat just above the location of the former ferry service that connected Brooklyn to Manhattan before the construction of the Brooklyn Bridge and was an iconic location in American literature and art.

From Walt Whitman's poem *Crossing Brooklyn Ferry* in his classic 1856 collection of poetry, *Leaves of Grass* to Hart Crane's 1930 long poem on the same theme, *The Bridge,* the view of the East River entering New York harbor from Brooklyn Heights inspired writers, painters, and photographers. And what is considered the very first American experimental film, *Manhatta* (1921) by Charles Sheeler and Paul Strand contained views of the same part of the harbor.

The single most significant celebration of the view on film was surely Menken's own *Go Go Go* (1964) which contained multiple elements that influenced Mekas's work. Menken's eleven minute masterpiece was a precursor of *Walden* in many ways: its bursts of single frames, its diverse, sometimes eccentric, choice of subjects drawn diary-like from New York city life, its use of non-realistic sound, its use of time-lapse, the brief duration of its sequences.

When Mekas came to visit Menken and turned his camera towards the sun setting over New York harbor, he may have been paying conscious homage to *Manhatta* and *Go Go Go* but also perhaps thinking of his own first glimpses on the harbor as he approached his future home by ship in 1949.

103 MARIE MENKEN

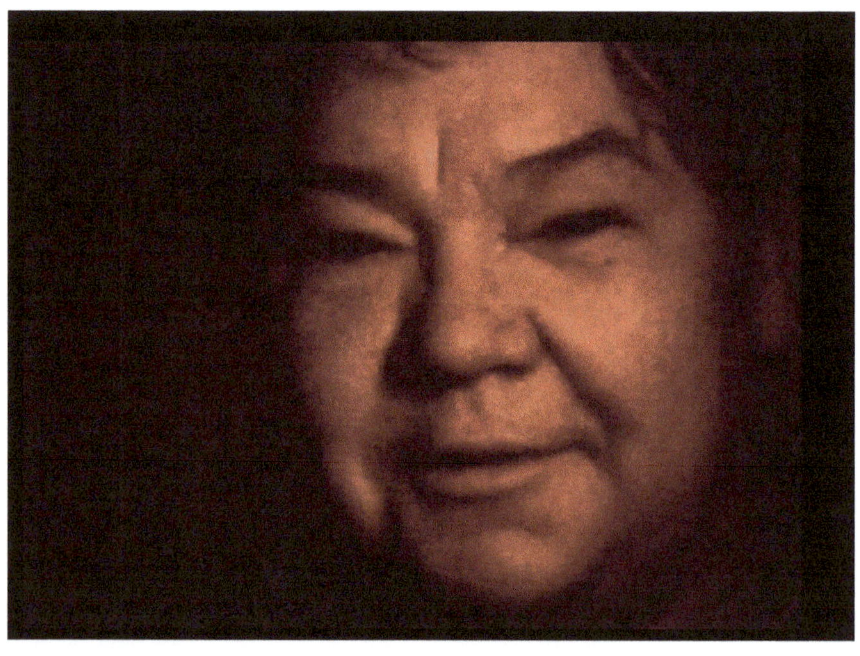

Reel 6 16:55

> There is no why for my making films. I just liked the twitters of the
> machine, and since it was an extension of painting for me, I tried it
> and loved it. In painting I never liked the staid and static, always
> looked for what would change the source of light and stance, using
> glitters, glass beads, luminous paint, so the camera was a natural for
> me ...[1]

Reading her words or looking at the list of films made by Marie Menken give little hint of the extent of her influence on American experimental film. "Her first public personal appearance" according to an ad in the *Village Voice* on December 28, was at midnight on Friday, December 29, and Saturday, December 30, 1961, at the Charles Theater. Mekas organized "a retrospective screening of Marie Menken's films."

The *Village Voice* ad quoted another artist "Stan Brankhage" (sic) as stating that "She, Gertrude Stein and my wife have been the three women who have most influenced my work." Even though Brakhage was not himself well known at the time (or at least not well enough for the *Voice* to spell his name correctly), it was still apparently considered necessary that Menken be endorsed by a male artist.

Such praise would later carry more weight as Brakhage's own reputation increased and he repeated it when interviewed for an excellent film on her life by Martina Kudlácek, *Notes On Marie Menken* (2006): "If there is one single filmmaker that I owe the most to for the crucial development of my own film making it would be Marie Menken."

Another early indication of her importance came from Mekas's *Village Voice* comments on the Charles Theater program published on January 4, 1962:

PRAISE TO MARIE MENKEN, THE FILM POET

Menken sings. Her lens is focused on the physical world, but she sees it through a poetic temperament and with an intensified sensitivity.

She catches the bits and fragments of the world around her and orga-
nizes them into aesthetic unities which communicate to us. Her filmic
language and her imagery are crisp, clear, wondrous.[2]

While Mekas's praise was deserved, he gave it in the context of his
larger argument that non-narrative film was analogous to poetry and,
perhaps not coincidentally, Menken's husband Willard Maas was
indeed a poet. But analogies to her husband's medium is not a particularly useful way to describe her work. She did not do so herself,
saying instead, "it was an extension of painting for me."

To support her painting, Menken had worked as an assistant to
another unsung pioneer of modern art, the German painter Hilla
Rebay, who had been hired by Solomon Guggenheim to advise him on
building his collection of "non-objective art." Menken attended "Concerts of Non-Objectivity" organized by Rebay which included films by
Hans Richter and Oskar Fischinger.

In a perceptive article on Menken, critic Melissa Ragona pointed out
that:

Her strategies are more deeply concerned with ungrounding the easel-
based practices of drawing and sculpture through film. Film not only
freed her from canvas and brush but allowed her to critique the verti-
cality and stasis of 1940s painting and object-based practices. Her
handheld camera produced a frenetic vertigo on sculptural, architectural, natural, and domestic objects, while her play with animation
stretched the borders of film frame and event.[3]

104 STONEWALL

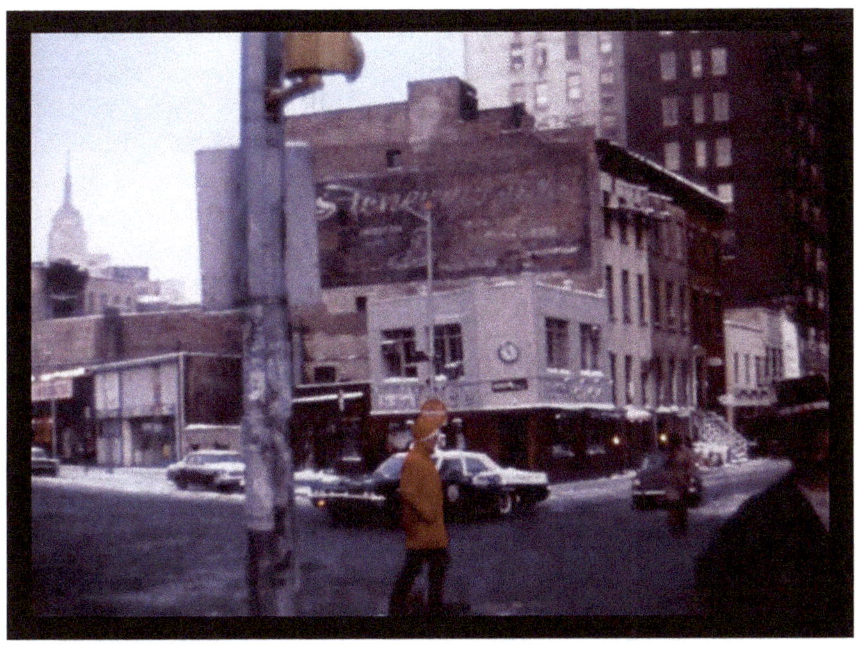

Reel 6 17:56

On his way down Christopher St. to deliver his weekly "Movie Journal" column to the *Village Voice* offices at the corner of 7th Ave, Mekas passed in front of the Stonewall Inn. It was unlikely that he ever entered but he could not have been unfamiliar with the tensions that boiled over there in the summer of 1969 - as he was editing the final version of *Walden*.

The Stonewall was a "gay bar," the kind of establishment that had been an object of increasing police harassment since 1963 at the same time that Mekas had been arrested for his showing of *Flaming Creatures* (1963). At the time authorities had decided to "clean up" the city's image in preparation for the 1964 World's Fair and their targets included both films like Jack Smith's which portrayed homosexual activity and bars where gay people congregated.

Just as obscenity laws had allowed the police to shut down the Film-Makers' Cinematheque, New York State Liquor Authority regulations gave the police freedom to arbitrarily close bars where gay people gathered on the grounds that their behavior was "disorderly."

By 1969, such actions had become so oppressive that some of the bars' clients finally rebelled. A routine police raid on the Stonewall Inn on June 28 provoked active resistance from the local gay community and demonstrations stretched over the next four nights in the surrounding neighborhood, including the sidewalk directly in front of the *Village Voice* offices where Mekas delivered his columns.

The events which came to be known as the "Stonewall Riots," were a turning point, the beginning of the LGBT community's refusal to accept denial of their basic civil rights.

As a champion of avant-garde film, Mekas had been engaged with the subject for years. Before his arrests for showing *Flaming Creatures*, and subsequently another work with homosexual themes, Jean Genet's *Un chant d'amour* (1950), in his *Village Voice* column of May 2, 1963, he had written:

A thing that may scare an average viewer is that this cinema is treading on the very edge of perversity. These artists are without inhibitions, sexual or any other kind. These are, as Ken Jacobs put it, 'dirty-mouthed' films. They all contain homosexual and lesbian elements. The homosexuality, because of its existence outside the official moral conventions, has unleashed sensitivities and experiences which have been at the bottom of much great poetry since the beginning of humanity.[1]

On July 3, 1969, Mekas's *Village Voice* colleague Lucian Truscott IV reported on a chance meeting in the neighborhood with a Mekas friend and frequent presence in *Walden*, Allen Ginsberg:

'Gay power! Isn't that great!' Allen said. 'We're one of the largest minorities in the country - 10 per cent, you know. It's about time we did something to assert ourselves'….We reached Cooper Square, and as Ginsberg turned to head toward home, he waved and yelled, 'Defend the fairies!' and bounced on across the square. He enjoyed the prospect of 'gay power' and is probably working on a manifesto for the movement right now. Watch out. The liberation is under way.[2]

Thirty years later, the Stonewall Inn became the first LGBT site in the country to be listed on the National Register of Historic Places in 1999 and as a National Historic Landmark in 2000.

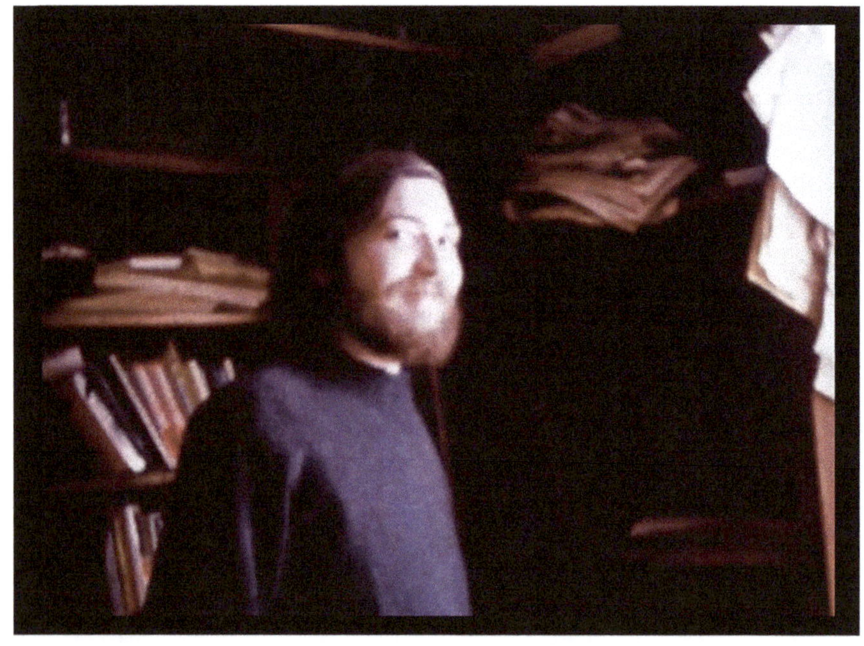

Reel 6 18:03

The split-second glimpse of James Stoller in *Walden* shows him smiling enigmatically in the office of the *Village Voice*. He is in the center of the room but still somehow elusive - a useful description of his entire professional life.

His official job was as a copy editor but the editorial policy of the *Voice* was not to edit its writers' copy. He also wrote criticism but he was never officially listed as a critic.

While still a student at Columbia, Stoller wrote on film for the student newspaper, the *Columbia Daily Spectator* and the writer Phillip Lopate would remember that:

> His articles were so stylistically mature and so informed that they
> seemed to me to be written by a professional quarterly critic rather
> than a college student. I developed an intellectual crush on this Stoller:
> if his opinion differed from mine, I would secretly revise my own.[1]

In the mid-1960s Stoller edited his own magazine called *Moviegoer* which was highly admired by other critics but only lasted a couple of years.

Mekas and Andrew Sarris were the official movie critics for the *Voice*. Even though for a short period, around the period of *Walden*, Stoller did write a column on film called "16mm," he never held the title of critic himself.

But Stoller's reviews were so articulate that, long after their publication, phrases from them were still regularly quoted to describe the films he reviewed. Speaking of those who had impacted him, critic Jonathan Rosenbaum wrote: "Undoubtedly even more influential was the passionately sincere and hypersensitive critical writing of James Stoller, a *Voice* proofreader in the 1960s and 1970s."[2]

Stoller was equally interested in music. The pioneering rock music critic Robert Christgau, who reviewed albums in a popular *Village Voice* column called "Consumer Guide," wrote off-handedly that when the *Voice* gave him a column, "master copy editor James Stoller thought of a title."[3] He also named Stoller as one of the few critics "who do write good things about rock and keep my hopes up."[4]

He was so self-effacing that it is difficult to appreciate Stoller's talent for both music and film except through fragmentary mentions by others. In his memoir Rosenbaum recollected an occasion when "Jim Stoller provided one of our most memorable evenings by agreeing, after lengthy persuasion, to play piano behind Pabst's *The Love of Jeanne Ney* (1927); it was a treat to see him overcome his compulsive modesty and perform in public."[5]

106 ED FANCHER

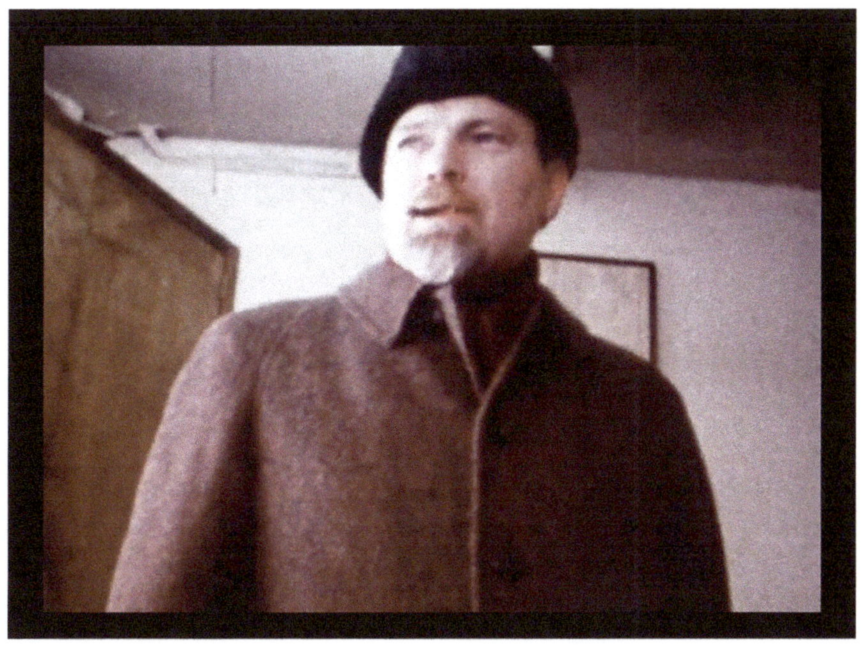

Reel 6 18:09

When they founded the *Village Voice,* Ed Fancher and his business partner Dan Wolf were students at the New School, a progressive university whose main campus was in the heart of Greenwich Village. Clark Whelton, a writer who had contributed to the *Voice* recalled:

> If 'location' is the secret of real estate, then timing is the secret of starting a newspaper - and the secret of selling it, too. The *Village Voice*'s three founders - Ed Fancher, Dan Wolf, and Norman Mailer - timed things exactly right. When the *Voice* hit the streets in 1955, its competition was the *Villager*, a great news source for bake sales and flower shows. The *Voice* focused on the disconnected segments of downtown arts and politics. Suddenly, the shadow world of Greenwich Village counterculture, with its roots in the nineteenth century, had a clearinghouse, a way of keeping in touch with the public and with each other.[1]

None of the partners really knew how to run a newspaper but they soon found a fourth partner, who did, Jerry Tallmer, who they engaged to be the culture editor and to find writers on the subject. One day, Mekas stopped by:

> It was a new, young paper, and a lot was happening. There was already a lot of coverage of what was going on in poetry readings, galleries, presented freshly with new sensibilities, but there was no coverage of cinema. And of course theater was already covered by Jerry Tallmer. I asked Jerry, 'Why don't you cover cinema?' I was already publishing *Film Culture,* so I was very much involved in the whole movie scene - not Hollywood, but independent. He said, 'Oh, we have nobody here, you want to do it?' I said, 'Sure, I will do it.'[2]

Mekas's tenure under Tallmer and Fancher was a long and hugely productive one. His reach expanded hugely in December 1962 when a newspaper strike silenced the *Voice*'s mainstream rivals for almost four months and made Mekas's column temporarily almost the only film criticism available in New York. Many future film artists were to credit their discovery of the medium to his weekly column.

In 2017, the *New York Times* reported on their reunion sixty years later:

> In the noisy front room, Jonas Mekas, who wrote about film for the *Voice* from 1957 to 1977, huddled with Ed Fancher, the founding publisher. Mr. Mekas and Mr. Fancher were both 94 and still read the *Voice* regularly.[3]

107 JULIAN BECK

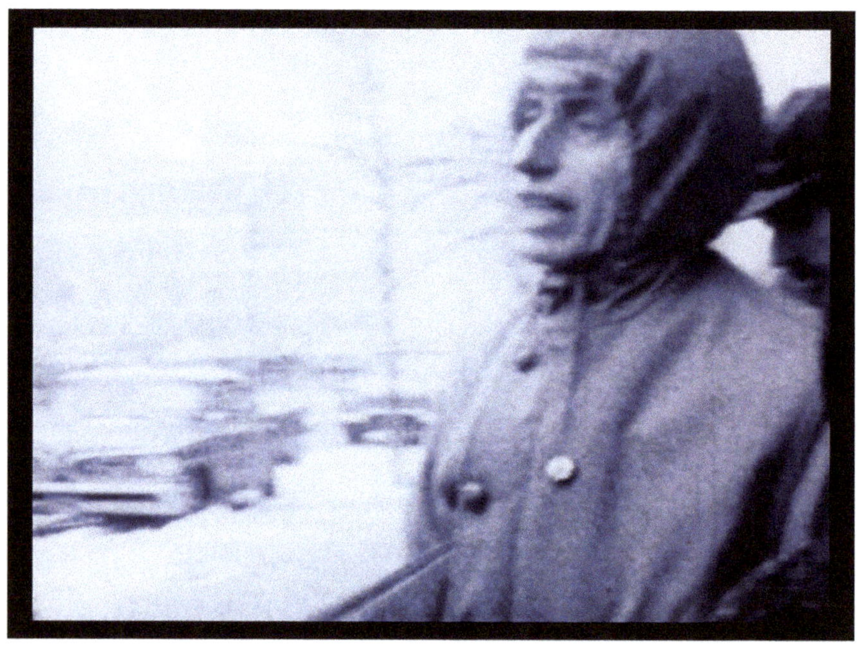

Reel 6 18:46

Julian Beck was a native New Yorker and a painter when he met the German-born Judith Malina and discovered that he shared her passion for theater. They founded the Living Theatre together in 1947.

One of their objectives was to break down the lines between theater and life, audience and performer, performance and public political action. So surely neither they nor Mekas were averse to the publicity that attended the forced closure of their production *The Brig*.

When their landlord announced the closure, ostensibly for unpaid taxes, Mekas resolved to preserve a record of the play on film. The company's directors arranged for a final private performance after the last public one for Mekas to film.

The resultant film, *The Brig* (1964), was better received than Mekas's first feature, *Guns of the Trees* (1962). But the Becks fared less well. Charged with tax evasion, they defended themselves without lawyers in a well-publicized trial. When they were found guilty, they fled the country.

With the Living Theatre in Europe, Beck and Malina were not visible on the streets of New York while Mekas was shooting *Walden*. But he clearly wanted them in his panorama of New York life so he inserted two black and white "flashbacks." The first showed only Malina; the second also included Beck.

Their paths crossed again in 1966 when Jerome Hill arranged a performance of the Living Theatre's *Frankenstein* at his outdoor theater overlooking the Mediterranean. Hill invited Mekas to record the production as he had with *The Brig*. But it was not included in Mekas's lyrical Cassis sequence in *Walden*. Only thirty years later did he edit his footage and present it as *Memories of Frankenstein* (1996).

108 LINDSAY SNOWSTORM

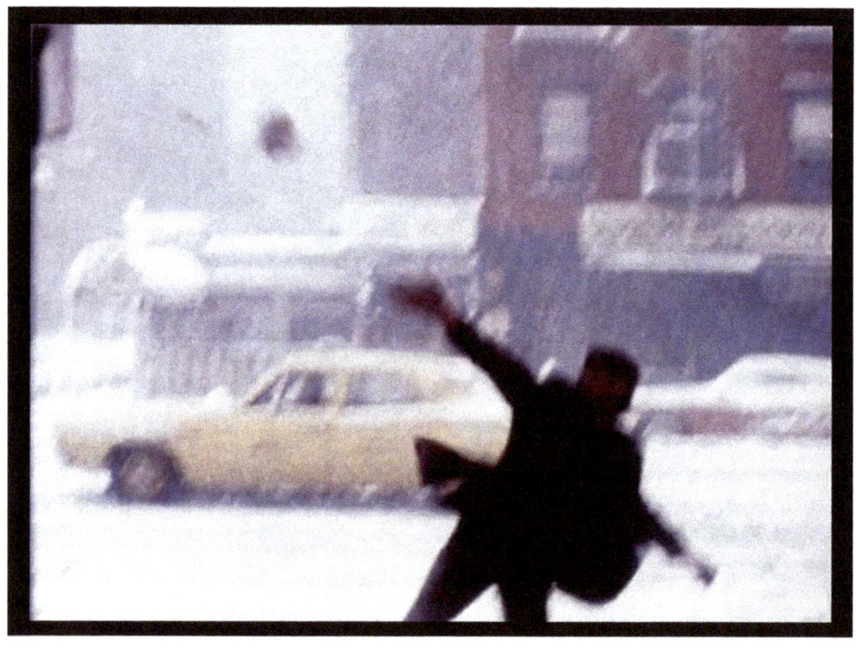

Reel 6 19:30

For three weeks in February 1969, Mekas's "Cinematheque in Exile" found a refuge at the Elgin Theater. Programs were at the awkward time of 11:15 on Sunday mornings. It was a "temporary arrangement," Mekas commented later, and "not the happiest time."[1]

Unhappier than usual was the program scheduled for the morning of February 9th. It was to consist of several documentaries by the radical film collective Newsreel. When an unpredicted winter storm dumped over fifteen inches of snow on the city, it had to be cancelled.

Budget problems had resulted in poor maintenance of the city's snow removal equipment and reportedly almost half of it was defective. And Sanitation Department employees were already disgruntled with the mayor for his resistance to their wage demands during a bitter strike the year before.

The result was that streets outside Manhattan, particularly in the borough of Queens, were impassable for days after the storm, paralyzing public transportation and essential services.

The problems were blamed less on the unpredicted storm than on the city's beleaguered mayor John Lindsay and the meteorological crisis became a political one that severely weakened his ability to govern the city and damaged his re-election campaign later in the year. Lindsay was abandoned by the Democratic Party and only barely won re-election by running as an independent. The blizzard took its place in New York City political history as "The Lindsay Snowstorm."

However for Mekas, a lover of city snowstorms, the joy of seeing New York turned white may have outweighed the disappointment of the cancelled screening. His sequence in *Walden* shot from under the marquee of the Elgin was one of his most lyrical snow scenes.

109 ELGIN THEATER

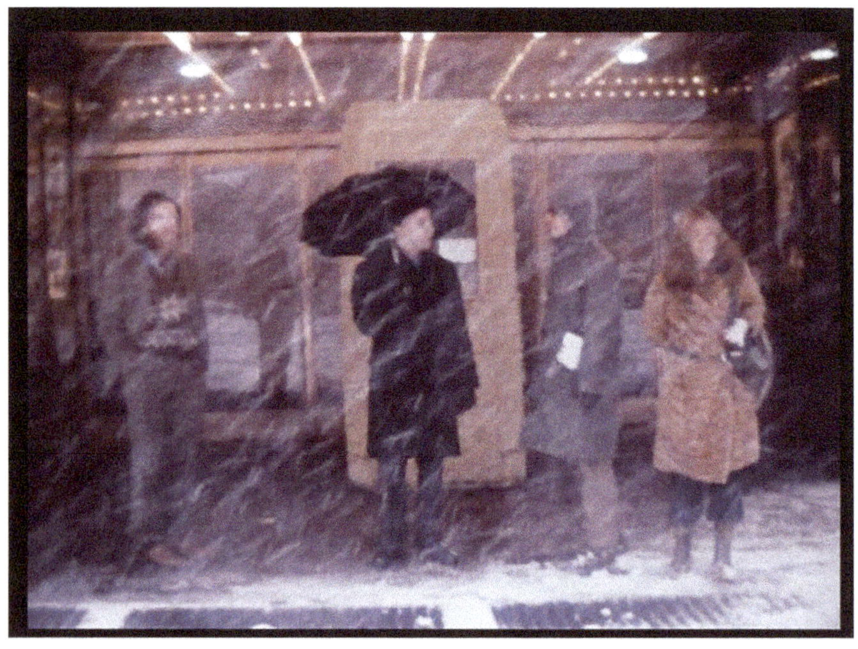

Reel 6 20:05

The Elgin Theater on 8th Ave at 19th St. was just around the corner from the Chelsea Hotel, Mekas's home from 1967 to 1974. And when the city authorities closed his 80 Wooster St. space in July 1968, the Elgin offered the Cinematheque a temporary home.

The Elgin's new manager was Ben Barenholtz, a native of Poland who, like Mekas, had lived in a refugee camp after the war before emigrating to Brooklyn. Barenholtz began to show foreign and independent features and, although the films programmed by the Cinematheque were never financially viable for a large commercial theater, Barenholtz was willing to help Mekas get them shown.

An initial series of Cinematheque programs began in the winter of 1969 on Sunday mornings when the theater was normally closed. The third of these, on the morning of February 9th, had to be cancelled because of the "Lindsay Snowstorm" so lyrically portrayed in *Walden*.

Another series of Cinematheque programs was scheduled at midnight - an hour presumably too late for most moviegoers. An unnamed Warhol film was announced for June 12th in a benefit show for Mekas's *Film Culture*. The film was in fact *Blue Movie* (1969), and, a few months later at another theater, it would achieve notoriety for its depiction of unsimulated sex and its confiscation by the police as obscene.

Three more midnight programs were presented by the Cinematheque in September - Kenneth Anger, Michael Snow and a selection of films from the Italian avant-garde. While not commercially successful in themselves, the Cinematheque programs did inspire Barenholtz to try showings of other films at midnight. The "midnight movies" formula would eventually become a popular phenomenon and attract such crowds to the Elgin that it would be widely copied in other theaters across the country.

Mekas's last experiment at the Elgin was billed as an alternative to the official 7th New York Film Festival uptown at Lincoln Center; he called it the 7½ New York Film Festival and it ran from December 16 to 24, 1969.

In retrospect, the festival's most significant event was the premiere of the final version of the diary film Mekas would eventually call *Walden*.

He had shown a first version in March of 1968 at the museum that had originally commissioned the project, the Albright-Knox Gallery in Buffalo. But over the following year, he had continued to edit the footage and shoot new sequences. By the end of 1969, he had a new version and presented it at the Elgin on Saturday Dec 20th at 9 PM, with a second showing as the closing event of the festival on Christmas Eve. Its description in the festival program read:

Diaries, Notes and Sketches by Jonas Mekas (3 hours) Starring New York City and the Four Seasons of the Year.

110 MARTA MENUJÍN

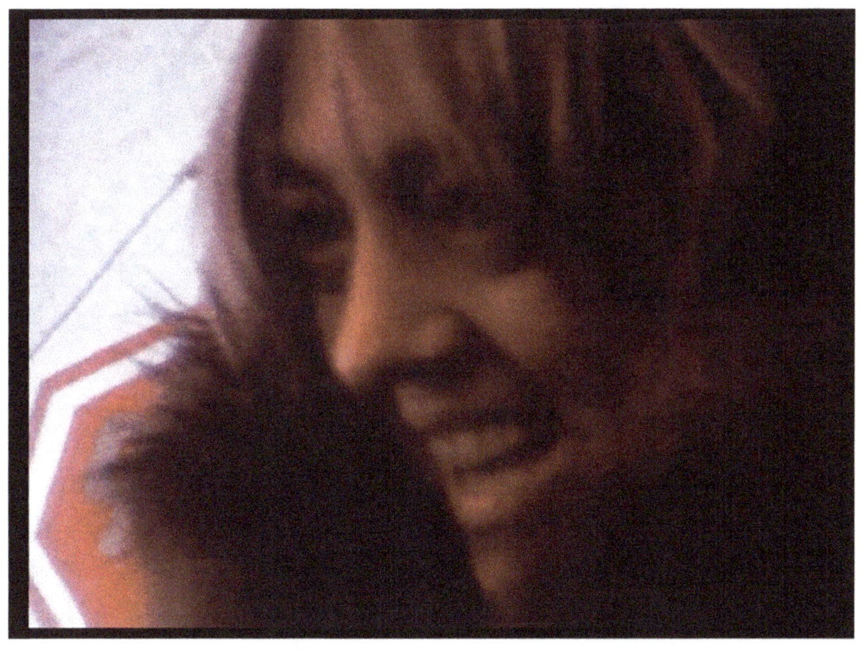

Reel 6 20:36

On the poster for *Walden*, Mekas explained that the young woman making her way across 8th Avenue in the blizzard is:

MARTHA WHOM I HADN'T SEEN FOR SOME TIME

.It was a period when the artist Marta Minujín was dividing her time between New York and her native Argentina so perhaps she had just come back from a time in Buenos Aires. In New York she was likely involved in preparations for an upcoming show at the Howard Wise Gallery - "TV As A Creative Medium" - that would later be seen as the first exhibition of video as art.

Minujín was barely 20 years old when she won a scholarship to study in Paris in 1962. Her work incorporated found objects such as discarded mattresses which she would then transform:

> ... I bought fabric and a glue pen and managed to borrow a sewing machine ... It was a kind of mattress-house, a construction of about three square meters of wood covered with overlapping, twisted-up, embracing mattresses, their stripes painted with bright fluorescent colors... that construction I hung in the center of the studio and people could enter and leave it as they wished.[1]

Then she decided to celebrate its destruction.

Minujín's artist friends Niki de Saint Phalle, Jean Tinguely, and Larry Rivers agreed to let her use an empty lot that bordered their studios and she sent out invitations to galleries and museums. Other artists were invited to add to, modify, or transform her work with their own before everything would be set on fire. *La Destrucción* was Minujín's first happening.

In 1966 a Guggenheim fellowship allowed Minujín to go to New York, where she would live for the better part of ten years. There she connected with the artists and engineers of E.A.T. (Experiments in Art and Technolgy) and create the "Minuphone," a telephone booth which allowed viewers to generate their own image and sound sequences with its push button dial while seeing themselves on a video monitor on its floor. Minujín constructed it with the help of an engineer at the Bell Telephone Laboratories, Pier Biorn, and installed it at the pioneer gallery for electronic art, the Howard Wise Gallery.

Three months after her snowy encounter with Mekas in front of the Elgin Theater in *Walden*, Minujín participated in the ground-breaking show "TV As A Creative Medium." Four decades after it, she was still creating flamboyant events and monumental sculpture around the world including for her own 70th birthday celebration in Buenos Aires in 2013.

111 WOOSTER STREET

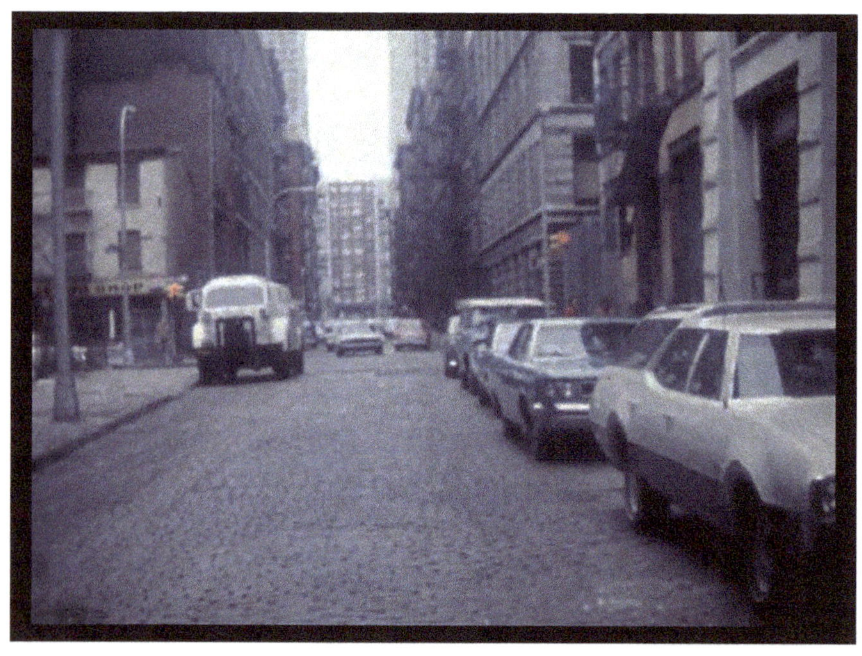

Reel 6 22:43

Mekas and his friend and fellow Lithuanian expatriate George Maciunas were both about to fulfill a dream.

By purchasing an empty building on Wooster St. in Lower Manhattan in August 1967, Maciunas moved closer to realizing the vision he had proposed in 1963: "FLUXHOUSE, A PLAN FOR AN ARTIST CONDOMINIUM IN NEW YORK CITY." For Mekas, it was the dream of a permanent home for the Film Makers' Cinematheque.

The building at 80 Wooster Street was in a desolate neighborhood referred to as "Hell's Hundred Acres" and was directly in the path of the proposed Lower Manhattan Expressway. In the 1965 mayoral election, the incumbent Mayor Wagner supported the plan of the all-powerful highway builder Robert Moses to begin demolition immediately.

Owners in the area, already lacking commercial tenants, were eager to sell. But Wagner's opponent John Lindsay opposed the plan and sued to stop demolition before the election. When Lindsay won and became mayor, the expressway work stopped but many of the buildings in its path were already empty.

George Maciunas, a skillful navigator of bureaucracy, was ready. He obtained funding from the U.S. Federal Housing Authority for his plan to convert abandoned buildings into artists' studios and then cleverly registered them as "agricultural cooperatives" to circumvent New York State restrictions on residential property.

On August 9, 1967, the "Fluxhouse Cooperative" concluded its purchase of 80 Wooster St. With backing from Jerome Hill, Mekas was able to buy its basement and ground floor, a little over a quarter of the building, in the name of the Film-Makers Cinematheque. A month later, Mekas announced in a *Village Voice* ad that the "Cinematheque is moving downtown, out of the 'commercial' sphere," to what he described as "a new borough of New York which from now on will be called The South Village."[1]

Mekas had obtained temporary approval from the city authorities to begin programs while he sought funding to make the improvements necessary for compliance with municipal regulations. Through the first months of 1968, as Mekas appealed for donations, the space was alive with not just films, but avant-garde music, dance and theater, including Fluxus performances, Richard Foreman's Ontological-Hysteric Theater, and music by Philip Glass.

But by July the temporary authorization to use the space expired and it had to be closed to the public. "The Cinematheque in Exile" continued at various locations - the Methodist Church on West Fourth Street, the Bleecker Street Cinema, the Elgin, the Gallery of Modern Art at Columbus Circle, and the Jewish Museum - until it found a permanent home in 1970 as Anthology Film Archives at the Public Theater on Lafayette St.

Mekas's dream for 80 Wooster Street had proved no more durable than the name he had announced for its neighborhood, the South Village. Instead the area south of Houston became known as Soho.

112 PETER KUBELKA

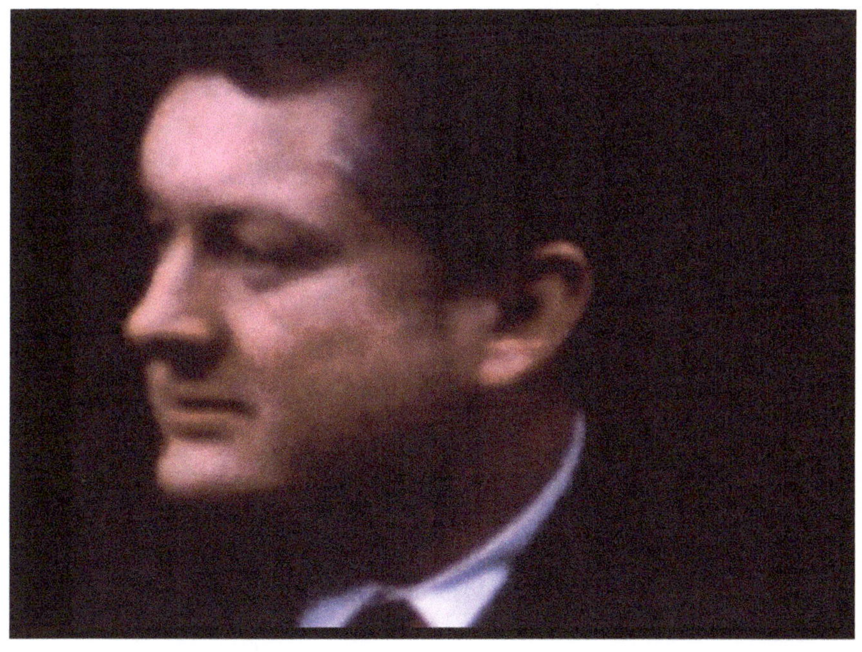

Reel 6 22:55

Mekas met the Austrian Peter Kubelka at the film festival at Knokke-le-Zoute in Belgium in December 1963 where the jury's decision to prevent Mekas from showing *Flaming Creatures* (1963) had sparked chaos. But before his own troubles began, Mekas had witnessed the audience's hostile reaction to another film.

Consisting only of a relentless alternation of solid black and white frames, *Arnulf Rainer* (1960) by Peter Kubelka did not please the audience at Knokke-le-Zoute. Outside the theater Mekas identified the distraught Kubelka and introduced himself. Their friendship would last the rest of their lives.

The next year Jerome Hill asked Mekas to choose twelve filmmakers to receive grants from his Hill Foundation. Mekas included Kubelka among them and convinced Kubelka to complete the extraordinarily intricate editing of footage he had shot when hired to accompany a hunting expedition to Africa, *Unsere Afrikareise* (1966).

In 1966, Mekas and Brakhage (whom Kubelka had met at the first Belgian experimental film festival in 1958) invited Kubelka to the U.S. to lecture about his work and Kubelka's life changed:

> After fourteen years of barely surviving - from 1952 to 1966, I had not
> earned a cent from my own work…After fourteen years of never
> having acknowledgment, nor receiving pay for what I did, my work
> paid my way. I will never forget that moment. It was a beautiful day
> ….[1]

But life for film artists in the U.S.was not so simple: it was possible for them to make money by speaking about their work but not necessarily just by showing it. When Kubelka accepted an invitation to Harvard but expressed doubts about talking, he was informed: "Either you do a lecture or we cannot pay you to come, because this is a lecture series."[2]

Kubelka learned the lesson well and would become, in P. Adams Sitney's words:

> ...the most determined theoretician within the avant-garde since Stan Brakhage; he is also a fierce exponent of his own originality, priority, and purity of influence...[3]

Henceforth Kubelka would spend less time filmmaking than theorizing, teaching, and lecturing about the five short films he had made between 1954 and 1966 (whose total running time was little more than half an hour). He established the Austrian Film Museum in Vienna in 1966 and was a founding member of Anthology Film Archives in New York. Again with Jerome Hill's help, it opened in November 1970 in a radically designed viewing space conceived by Kubelka.

His brief appearance in *Walden* was at a planning meeting with his fellow members of the selection committee that would determine the works of the "Essential Cinema," the core of Anthology's programming. In the following decade he would have a comparably central role in the establishment of a film collection at the new home of the Musée national d'art moderne at the Centre Pompidou in Paris.

113 JAMES BROUGHTON

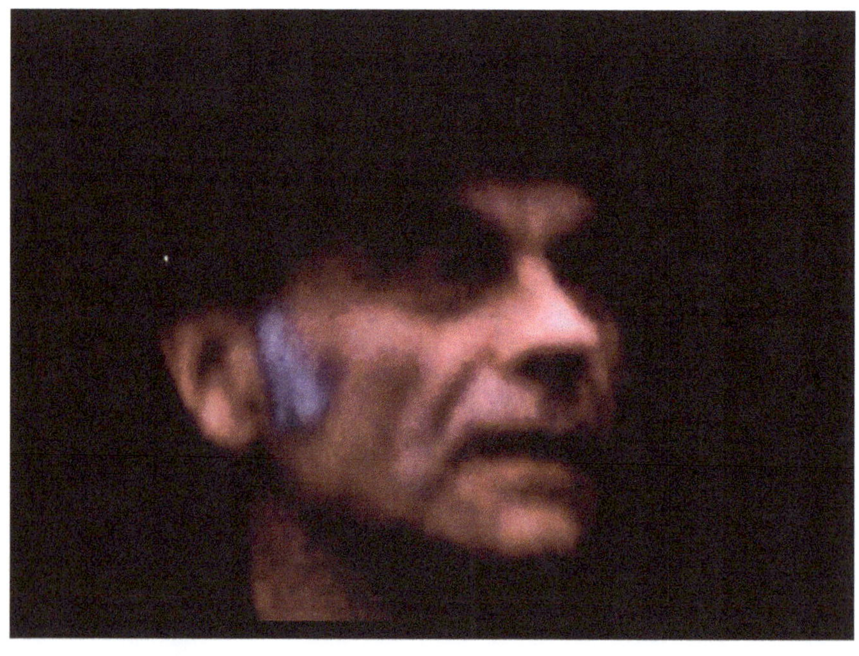

Reel 6 22:58

When Anthology Film Archives was founded, a five member selection committee was tasked with defining "The Essential Cinema" to be preserved and exhibited. It consisted of Mekas, Ken Kelman, James Broughton, Peter Kubelka, and P. Adams Sitney.

Of the five, three were New Yorkers, another, Kubelka, was from Austria but had lived in New York and stayed there when he visited the U.S. Only one, James Broughton, came from west of the Hudson River.

Seen through *Walden* - or through Mekas's writing or any of his other films, New York was the center of avant-garde film. Only once in *Walden* does Mekas venture into the American West - his visit to the Brakhages' home in the Rocky Mountains in Colorado. There was no indication that on the other side of the mountains, there was another center where film artists were just as active as in New York, Broughton's home of San Francisco.

In fact, the history of American experimental film can be said to have begun in San Francisco. In September of 1946, the San Francisco Museum of Art launched the "Art in Cinema" series by local artist, Frank Stauffacher. It was the first manifestation of a revival of the avant-garde film after it had been nearly extinguished by the rise of fascism in Europe.

Along with works of the first European avant-garde by Hans Richter and Man Ray, Stauffacher programmed films made in post-war America including Maya Deren's *Meshes of the Afternoon* (1943) and the first work of two San Francisco artists, Sidney Peterson and James Broughton, *The Potted Psalm* (1946). The next year Stauffacher would be the cinematographer for Broughton's second film, *Mother's Day* (1948).

Broughton always considered himself primarily a poet but he remained a leading light of the "San Francisco school" of filmmakers that emerged during the 1950s and 1960s and included among many others, Harry Smith, Bruce Baillie, and Jordan Belson. While it might not have been evident from a New York perspective, avant-garde film was just as alive on the West Coast as in Manhattan.

But in the early 1950s San Francisco was better known as a center for "Beat" poetry, with its headquarters at the City Lights Bookshop. It was that reputation which had, in 1953, drawn the 20 year-old Stan Brakhage to the city. Arriving in San Francisco as an aspiring poet, he met and began a lifelong friendship with Broughton.

Brakhage would soon move on to New York and, influenced by the artists Marie Menken and Joseph Cornell, decide to devote himself to filmmaking. Curiously, at the same time Broughton, back in San Francisco, decided to give up filmmaking entirely for poetry.

When, fifteen years later, Broughton eventually made another film, *The Bed* (1967), he credited his friendship with Brakhage as his inspiration.[1] Brakhage in turn had spoken to Mekas and Jerome Hill about providing Broughton with financial aid to continue with his film projects.

Hill was in the process of assembling the selection committee for the "Essential Cinema" collection of Anthology Film Archives and Broughton received an invitation to join. He accepted and travelled east for the first meeting of the Anthology committee. That meeting, in the winter of 1969, was the occasion for Mekas to capture images of the lone Californian on the icy sidewalks of New York.

114 JOYCE WIELAND

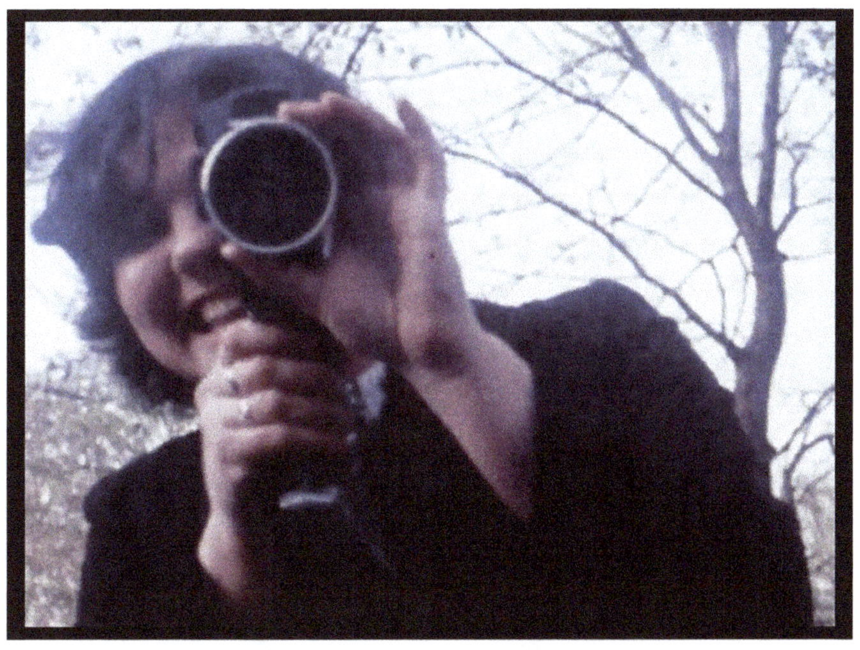

Reel 6 23:53

Joyce Wieland appeared in *Walden* near the entrance to Central Park at Columbus Circle at about the time her 1968 work *Rat Life And Diet In North America* premiered at the Cinematheque hosted by the Jewish Museum. The film was, in Mekas's words:

> a parable, a satire, an adventure movie, or you can call it pop art or any art you want - I find it one of the most original films made recently.[1]

When she arrived in New York in 1962 with her husband Michael Snow, she had already established a career as a painter in her native Toronto. She had met Snow, just back from traveling and working as a musician in Europe, at an animation studio where she had learned basic filmmaking techniques. As a painter, she had her first solo show in Toronto in 1960.

When the couple arrived in Manhattan in the summer of 1963, Mekas's Cinematheque (then still called the Film-Makers' Showcase) had just moved to the Gramercy Arts Theater at 138 East 27th St. There Wieland met film artists who showed up with their unfinished work for informal screenings - including Shirley Clarke, George and Mike Kuchar, and Ken Jacobs - and was caught up in the censorship battles that were brewing around screenings of Jack Smith's *Flaming Creatures* (1963).

For Wieland, Smith's film brought a kind of liberation:

> It really opened the door for me. My God, it *allowed* me to do this kind of thing. This guy was making very personal, very painful statements about his private life. It meant that I could express anything I wanted to express.[2]

Echoes of Wieland's reaction to Jack Smith's film can be heard in P. Adams Sitney's comments on one of her own films made near the end of her time in New York, *La Raison Avant la Passion* (1969):

Joyce Wieland's major film so far. With its many eccentricities, it is a glyph of her artistic personality; a lyric vision tempered by an aggressive form and a visionary patriotism mixed with ironic self parody. It is a film to be seen many times.[3]

In 1987, fifteen years after she had moved back to Canada and returned exclusively to painting, Wieland reflected on her time in the 1960s New York avant-garde by re-editing some footage she had shot with filmmaker Hollis Frampton in 1967. In *A and B in Ontario* (1984):

She wittily reviewed the war between the sexes (and parodied the navel-gazing insularity of the avant-garde) by turning herself and the late Hollis Frampton loose with movie cameras; they spend the entire film playing cinematic hide-and-seek with each other.[4]

115 MICHAEL SNOW

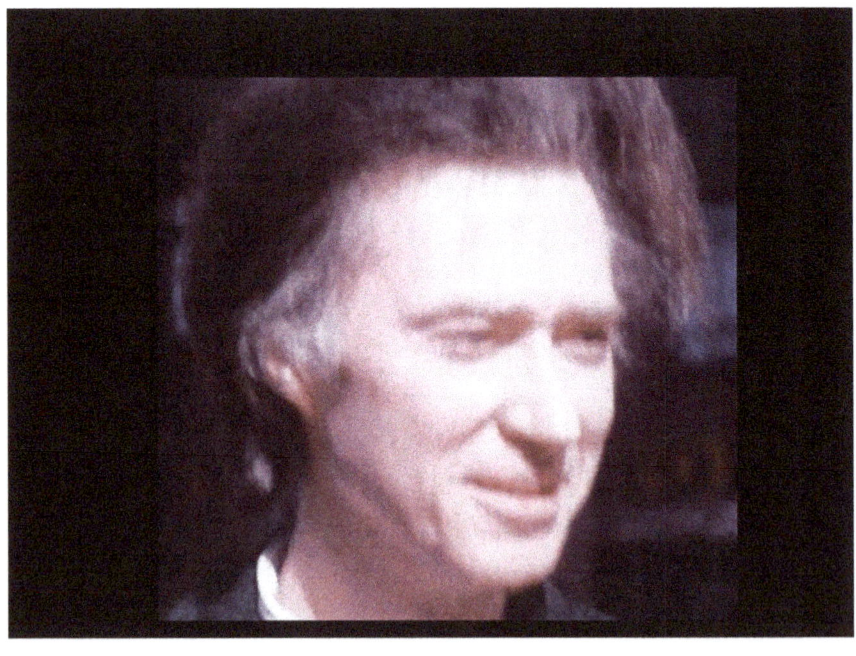

Reel 6 24:22

Michael Snow and his wife the artist Joyce Wieland came to New York from Canada in the early 1960s and would live there for the next ten years before returning to Canada. Snow had been a professional jazz musician and continued to perform while also making films, paintings, sculptures, and photographs.

Mekas remembered:

> At the Film-Makers Cinematheque on 41st street, one evening maybe in early November of 1967, Ken Jacobs said, 'Oh! Michael has a new film and he would like to check it by screening it just for some friends.' So after the regular program, he came and he screened it and the film was *Wavelength*.
>
> When I saw it, I said, 'Oh boy' and it was just then that Jacques Ledoux, the director of the Royal Film Archive of Belgium, had written to me and asked me if I had any films to suggest for his experimental film festival at Knokke-le-Zoute at the end of December 1967. So I said to Michael 'This is it, this is it! I mean this is the film' and Michael said 'Yeah but I have no money and I have no print, this is just like a working print' and I said, 'You have two weeks to make the print for the festival...and I will pay for it,' 'You will pay for it?' 'Sure, I will pay for it because this is it, this is the film.'
>
> And so, he made the print and I paid for it, it went straight to the festival and it got the grand prize. It was obvious that *Wavelength* was a masterpiece, there was no doubt about it for me.[1]

At around the time Mekas filmed Snow and Wieland in Central Park in *Walden,* he reported on the premiere at the Whitney Museum of two new works by Snow, *One Second in Montreal* (1969) and *Back and Forth* (1969) in the *Village Voice*. For once he seemed to be at a loss for words:

I have neither space nor a real way of talking about this film. But I feel that it's full of all kinds of ideas and implications concerning the subject matter, the content and form of cinema.[2]

Then, just a week later, he tried again:

I keep rambling, forgive me, dear reader: You certainly don't expect me to speak very clearly about matters which I do not exactly understand? I'm only trying to understand them. The exact processes, how a work of art works, will always escape us. Yes, we react to the form of the film. We react kinesthetically, too, to the movements, to the light. But through the form we reach deeper, into the indescribable, into the invisible: We reach into the area of relationships, proportions. You can't put your finger on it.[3]

Mekas was far from alone in not being able to put his finger on Snow's work. Its enigmatic, multi-faceted qualities made critical precision difficult and seemed to frustrate all who tried to write about it. It seemed that critics knew there was something extraordinary there but had trouble specifying what.

For Scott MacDonald it sufficed to say that:

Few filmmakers have had as large an impact on the recent avant-garde film scene as Canadian Michael Snow, whose *Wavelength* is probably the most frequently discussed 'structural' film."[4]

And Annette Michelson wrote simply of "the profound effect it had upon the broadest spectrum of viewers...."[5]

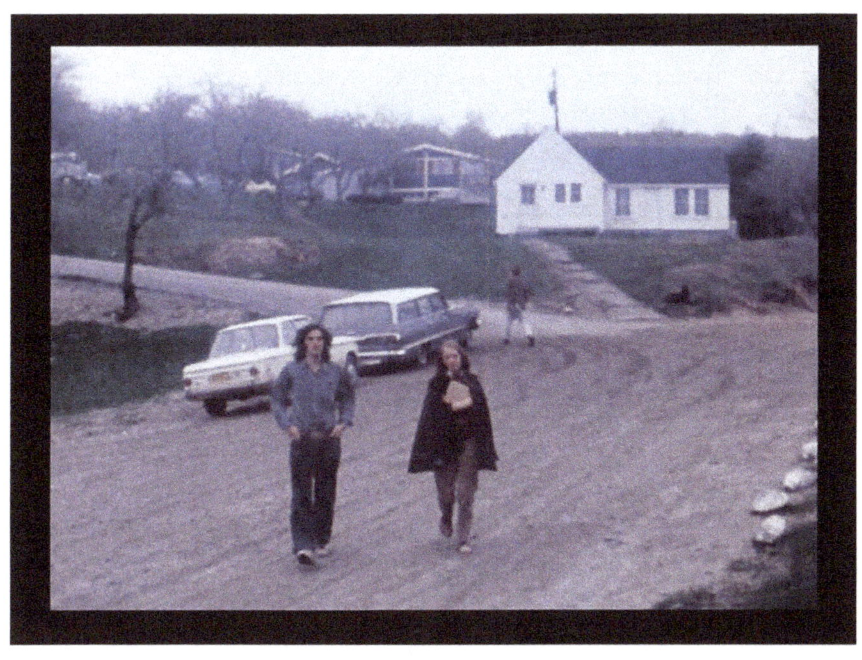

Reel 6 25:08

Although it is not always acknowledged explicitly, many, if not most, of Mekas's trips outside New York in *Walden* were to college campuses.

On the *Walden* poster Mekas noted a sequence in the first reel, "COMING HOME FROM ST. VINCENT COLLEGE," in Latrobe, Pennsylvania; in its fourth reel there is the University of Louisiana "at Monroe, the girl with flowers, at the railroad station," at the University of Texas there are "Austin film-makers, shooting in the park, fooling around." In the fifth reel, "leaves, autumn trees & park at the University of Delaware," in the sixth, "COMING BACK TO NEW YORK" from the State University at Buffalo, "A GIRL WAITING FOR SPRING, AT RUTGERS," in New Brunswick, New Jersey and then finally, "students at Marlboro College" in Vermont.

Marlboro College was a small liberal arts school in rural Vermont not atypical of the many campuses Mekas visited but perhaps more hospitable than most. As a small private institution, Marlboro would have been both freer in its teaching methods and more expensive to attend. Its students tended to be from more affluent families and under less pressure to earn a college degree that would help them quickly find jobs. They had more time for art.

Lecturing and teaching at such institutions were one of the few ways film artists could earn a living related to their work. Some artists such as Stan Brakhage were naturally gifted at this and flourished in the classroom; others found it painful. But those who were not independently wealthy did not have much choice.

Mekas never accepted a permanent academic post such as his brother Adolfas had at Bard College in Annandale-on-Hudson, New York. But he seemed to have genuinely enjoyed both the extensive travel and his contact with students. An eternal optimist he was convinced that the rebellious spirit on the campuses of the 1960s was the harbinger of a better era: "Wherever I go, I meet little groups of beautiful people (there is no other name for them) and they constitute the cells of the new millennium."[1]

Mekas managed to survive without talking about his work full-time to college students. But if he had convinced any of them at Marlboro College in 1969 to become artists, they were likely soon to be themselves looking for teaching jobs. In an uncharacteristically cynical moment he reflected that the 1950s, not the 1960s, were the truly creative years: "in the sixties the filmmakers were teaching and it was just their students repeating their professor's ideas."[2]

117 HOWARD SCHULMAN

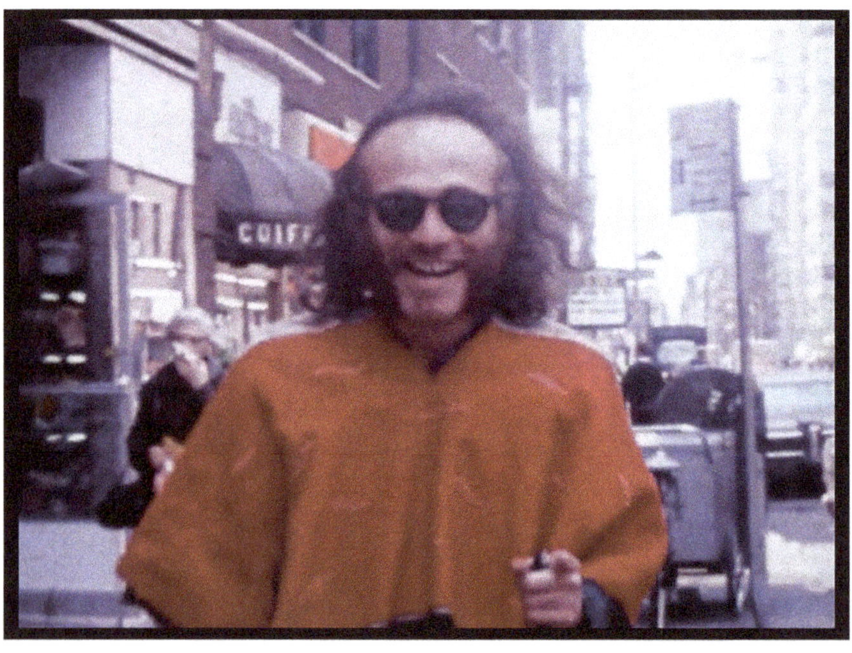

Reel 6 25:27

The *Walden* poster parenthetically identified him as "Rasputin" and it was easy to imagine Howard Schulman as a mad monk as he careened toward Mekas's camera on 8th St.

He was a poet and political radical, a member of "The League of Militant Poets." He published a journal called *Pa'lante* whose first and only issue appeared in May 1962. In it Schulman announced: "America, we are Yankee poets who believe that socialism will make you more beautiful, hundreds of times richer and sane."

Pa'lante included contributions from poets and playwrights of the literary avant-garde - such as Amiri Baraka (then known as LeRoi Jones), William Burroughs and Michael McClure. Among them were some who were particularly close to Mekas including Allen Ginsberg who had helped in the protest against the censorship of *Flaming Creatures* (1963), Diane di Prima whose New York Poets' Theater had shared space for a time with the Film-Makers' Cinematheque at 4 St. Mark's Place, and Warhol's ubiquitous assistant Gerard Malanga who appeared throughout *Walden*.

Mekas's radicalism had a mostly cultural focus and his quarrels with the state were local - the building regulations which kept him from showing films at 80 Wooster St. and censorship actions by the police department. They did not extend to eradicating international capitalism.

But for Schulman the struggle was not limited to lower Manhattan. Schulman explained that *Pa'lante* was "devoted to the American Renaissance and the writing of a new world. This new world is the world of the future whose image may be found in the fraternal socialist countries..."

He was a member of the Fair Play for Cuba Committee, an organization considered subversive by the FBI. Agents noted his support of Fidel Castro and tracked his travel to Cuba. In the hysteria following the assassination of President Kennedy in November 1963 Schulman was purportedly briefly arrested in Morocco in connection with the President's murder.[1]

By the time of what seems to have been a chance encounter on 8th St. recorded in *Walden*, Schulman was apparently no longer a threat to the American government but his Rasputin-like energy seemed undiminished.

118 MONTREAL BED-IN

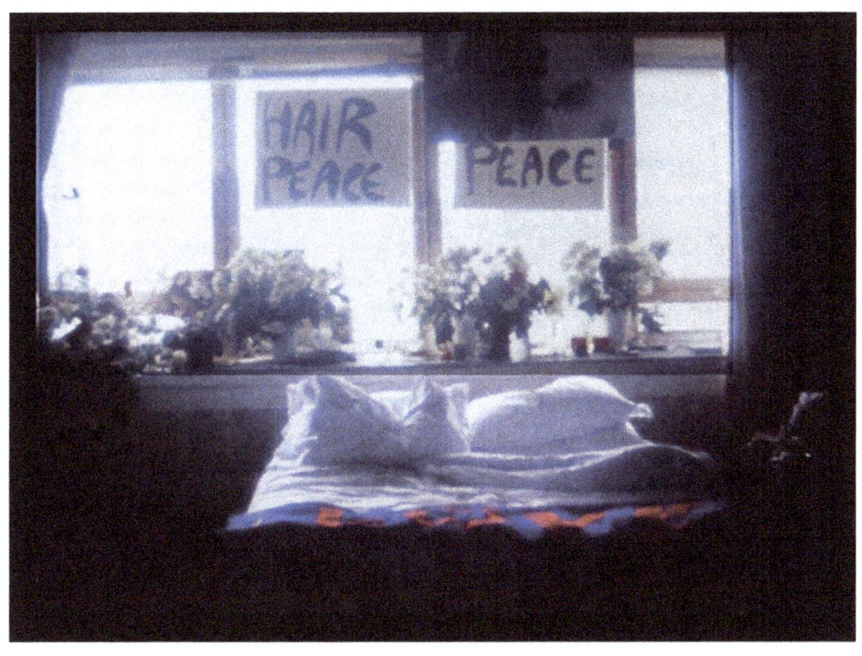

Reel 6 26:46

The Fluxus artist Yoko Ono had already created scores for performance art events such as the one she had performed in 1964 in Tokyo, "Cut Piece." Her score read:

> Performer sits on stage with a pair of scissors in front of him. It is announced that members of the audience may come on stage - one at a time - to cut a small piece of the performer's clothing to take with them. Performer remains motionless throughout the piece. Piece ends at the performer's option.[1]

Although it was never mentioned in the frenzy of media attention, the Montreal "Bed-In for Peace" five years later in May of 1969, was essentially a variation on "Cut Piece."

A bed had replaced the stage, the audience were journalists who, one at a time, sought to extract not pieces of clothing but pieces of information about the couple's personal life. Yoko Ono later pointed out that the information the journalists took away was no more significant than a small scrap of clothing. The worst scandal to report was: "Married couple are in bed."[2]

The difference of course was "Beatlemania." Sharing the bed/stage with Yoko Ono was Beatle John Lennon and anything a Beatle did or said was automatically international news. And they were professionals; the Montreal Bed-In was promoted and managed by the group's publicist and press officer, Derek Taylor.

In addition to the crowd of journalists, Taylor had also invited a number of celebrity guests to stimulate the media's interest. Among them were the guru of psychedelic drugs, Timothy Leary, irascible right-wing cartoonist Al Capp, comedian and radical activist Dick Gregory, political columnist Nat Hentoff and poet Allen Ginsberg. Perhaps at the suggestion of his Fluxus friend Yoko Ono, Mekas was also invited.

Never before had he been surrounded by so many other cameras all focussed on the same subject he was filming. As Mekas clicked off short bursts of single frames, the television cameramen around him filmed at the speed which reproduced "normal" motion, 24 frames per second. While he preserved a moment for his private diary, the others fed the public's voracious appetite for celebrity news.

Mekas clearly found media events interesting but never more than more mundane ones. Just as Peter Beard's lavish Newport wedding was followed by scenes of urban blight in Boston, the Beatlemania in Montreal recorded in *Walden* was followed by views from the back of a city bus on 8th Avenue.

119 YOKO ONO

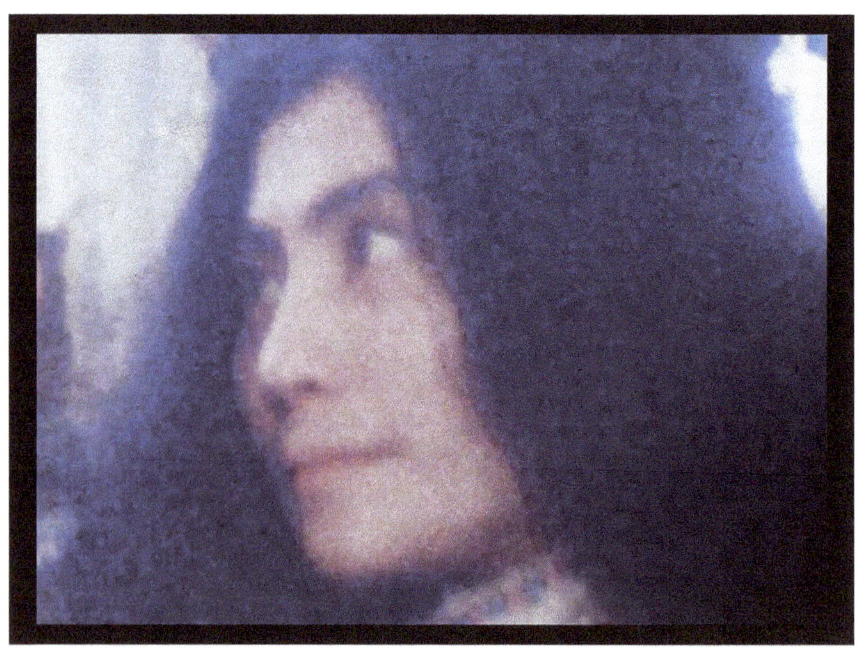

Reel 6 26:54

Mekas recalled:

> I had met Yoko with George Maciunas at his first New York gallery, the
> AG Gallery at Madison Avenue and 74th Street and that's where Yoko
> Ono had her first public show in New York, besides her loft events on
> Chambers Street.
>
> And one day, even before the show, George asked if I could help her
> move to another apartment. It was in 1961 I think. And then later,
> Yoko went back to Japan, and she decided that she wanted to help to
> bring in some films, some filmmakers that she knew in Japan. We tried
> to do something but it never really materialized, and then she decided
> to run away from Japan and she needed a job to get a green card to
> work in the U.S. So I gave her a job at the office of *Film Culture* maga-
> zine and that's how she managed to get into the United States. I did
> not ask her to do anything. It was just a formality.[1]

In 1966, Yoko Ono left New York for London where she participated
with other Fluxus artists in the "Destruction in Art Symposium" in
September and organized a number of well-publicized performance art
events around the U.K. The *Liverpool Daily Post* proclaimed her "The
High Priestess of the Happening." In November she had a solo exhibition at the Indica Gallery, a meeting place for London's counter-
cultural elite. There she met the Beatle John Lennon.

Suddenly Yoko Ono was no longer a figure in the relatively marginal
domain of contemporary art but an auxiliary member of the Beatles,
one of the most intensely observed phenomena of the 20th century.
When it was widely reported that the group was about to split up, she
was cited as one of the reasons. The group's dissolution, speculated
CBS News, was an event that "historians may, one day, view as a landmark in the decline of the British Empire."[2]

The 1963 Fluxus "Manifesto" drafted by its founder George Maciunas
had pledged to "purge the world of professional and commercialized

culture."[3] But when Yoko Ono arrived in Montreal with her husband John Lennon in 1969, their "Bed-In" used every tool of professional and commercialized culture available. The effort was renewed in December with a billboard campaign in major cities around the world declaring WAR IS OVER! If You Want It – Happy Christmas From John and Yoko".

And though it may not have been purged of commercialized culture as Maciunas's manifesto demanded, it did respect another Fluxus requirement: it was truly "living art, anti-art…NON ART REALITY to be fully grasped by all peoples, not only critics, dilettantes and professionals."[4]

120 JOHN LENNON

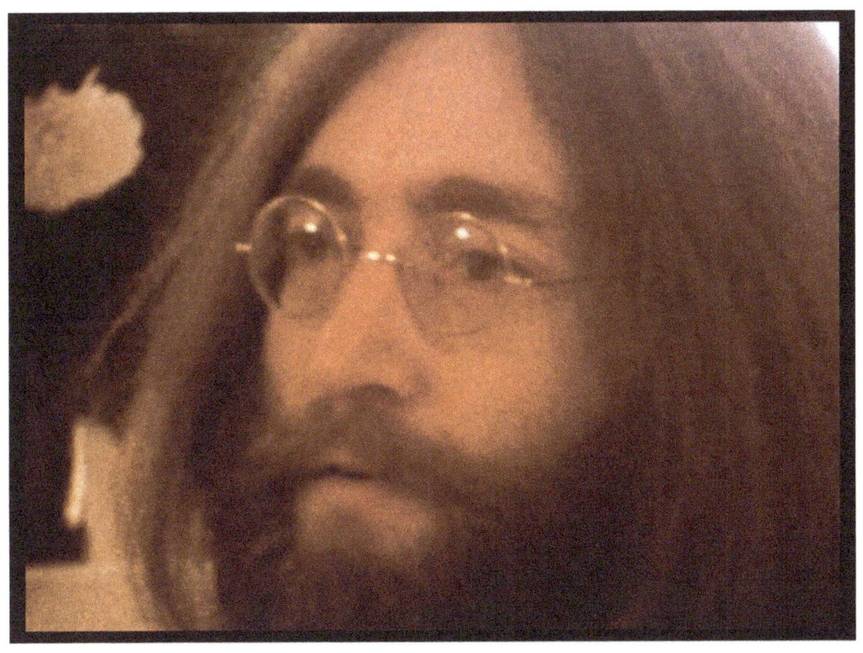

Reel 6 26:54

With the possible exception of Andy Warhol, no one visible in *Walden* was nearly as famous as John Lennon. And the addition of his name was certainly useful for promotion. The first version that Mekas showed in March 1968 had not included him and the sequences of Lennon and Yoko Ono at their Montreal Bed-In in May of 1969 were added later to the final version that premiered in December of that year.

But Lennon was genuinely interested in Mekas's world and a year after the event in Montreal, Lennon and Ono would move to New York from London. Mekas recalled their arrival:

> They landed at JFK and Yoko called me from the airport and said, 'John wants espresso. Do you know a good espresso place?' This was New York in 1970 and it was after midnight so there was only maybe one place in the whole of New York that was open at that hour. But I knew it! So I said 'Sure I know where: Emilio, 6th Avenue and 4th Street, next to the movie theater.' It's no longer there, but that's where we met at one o'clock in the morning and John had his coffee and we stayed there for an hour or so.[1]

Mekas would later use celebrity in a more overt way in the extracts from his diary that he would release as separate films. They included not just Lennon - *Happy Birthday to John* (1996) but also Warhol - *Scenes from the Life of Andy Warhol* (1990) and Jacqueline Kennedy Onassis and her children - *This Side of Paradise* (1999).

121 AL CAPP

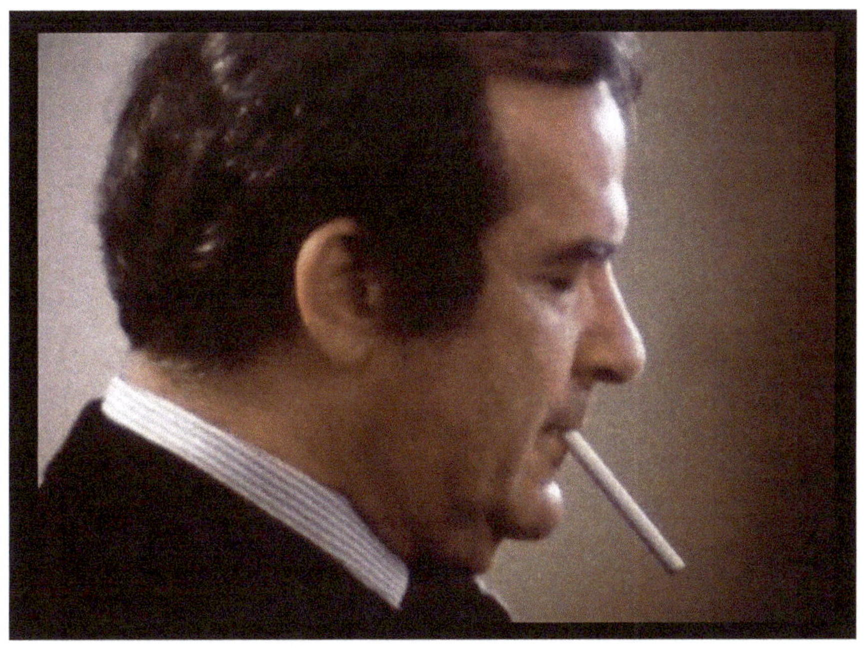

Reel 6 28:41

When Yoko Ono, John Lennon, and the Beatles' press secretary Derek Taylor organized their "Bed-In" in Montreal, the objective was to exploit their celebrity to plea for world peace. But it was the Beatles, not world peace, that attracted the media and, in particular, rumors of their imminent break-up. The challenge then was how to change the subject from rock stars to non-violent war resistance.

To this end, they invited a number of non-Beatles who were prominent figures in popular culture. Most of them - including psychedelic drug guru Timothy Leary, television comedian Tommy Smothers, and poet Allen Ginsberg - could be relied upon to provide sympathetic reinforcement. But one invitee, Al Capp, was different.

Capp was the most popular cartoonist in America. The characters he had created for his daily comic strips - Li'l Abner, Daisy Mae, Mammy Yokum and their imaginary Southern town Dogpatch - were as well known as Walt Disney's. And since 1969 they too had their theme park: Dogpatch U.S.A. in Arkansas.

Although famous for his caricatural portrayal of rural mid-America, Capp was from Connecticut, a grandson of Eastern European Jewish immigrants. He achieved success in New York City from where, starting in 1932, his Li'l Abner comic strip was syndicated to newspapers around the world.

Over the decades, Capp had brilliantly satirized the pomposity and hypocrisy of politicians and plutocrats but by the 1960s he was seeing similar traits in their critics. He began visiting college campuses to publicly antagonize the heroes of the counter-culture and was invited to enliven the Bed-In as a comic book villain from the war-mongering establishment. Playing the role perfectly, he approached Ono and Lennon's bed and introduced himself: "I'm that dreadful Neanderthal fascist. How do you do?"

With all the cameras, including Mekas's, turning, a predictably ill-tempered and insult-laden dialogue ensued. After a while, the Beatles' press secretary Taylor seemed to have had enough and ordered Capp to leave. But Lennon remembered that the confrontation had been their idea in the first place: "Leave it," he told Taylor, "We asked him here."

122 NAT HENTOFF

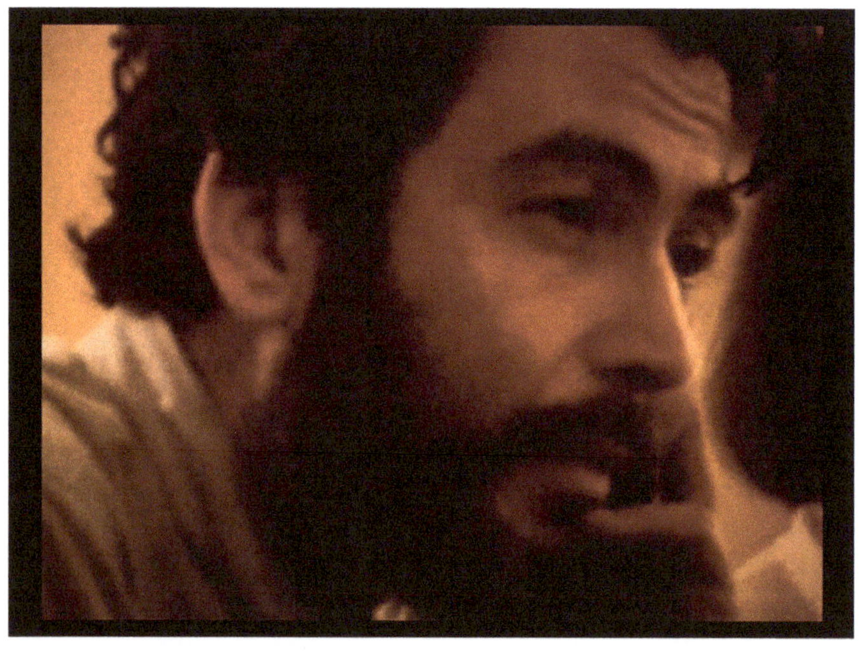

Reel 6 29:09

Some of the invitees to Yoko Ono and John Lennon's Montreal Bed-In were famous enough themselves to boost the event's visibility. Counter-culture icons such as Timothy Leary and Allen Ginsberg added to their charisma while cartoonist Al Capp played his assigned role of establishment villain.

But what motivated the invitations to Mekas and his *Village Voice* colleague Nat Hentoff is less clear. Mekas's column in the *Voice* was about avant-garde film and the films he made were not commercially distributed. Hentoff wrote about jazz and libertarian politics and was a ferocious defender of civil liberties. None of these subjects were particularly relevant to the Bed-In.

As a jazz critic and historian, Hentoff had reflected on how the "British Invasion" of American popular culture had exposed young white Americans to the African-American roots of rhythm and blues music. British groups such as The Beatles and the Rolling Stones had:

> …turned millions of American adolescents on to what had been here hurting all the time…but the young here never did want it raw so they absorbed it through the British filter.[1]

Hentoff seemed as bemused as anyone when he recalled in 2012:

> When John Lennon and Yoko had a bed-in for peace in their hotel room in Montreal, I was invited. So I went. My wife and I spent a very amiable hour or so talking to both of them …Some people are stunned that I was actually in his presence.[2]

After his move to New York in 1971, Lennon's commitment to radical politics deepened and, had his life not been cut short in 1980, he and Hentoff may have had better occasions than their short hour together in Montreal to explore the values and ideas they held in common.

123 NEW YORKER THEATER

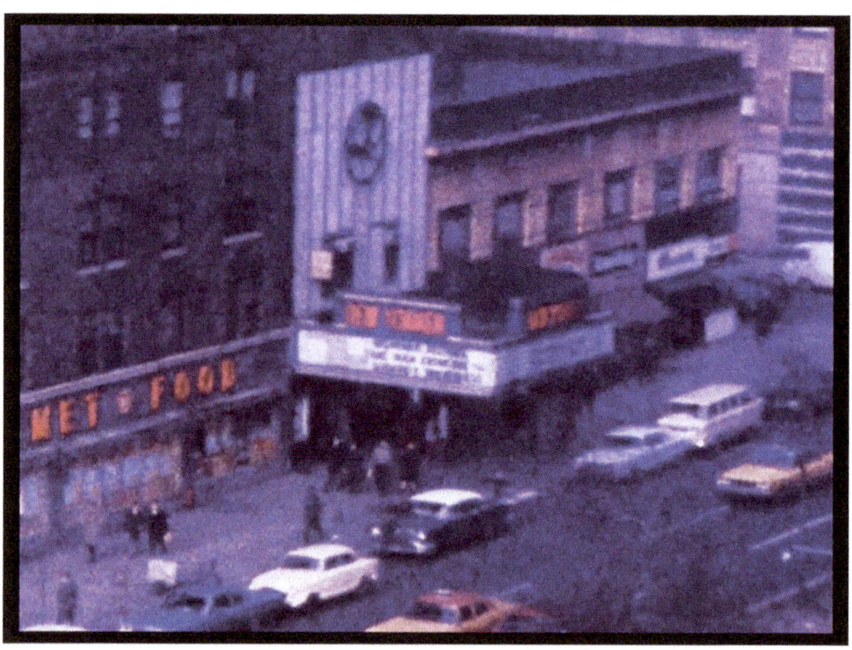

Reel 6 32:10

Pointing his camera out the window of Barbara and David Stone's apartment on the Upper West Side, Mekas captured views of the New Yorker Theater, a landmark in the history of American film criticism.

It had opened in 1927 as the Roxy Theater but started a new life as the New Yorker in March 1960 when it was leased by Daniel Talbot, a young film critic who had just published one of the first American books to take the academic study of film seriously, *Film: An Anthology*.

Included in Talbot's anthology was a long essay by the artist and film critic, Manny Farber, entitled "Underground Films" which championed the then unfashionable work of Hollywood film industry directors such as Howard Hawks and John Ford. In his new role as a film exhibitor, Talbot used the New Yorker to encourage a re-evaluation of their films and his programming would inspire a new generation of American film critics to defend Hollywood films. Notable among them was the critic Mekas would hire to help cover film at the *Village Voice*, Andrew Sarris.

A few months after Talbot opened the New Yorker, Mekas and the producer Lewis Allen called a meeting to form the "New American Cinema Group" and Talbot attended. The group's "First Statement" declared its intention to:

> ...establish our own cooperative distribution center...The New Yorker Theatre, The Bleecker St. Cinema,....are the first movie houses to join us by pledging to exhibit our films. [1]

But It was not long before it was clear that the members of the group did not all have the same interpretation of "Underground Films."

For some in the New American Cinema Group it meant a revalorization of certain directors who worked in the Hollywood movie factory. But for Mekas it was a clandestine resistance movement opposed to Hollywood. Dan Talbot wanted to run a sustainable business by exhibiting feature-length narrative films. Mekas wanted to show films as liberated from formal constraints as free verse poetry or abstract painting.

During the period covered by *Walden*, the New Yorker Theater flourished by reviving classic Hollywood films and importing unorthodox feature films from Europe and Asia. And, very briefly, it also provided a refuge for Mekas's never-profitable avant-garde.

In November 1964 Mekas had announced the formation of the "Film-Makers' Cinematheque" as the home of "independent, underground, avant-garde cinema." It was to be at 83 East 4th St. in the East Village. But he had not yet obtained the necessary permits to open the space as a public movie theater. So Talbot agreed to show Cinematheque programs at the New Yorker, but only at a time when he could not otherwise attract a paying audience: Monday at midnight.

Mekas issued a press release in December that read:

> WE ARE GREATLY AWARE that our current Monday midnight screenings are making it either undesirable or impossible for many to attend our screenings at the New Yorker Theater.

> But neither could he move back downtown because, he explained, "the wheels of bureaucracy are turning slowly."

In fact, they did not appear to be turning at all.

The Cinematheque on East 4th St. never opened and Mekas moved on from the New Yorker to various other locations, settling for a time in the Wurlitzer Building on 42nd St. Finally, in 1970, through the philanthropy of Jerome Hill, it found a permanent home under a new name: Anthology Film Archives.

INDEX OF NAMES

ACKNOWLEDGMENTS

This book was made possible by Sebastian Mekas and Pip Chodorov who supported it at every step of its creation.

Pip encouraged me to write the first chapters. At my request, he solicited recollections from Jonas himself over two hot summer days in Brooklyn in 2017. Several years later, he completed the exhausting task of correcting and improving my first draft.

Marie-Hélène Hammen then found the courage to proofread and correct the final result.

The mistakes that remain were doubtless added by me after they both had finished.

NOTES

PREFACE

1. *Village Voice* ad, 11 December 1969, p. 54.
2. https://www.flickeralley.com/jonas-mekas-was-definitely-the-driving-force-of-that-movement-in-his-quiet-interview-with-wendy-clarke/
3. Scott MacDonald, *A Critical Cinema 2*, University of California Press, 1992. p. 102.
4. Ibid.

PROLOGUE: STILL WINTER

1. "The First Statement of The New American Cinema Group." *Film Culture*, 22–23, 1961, p.131.
2. Jonas Mekas, "Movie Journal," *The Village Voice*, April 18, 1963, p. 13).
3. Festival Program EXPRMNTL 3, Knokke-le-Zoute, December 1963.
4. Leslie Trumbull, "Movie Journal: Report from Belgium," *The Village Voice*, January 9, 1964.
5. Jonas Mekas, "Movie Journal," *The Village Voice*, January 16, 1964, p. 13.
6. "Mekas Jailed: City Sleuths Douse Flaming Creatures," *The Village Voice*, 12 March, 1964, p. 3, 13.
7. "Mekas Gaoled Again, Genet Film Does It," *The Village Voice*, March 19, 1964, p. 13.
8. First ad for the Film-Makers' Cinematheque in the *Village Voice*, 12 November 12, 1964, p. 15.
9. Quoted in Calvin Tomkins, "All Pockets Open," *The New Yorker*, January 6, 1973.
10. Jonas Mekas, *I Had Nowhere to Go*, Spector Books, 2017, p.21.

2. SNOW

1. Quoted in Calvin Tomkins, "All Pockets Open," The New Yorker, January 6, 1973.

3. FILM-MAKERS' CINEMATHEQUE

1. Reproduced in Gary Comena's invaluable chronology of the Film-Makers' Cinematheque at https://warholstars.org/filmmakers-cinematheque-1-1961-62.html

5. BARBARA & DAVID STONE

1.   http://anthologyfilmarchives.org/film_screenings/series/38043

8. GIRLS IN THE PARK

1.   Scott MacDonald, Interview with Mekas in *A Critical Cinema 2*, University of California Press, 1992, p.100.

10. GENERAL POST OFFICE

1.   Vincent Scully quoted in Herbert Muschamp, "Architecture View: In This Dream Station Future and Past Collide," *New York Times*, June 20, 1993.

11. DAVID BROOKS

1.   Jonas Mekas, *Movie Journal*, New York, Columbia University Press, second edition, 2016, p. 331.

12. HARRY SMITH

1.   Jonas Mekas, *Movie Journal*, New York, Columbia University Press, second edition, 2016, p. 189.

13. WEDDINGS

1.   Scott MacDonald, *A Critical Cinema 2: Interviews with Independent Filmmakers*, University of California Press, 1992. p.99.

15. ADOLFAS MEKAS

1.   ADOLFAS MEKAS (1925–2011), *The Brooklyn Rail*, July-August 2011.

16. ED EMSHWILLER

1.   John J. O'Connor, "TV: Ed Emshwiller's 'Scape-Mates' Moves Briskly," *New York Times*," March 23, 1973.

17. LEO ADAMS

1. "July 18, 1950," *I Seem to Live: The New York Diaries, 1969-2011, Volume 2*, Spector Books, 1991, p. 321.

18. ALGIRDAS LANDSBERGIS

1. Stasys Gostaurus in *Litanus Lithuanian Quarterly Journal of Arts and Sciences*, Volume 51, No.1 - Spring 2005.

20. CASSIS

1. Scott MacDonald, *A Critical Cinema: Interviews with Independent Filmmakers, Volume 2*, University of California Press, 1992.

21. STAN BRAKHAGE

1. Jonas Mekas, *Movie Journal*, New York, Columbia University Press. 2016, p. 42.

22. CARL DREYER

1. *New York Times*, June 3, 1966.
2. Jonas Mekas, *Movie Journal*, New York, Columbia University Press, 2016, p. 214.

23. THOREAU'S WALDEN

1. "The Emerson-Thoreau Correspondence: The Dial Period," edited by F. B. Sanborn, *The Atlantic Monthly*, Vol. LXIX, N° CCCCXV, May 1892. p. 588.

24. AMY TAUBIN

1. Amy Taubin, "Jonas Mekas's MOVIE JOURNAL," *Artforum*, April 2017.
2. "PASSAGES: Amy Taubin on Jonas Mekas," *Artforum*, March 2019.
3. Ibid.
4. The first screening was on July 1, 1963 and lasted until February 3, 1964.
5. Unpublished interview with Pip Chodorov, August 27, 2017.
6. *Village Voice* ad, 11 December 1969, p. 54.

25. MILLBROOK

1. Alina Cohen, "When Timothy Leary Got Artists to Take LSD," *Artsy,* June 18, 2018.
2. *Village Voice* ad, 27 July 1967, p. 19.
3. *Village Voice* ad, 27 July 1967, p. 19.

26. TIMOTHY LEARY

1. Quoted in the "The Plot to Turn On the World: The Leary/Ginsberg Acid Conspiracy," *Multidisciplinary Association for Psychedelic Studies*, April 21, 2011.

30. GREGORY MARKOPOULOS

1. Jonas Mekas, *Movie Journal*, New York, Columbia University Press, second edition, 2016, p. 271.
2. ibid (p. 92).
3. Ibid (p. 271).
4. http://www.thetemenos.org/temenos-screenings/background/

31. BOLEX

1. If accurate, his birthdate was almost simultaneous with the first public exhibition of motion pictures by the Lumière brothers in Paris which occurred on 28 December.
2. He would use this footage in the next segment of his diaries *Lost, Lost, Lost* (1976) that he released after *Walden*.

32. BLEECKER STREET

1. Jonas Mekas, *Movie Journal*, New York, Columbia University Press, second edition, 2016, p. 93.

34. LOUIS BRIGANTE

1. P. Adams Sitney, *The Cinema of Poetry*, Oxford University Press, 2015, p. 2.
2. William C. Wees, *Recycled Images: The Art and Politics of Found Footage Films*, New York, Anthology Film Archives, 1993.

35. MIKE JACOBSON

1. Wheeler W. Dixon, *The Exploding Eye: A Re-Visionary History of 1960s American Experimental Cinema*, SUNY Press, 1998.
2. Jonas Mekas, *Movie Journal*, New York, Columbia University Press, second edition, 2016, p. 343.
3. http://unbrokenjournal.com/?s=Jacobson

36. CIRCUS

1. Roger Angell, "The Last Show: A Farewell to the Ringling Brothers and Barnum & Bailey Circus," *The New Yorker*, June 1, 2017.

37. BARBARA RUBIN

1. J. Hoberman, "Barbara Rubin, Shameless Angel of Avant-Garde Cinema," *The New York Review of Books*, https://www.nybooks.com/daily/2019/05/21/barbara-rubin-shameless-angel-of-avant-garde-cinema/
2. Jonas Mekas, *Movie Journal*, New York, Columbia University Press, second edition, 2016, p. 95-96.
3. J. Hoberman *The New York Review of Books*, https://www.nybooks.com/daily/2019/05/21/barbara-rubin-shameless-angel-of-avant-garde-cinema/

38. AL ARONOWITZ

1. "Kreplach to Invade London": https://content.wisconsinhistory.org/digital/collection/p15932coll8/id/57763
2. "BOB DYLAN AND THE BEATLES VOLUME ONE OF THE BEST OF THE BLACKLISTED JOURNALIST" *Kirkus Book Reviews*: Review Posted Online: May 23, 2010.

39. TULI KUPFERBERG

1. Jon Pareles, "At a Reunion With the Fugs, Teenage Days Have Moved On," *The New York Times*, Oct. 9, 2004.
2. Ben Ratliff, "Generations of Admirers Play Their Respects," *The New York Times*, Jan. 25, 2010.

40. ALLEN GINSBERG

1. Interview with Pip Chodorov, August 26, 2017. Published in the booklet accompanying the Re:Voir DVD release of *He Stands in a Desert Counting the Seconds of his Life*.

42. ED SANDERS

1. Ben Ratliff, "Present at the Counterculture's Creation," *The New York Times,* Jan. 11, 2012.
2. "Still Happening: A Conversation with Ed Sanders," Jennifer Seaman Cook interviews Ed Sanders, *Los Angeles Review of Books*, July 18, 2018.

43. RONNA PAGE

1. Andy Warhol's "The Chelsea Girls". Edited with text by Geralyn Huxley, Greg Pierce. D.A.P./THE ANDY WARHOL MUSEUM, 2018.

44. ANDY WARHOL

1. Unpublished interview with Pip Chodorov, August 26, 2017.
2. Jonas Mekas, *Movie Journal*, New York, Columbia University Press, second edition, 2016, p. 103.
3. Unpublished interview with Pip Chodorov, August 26, 2017.

45. WALTER BOWART

1. Margalit Fox, "Walter Bowart, Alternative Journalist, Dies at 68", *The New York Times*. January 14, 2008.

47. STORM DE HIRSCH

1. "Interview with Shirley Clarke," *Film Culture* 46, October 1968.
2. Jonas Mekas, *Movie Journal*, New York, Columbia University Press, second edition, 2016, p. 156.
3. Ibid. p. 95.

50. MARTY GREENBAUM

1. Catalog for *Things I see: Pastels,* The Butler Institute of American Art, Youngstown, Ohio, 2008.
2. Edward Bryant, *Marty Greenbaum,* catalog for The Picker Art Gallery, Colgate University, February 1977.
3. Ed McCormack, "Marty Greenbaum: Visionary Mojo Man in the Postmodern Age," *Gallery & Studio,* December 2001.
4. Ibid.

51. JEROME HILL

1. Jonas Mekas Interview by the Jerome Foundation, 2005, https://vimeo.com/115010148

52. KEN KELMAN

1. Gene Youngblood, *Expanded Cinema,* E.P. Dutton; 1st edition, January 1970.
2. Ken Kelman, "Anticipations of the Light," *The New American Cinema,* ed. Gregory Battcock, New York: Dutton Paperbacks, 1967, pp. 24, 25.
3. Gary Comenas, https://warholstars.org/filmmakers-cinematheque-5-1968.html
4. Introduction by Ken Kelman of Carl Dreyer's "Gertrud" at Carnegie Museum of Art, 11/27/1973. https://records.cmoa.org/things/0cf72c18-589f-43b9-b729-f2e02402856f/

53. TIMES SQUARE

1. Mekas diary quoted in Calvin Tomkins, "All Pockets Open," *The New Yorker,* January 6, 1973.

54. BARBET SCHROEDER

1. Jonas Mekas, *Movie Journal,* New York, Columbia University Press, second edition, 2016, p. 20.
2. Ibid. p. 45.
3. Ibid. pp. 147-148.

55. CAFETERIAS

1. John Clellon Holmes, *Go: A Novel*, Open Road Media, Google Books, 2015.
2. "The Impotent Decoration: An Interview with P. Adams Sitney,"
    Nassau Literary Review, February 7, 2015.

56. JEROME HILER

1. https://textoflight.files.wordpress.com/2014/03/return-to-form-jerome-hiler.pdf
2. https://openspace.sfmoma.org/2020/02/jerome-hiler-and-mac-mcginnes-in-conversation/
3. Ibid.
4. https://nathanieldorsky.net/tagged/ingreen
5. https://textoflight.files.wordpress.com/2014/03/return-to-form-jerome-hiler.pdf

57. JOHN CAVANAUGH

1. P. Adams Sitney, *Eyes Upside Down: Visionary Filmmakers and the Heritage of Emerson*,
    Oxford University Press, 2008 p. 175.
2. Hannah Higgins, *Fluxus Experience*, Berkeley, University of California Press, 2002,
    p.17.
3. Jonas Mekas, *Movie Journal*, New York, Columbia University Press, second edition,
    2016, p. 306.

59. NATHANIEL DORSKY

1. https://nathanieldorsky.net/tagged/ingreen
2. Quoted by P. Adams Sitney in "Tone Poems: P. Adams Sitney on the Filkms of
    Nathaniel Dorsky," *Artforum*, November 2007.
3. Nathaniel Dorsky, *Devotional Cinema*, Tuumba Press, 2005.
4. Manohla Dargis, "For Nathaniel Dorsky and Jerome Hiler, Film is the Star," *The New
    York Times*, September, 27, 2015. https://www.nytimes.-
    com/2015/09/27/movies/for-nathaniel-dorsky-and-jerome-hiler-film-is-the-
    star.html

60. THEATER DISTRICT

1. Hidden in Plain Sight: Jerome Hiler and Mac McGinnes in Conversation, February
    27, 2020, San Francisco Museum of Modern Art, https://openspace.sfmo-
    ma.org/2020/02/jerome-hiler-and-mac-mcginnes-in-conversation/

61. STEPHEN SHORE

1. https://www.wsj.com/articles/stephen-shores-never-before-seen-photos-of-andy-warhols-factory-1475075231
2. Stephen Shore, LynneTillman, *The Velvet Years: Warhol's Factory 1965-67*, New York, Thunder's Mouth Press, 1995.
3. A conversation with Stephen Shore, *FT Series Photo London 2019*, https://www.ft.com/content/e81096de-726b-11e9-bf5c-6eeb837566c5

62. NICO

1. Quoted by Gerard Malanga, *Up-tight: The Velvet Underground Story*, London: Omnibus Press, 1983, p. 114.

63. JACK SMITH

1. https://www.gladstonegallery.com/sites/default/files/Thelmagazine_Nov011.pdf

64. MARIO MONTEZ

1. Douglas Martin, "Mario Montez, a Warhol Glamour Avatar, Dies at 78," *New York Times*, Oct. 3, 2013.
2. Andy Warhol and Pat Hackett, *POPism: The Warhol Sixties*, New York, Houghton Mifflin Harcourt, 2009, p.228.

65. EDIE SEDGWICK

1. Christopher Knight, "Seeing double wasn't even the half of it," *Los Angeles Times*, January 7, 2007.
2. Rhoda Koenig, "Edie Sedgwick: The life and death of the Sixties star," *The Independent*, January 9, 2007.
3. Ibid.
4. Nora Ephram, *New York Post Magazine*, September 5, 1965.

66. LOU REED

1. Conrad quoted in Gerard Malanga, *Uptight: The Velvet Underground Story*, London, Omnibus Press, 1983, p. 123.
2. Cale quoted in Gerard Malanga, *Uptight: The Velvet Underground Story: The Velvet Underground Story*, London, Omnibus Press, 1983, p. 125.

3. https://www.rollingstone.com/music/music-lists/500-greatest-albums-of-all-time-156826/the-velvet-underground-and-nico-the-velvet-underground-52023/
4. Patti Smith, "Lou Reed," *The New Yorker*, 4 November 2013, quoted by Alex Williams, "Who Was the Real Lou Reed?" in *The New York Times,* 31 October 2015.

67. VELVET UNDERGROUND

1. Jonas Mekas, *Movie Journal*, New York, Columbia University Press, second edition, 2016, p. 198.
2. Quoted by Gerard Malanga, *Up-tight: The Velvet Underground Story*, London, Omnibus Press, 1983, p.112.
3. Ibid.
4. Grace Glueck, "Syndromes Pop at Delmonico's," *New York Times*, January 14, 1966.
5. Ibid.

68. JOHN CALE

1. In Scott MacDonald, *A Critical Cinema: Interviews with Independent Filmmakers*, Volume 2, University of California Press, 1992.
2. Cale quoted in Gerard Malanga, *Up-tight: The Velvet Underground Story*, London, Omnibus Press, 1983, p. 115.
3. Ibid. p. 121.
4. Simon Price, "John Cale: The long reign of the alternative Prince of Wales," *The Independent,* 28 February 2010.

70. NAOMI LEVINE

1. Unpublished interview with Pip Chodorov, August 27, 2017.
2. July 25, 1963, reprinted in Jonas Mekas, *Movie Journal*, New York, Columbia University Press, second edition, 2016, p. 196.
3. December 24, 1964, reprinted in Jonas Mekas, *Movie Journal*, New York, Columbia University Press, second edition, 2016, p. 176.

71. FERRY STREET

1. Amy Taubin, "Ken Jacobs's The Sky Socialist," *Film Comment*, June 14, 2019.

72. FLORENCE KARPF JACOBS

1. Scott MacDonald, *A Critical Cinema 3: Interviews with Independent Filmmakers*, University of California Press, 1999.
2. Amy Taubin interview in Michele Pierson, *Optic Antics: The Cinema of Ken Jacobs*, Oxford University Press, Kindle Edition.

73. KEN JACOBS

1. https://conversations.berkeley.edu/jacobs_1999
2. Ken Jacobs Interview: *Conversations with History; Institute of International Studies*, UC Berkeley.
3. Unpublished interview with Pip Chodorov, August 27, 2017.
4. Michele Pierson, *Optic Antics: The Cinema of Ken Jacobs*, Oxford University Press, Kindle Edition.

74. JUDITH MALINA

1. Jonas Mekas, *Movie Journal*, New York, Columbia University Press, second edition, 2016, p. 201.

75. COLUMBUS CIRCLE

1. Ada Louise Huxtable, "Columbus Circle Gallery Will Open in Mid-March," *The New York Times*, February 25, 1964.
2. Ibid.
3. *Village Voice* ad, May 1, 1969.
4. Nicolai Ouroussoff, "Taming the Beast From 1965," *The New York Times*, October 4, 2004.

76. FILM-MAKERS' COOP

1. "The First Statement of the New American Cinema Group," *Film Culture*, No. 21-22, 1961.
2. Ibid.
3. Mekas recollection on the web site of the New York Film-Makers' Coop: https://film-makerscoop.com

77. HERMAN G. WEINBERG

1. Jonas Mekas, *Movie Journal*, New York, Columbia University Press, second edition, 2016, p. 335.

79. OLMSTED HIKE

1. Charles E. Little, *Greenways for America*, Baltimore, The Johns Hopkins University Press, 1990, p. 95.

80. JOHN LINDSAY

1. Jonas Mekas, *Movie Journal*, New York, Columbia University Press, second edition, 2016, p. 242.

81. THOMAS HOVING

1. Quoted in *Princeton Alumni Weekly*, Volume 77, 1977.

83. JANE WODENING

1. https://janewodening.com/about-the-author/
2. Quoted in Richard Deming, "Collage, Collaboration, and Material Quotation: The Scrapbooks of Jane Wodening and Stan Brakhage, 1962-66, in the Beinecke Library," *Yale University Library Gazette*, October 2006.
3. Barr, William R. (1999) "Brakhage: Artistic Development in Two Childbirth Films," *Film Quarterly: Forty Years, a Selection,* University of California Press, 1999, p. 536-541.
4. Winston, Archer, quoted in Wheeler W.Dixon, *Visions of Paradise: Images of Eden in the Cinema,* Rutgers University Press, 2006, p.19.
5. Jane Wodening, *Brakhage's Childhood*, New York, Granary Books, 2015.

84. RICHARD FOREMAN

1. Unpublished interview with Pip Chodorov, August 27, 2017.
2. "About Us," The Ontological-Hysteric Theater, http://www.ontological.com/history.html

85. HANS RICHTER

1. Unpublished interview with Pip Chodorov, August 27, 2017.

86. STANDISH LAWDER

1. Unpublished interview with Pip Chodorov, August 27, 2017.
2. Film-makers Coop Catalogue, https://film-makerscoop.com/catalogue/standish-lawder-sunday-in-southbury

87. RAY JOHNSON

1. Grace Glueck, "What Happened? Nothing." *The New York Times* October 22, 1965.
2. Oral history interview with Ray Johnson, Apr. 17, 1968, Smithsonian Archives of American Art.
3. Grace Glueck, "Gallery View; A Witty Master of the Deadpan Spoof," *New York Times*, February 19, 1984.
4. New York Correspondence School.
5. David Bourdon, "Cosmic Ray, An open letter to the founder of the New York Correspondence School, *Art in America*, October 1995.

89. PETER BEARD

1. Unpublished interview with Pip Chodorov, August 2017.
2. Leslie Bennetts, "African Dreamer," *Vanity Fair*, November 1996.

90. NEWPORT

1. "Minnie Cushing and Peter Beard Wed in Newport," *The New York Times*, August 13, 1967 p. 74.

91. ROXBURY

1. Susan E. Davis, "White Revolutionaries Settle in Roxbury," *Bay State Banner*," February 15, 1967.
2. http://www.forthill.com/profile-2/

92. MEL LYMAN

1. David Felton, "The Lyman Family's Holy Siege of America," *Rolling Stone*, December 23, 1971.
2. Ibid.

94. GIDEON BACHMANN

1. "Gideon Bachmann, New York Diary," published in booklet included with DVD, *Underground New York*, Re:Voir, 2016.

95. WILLARD VAN DYKE

1. Unpublished interview with Pip Chodorov, August 26, 2017.
2. https://assets.moma.org/momaorg/shared/pdfs/docs/press_archives/4158/releases/MOMA_1968_July-December_0090_132.pdf

97. WENDY CLARKE

1. https://www.flickeralley.com/jonas-mekas-was-definitely-the-driving-force-of-that-movement-in-his-quiet-interview-with-wendy-clarke/
2. Marjorie Rosen, "Shirley Clarke: Videospace Explorer," in *Ms.* April 1975, pp. 107–110.
3. https://dsps.lib.uiowa.edu/downtownpopunderground/person/wendy-clarke/

98. SHIRLEY CLARKE

1. "Shirley Clarke Interviewed by Gretchen Berg," *Dance Perspectives 30*, Summer 1967.
2. Ibid.
3. https://www.flickeralley.com/jonas-mekas-was-definitely-the-driving-force-of-that-movement-in-his-quiet-interview-with-wendy-clarke/
4. Jonas Mekas, *Movie Journal*, New York, Columbia University Press, second edition, 2016, p. 297.

99. JUD YALKUT

1. Jud Yalkut, Preface to *Electronic Zen: the Alternate Video Generation*, Eyewash Books/Paris Expérimental, 2022.
2. Quoted in Gregory Zinman, "DREAM REELER, Jud Yalkut (1938-2013)," *The Brooklyn Rail*, September 4, 2013.

101. ERNIE GEHR

1. Unpublished interview with Pip Chodorov, August 27, 2017.
2. https://www.fredcamper.com/Film/Gehr1.html
3. https://mubi.com/notebook/posts/a-playground-with-no-supervision-an-interview-with-ernie-gehr

103. MARIE MENKEN

1. Quoted by Robert Haller circa 1966,
    http://www.roberthaller.com/firstlight/menken.html
2. Jonas Mekas, *Movie Journal*, New York, Columbia University Press, second edition, 2016, p. 52.
3. Melissa Ragona, "Swing and Sway: Marie Menken's Filmic Events" in *Women's Experimental Cinema: Critical Frameworks* edited by Robin Blaetz, Duke University Press, 2007.

104. STONEWALL

1. Jonas Mekas, *Movie Journal*, New York, Columbia University Press, second edition, 2016, p. 91.
2. Lucian Truscott IV, "Gay Power Comes to Sheridan Square," *The Village Voice*, July 3, 1969.

105. JAMES STOLLER

1. Phillip Lopate, *Getting Personal: Selected Essays*, Kindle Edition.
2. Jonathan Rosenbaum, *Placing Movies: The Practice of Film Criticism*, University of California Press, 1995.
3. Robert Christgau "Can't Stop the Music," *Village Voice* October 18, 2005.
4. *Robert Christgau, Dean of American Rock Critics* :https://www.robertchristgau.com/xg/misc/71inbrief-72.php
5. Phillip Lopate, *Getting Personal: Selected Essays*, Kindle Edition.

106. ED FANCHER

1. Clark Whelton, "Exeunt Omnes: Farewell to The Village Voice," *City Journal*, September 4, 2018.
2. Quoted by Bilge Ebirir, 'I'm Like the Last Leaf of a Big Tree': A Conversation With Jonas Mekas, *The Village Voice*, September 21, 2017.

3. John Leland, "A Village Voice Reunion, and Nobody Got Punched," *New York Times*, September 10, 2017.

108. LINDSAY SNOWSTORM

1. Jonas Mekas, "Showcases I Ran in the Sixties" in *To Free the Cinema: Jonas Mekas & the New York Underground*, Princeton University Press, 1992. p. 324.

110. MARTA MENUJÍN

1. Marta Minujín, *Destruction of My Works in the Impasse Ronsin*, Paris, 1963, https://post.at.moma.org/sources/8/publications/129

111. WOOSTER STREET

1. *Village Voice* ad, September 7, 1967, p. 30.

112. PETER KUBELKA

1. In Scott MacDonald, *A Critical Cinema 4*, University of California Press, 2005, p.178.
2. Ibid.
3. P. Adams Sitney, *Visionary Film: The American Avant-garde, 1943-2000*, Oxford University Press, 2002. p. 284.

113. JAMES BROUGHTON

1. Kent State University Libraries, Special Collections and Archives, James Broughton papers, Collection 1, https://www.library.kent.edu/james-broughton-papers-collection-1#series1

114. JOYCE WIELAND

1. Quoted in the Film-Makers Coop catalogue: https://film-makerscoop.com/catalogue/joyce-wieland-rat-life-and-diet-in-north-america
2. Quoted in Iris Nowell, *Joyce Wieland: A Life in Art*, ECW Press, 2001, p. 201.
3. Quoted in the Film-Makers Coop catalogue: https://film-makerscoop.com/catalogue/joyce-wieland-la-raison-avant-la-passion
4. Jay Scott, "Full Circle," *Canadian Art*, March 1987. p. 63.

115. MICHAEL SNOW

1. Unpublished interview with Pip Chodorov, August 26, 2017.
2. Jonas Mekas, *Movie Journal*, New York, Columbia University Press, second edition, 2016, p. 352.
3. Ibid. p. 354.
4. Scott MacDonald, "*So Is This* by Michael Snow," *Film Quarterly* Vol. 39, No. 1, Autumn 1985, p. 34.
5. Annette Michelson, "About Snow," *October* Vol. 8, Spring 1979, p.118.

116. MARLBORO COLLEGE

1. Jonas Mekas, *Movie Journal*, New York, Columbia University Press, second edition, 2016, p. 287.
2. Unpublished interview with Pip Chodorov, August 27, 2017.

117. HOWARD SCHULMAN

1. John Edgar Hoover, FBI Memorandum to the Deputy Assistant Secretary for Security, Department of State, 20 December 1963, (NI) 105-32555. Cited in Lucy Bradnock, 'The New York Poetry Scene', in Lucy Bradnock (ed.), *In Focus:* Blood of a Poet Box *1965–8 by Eleanor Antin*, Tate Research Publication, 2019.

118. MONTREAL BED-IN

1. Quoted at: https://www.moma.org/learn/moma_learning/yoko-ono-cut-piece-1964/
2. Quoted in Nathalie Atkinson, "Give Peace a Chance: John Lennon and Yoko Ono's Iconic Montreal Bed-In Turns 51," May 22, 2020. https://www.everythingzoomer.com/arts-entertainment/2020/05/22/john-lennon-yoko-onos-montreal-bed/

119. YOKO ONO

1. Unpublished interview with Pip Chodorov, August 26, 2017.
2. CBS News report quoted in Keith Badman, *The Beatles Diary Volume 2: After the Break-Up 1970–2001*. London: Omnibus Press, 2001.
3. George Maciunas, *Fluxus Manifesto*, 1963 Offset lithograph, https://www.moma.org/collection/works/127947
4. Ibid.

120. JOHN LENNON

1. Unpublished interview with Pip Chodorov, August 26, 2017.

122. NAT HENTOFF

1. Quoted by Ned Rorem, in "The Music of the Beatles," *The New York Review of Books*, January 18, 1968.
2. John W. Whitehead, "An interview with Nat Hentoff," March 5, 2012, http://gadfly-online.com/home/index.php/impressions-people-i-knew-an-interview-with-nat-hentoff-by-john-w-whitehead/

123. NEW YORKER THEATER

1. The First Statement of the New American Cinema Group," *Film Culture*, 22–23, 1961, p.131–133.

www.ingramcontent.com/pod-product-compliance
Lightning Source LLC
LaVergne TN
LVHW051115180726
843512LV00012B/847